Praise for *Curative Magic*

"This is a much-needed book for witches who live busy lifestyles, living between the mundane and magical worlds. Packed full of valuable information and witchy tips to guide the discerning Witch in their day-to-day lives."

—Barbara Meiklejohn-Free, Highland Seer
and author of *Scottish Witchcraft*

"Rachel Patterson takes her readers on a practical magic, no fuss, empathetic journey through common mental health conditions, difficult emotions, and experiences we're all likely to experience. This Witch's guide to mind, body, and soul is packed to bursting with recipes, meditations, spells, and rituals. Read this book from one of the best; sit with it and allow the magic to soothe your soul."

—Samantha Leaver, author of *Pagan Portals: Hellenic Paganism*

T0341998

CURATIVE
MAGIC

About the Author

Rachel Patterson, also known as the "Kitchen Witch," is a High Priestess of the Kitchen Witch Coven and an Elder at the online Kitchen Witch School of Natural Witchcraft. Rachel is a popular contributor to several magazines including *Pagan Dawn*, *The Magical Times* and *Witchcraft & Wicca*. You will also find her "regular ramblings" on the Patheos Pagan channel, Moon Books, Witches & Pagans, and her own blogs. Her Craft is a combination of old religion Witchcraft, Wicca, wild Witchcraft, kitchen witchery, green witchery, and folk magic.

CURATIVE MAGIC

A Witch's Guide to Self Discovery, Care & Healing

Llewellyn Publications
Woodbury, Minnesota

RACHEL PATTERSON

First Edition
Third Printing, 2021

Book design by Samantha Penn
Cover design by Kevin R. Brown
Interior art on page 355 by Mary Ann Zapalac

Llewellyn Publications is a registered trademark of Llewellyn Worldwide Ltd.

A Kitchen Witch's World of Magical Plants & Herbs © 2014 Moon Books used with permission from John Hunt Publishing Ltd., Hampshire, UK.

Library of Congress Cataloging-in-Publication Data
Names: Patterson, Rachel, author.
Title: Curative magic : a witch's guide to self discovery, care & healing /
   by Rachel Patterson.
Description: First edition. | Woodbury, MN : Llewellyn Publications, [2020]
   | Includes index. | Summary: "Curative Magic shows you how to work with
   the tools that witchcraft provides, including spells, rituals, and herbs
   as well as meditation and recipe" —Provided by publisher.
Identifiers: LCCN 2020017391 (print) | LCCN 2020017392 (ebook) | ISBN
   9780738763286 (paperback) | ISBN 9780738763354 (ebook)
Subjects: LCSH: Witchcraft. | Self-care, Health. | Spiritual healing. |
   Healing—Religious aspects.
Classification: LCC BF1566 .P36 2020 (print) | LCC BF1566 (ebook) | DDC
   133.4/3—dc23
LC record available at https://lccn.loc.gov/2020017391
LC ebook record available at https://lccn.loc.gov/2020017392

Llewellyn Worldwide Ltd. does not participate in, endorse, or have any authority or responsibility concerning private business transactions between our authors and the public.

All mail addressed to the author is forwarded but the publisher cannot, unless specifically instructed by the author, give out an address or phone number.

Any internet references contained in this work are current at publication time, but the publisher cannot guarantee that a specific location will continue to be maintained. Please refer to the publisher's website for links to authors' websites and other sources.

Llewellyn Publications
A Division of Llewellyn Worldwide Ltd.
2143 Wooddale Drive
Woodbury, MN 55125-2989
www.llewellyn.com

Printed in the United States of America

*To my ever-patient and understanding
husband, Pete—more adventures to come!
With gratitude and thanks to my family, friends, and the
Kitchen Witch posse for being a part of my world.*

Disclaimer

If you have ailments or mental health issues, get them diagnosed by a medical professional. If it is advised, work out a course of medication. This book does not in any way replace the need for proper medical treatment, including medication or therapy for mental health issues. I do not advocate self-diagnosis. Always seek professional advice.

Never self-medicate, even with herbal remedies. Herbal remedies can be extremely potent; some are toxic. Others can react with prescription or over-the-counter medications in adverse ways. Please do not ingest any herbs if you aren't sure you have identified them correctly. If you are on medication or have health issues, please do not ingest any herbs without first consulting a qualified practitioner.

Note: Medical descriptions for all the emotional and mental issues were taken from the National Health Service guideline website.

Contents

Part One

A Beginning

Part Two

Magical Self-Care for Specific Conditions

Part Three

∽

Guidance and Moving Forward

PART ONE
A BEGINNING

CHAPTER ONE

Introduction and Working with This Book

I am a Witch, a working wife, and a mother to teenage children. Last year I also turned fifty. Life is pretty darn good all things considered, but it hasn't always been easy. Most people outside of my family probably believe me to be a strong and confident person who leads a blessed life. And I do have a wonderful life generally, but it takes work and has most definitely been earnt. What people see on the outside isn't always how I feel inside.

Probably somewhere around thirty years ago now, I found Paganism and Witchcraft—although, since I was born on Samhain, I guess my fate was sealed at birth! The Pagan pathway has changed me for the better. Paganism has helped me learn about who I am; I embrace and encourage my good qualities and recognise and acknowledge my bad ones. I even work with them to "adjust" how I react. Witchcraft has given me the tools to help myself. I use the term "help" rather than "cure" because personality traits and characteristics are not ailments, but we all suffer from stress, anxiety, panic, and other negative emotions at times. Having a magical first aid kit in hand really does make a huge difference.

I don't promise to have all the answers. I can't promise that the contents of this book are a quick fix (because they aren't). What I can do is offer the solutions I have come up with from my own experiences. I can present to you different options and ways of working to overcome some of the issues that most people have to deal with at some point. It probably won't be easy. And it will definitely take some time and effort on your part, but it really will be worth it.

Most importantly, remember that you are never alone, particularly with this online world. There is always someone somewhere that will listen.

You are important.

You are amazing, no matter what you think on a bad day. Remember that you are just experiencing that … a bad day. Underneath it all, you are amazing.

There is nothing that cannot be sorted, dealt with, or handled in some way.

Don't give up. It is OK to have a day off and start again the next day, or even the next week.

Be kind to yourself and be gentle. Learn to trust your intuition.

You are not broken. You do not need to be fixed. You just might need a bit of TLC and some fine-tuning.

Recognising, Acknowledging, and Accepting

One of the first steps to taking control of your emotions is to recognise the character traits that are causing issues or the bad habits or cycles you have gotten caught up in. Without recognising them, it is difficult to move forward. Some of them are there for good, others can be tweaked a little, and a few can be removed completely. You are who you are. DNA and the influences you had growing up will have set a few of them in stone. But by realising what they are and acknowledging them, you can choose what to do with them.

Each of us is an individual, and we are all motivated by different things.

Don't make yourself ill by doing what you think you ought to rather than saying no for the benefit of your mental and emotional health.

The world is full of people; some good, others not so much. You will meet a few difficult people along the way. They all have their own story. Remember their story is not yours.

Once you have worked out what your prompts are, then you can learn to recognise and deal with any issues, hopefully before they present themselves too strongly.

Remember to accept that "stuff happens" as well. You cannot be expected to deal with everything all at once, and even once you are familiar with it all, sometimes issues slip through the net. Once you catch them, you can deal with them.

Underlying Causes

Usually, but not always, there will be an underlying cause for any of the icky emotions such as stress, grief, anxiety, and all the other "band members." There are situations that trigger us into letting emotions take over. It may be obvious what the cause is, such as a death in the family, a miscarriage, loss of a job, or a busy schedule at work. But sometimes it isn't obvious, and those causes may take a little bit of research to uncover. Some issues, such as depression, can be deeply rooted and may even go back to your childhood. This is where shadow work comes into its own.

Shadow work is a process that uncovers that which lies hidden in the shadows of your mind, your psyche, and your past. Humans do tend to bury uncomfortable things and hide them in the dark. Shining light on to these "shadows" will help uncover them and allow you to deal with them.

Shadow work can bring up some unpleasant memories and stir up a heap load of emotions. Be prepared for a possible bumpy road ahead. Just keep bearing in mind that the work you put in will be rewarding at the end. Although I say "end," I have found shadow work is the gift that just keeps giving. Once you have started, the work continues and is always present. It puts you in a frame of mind that keeps you open to recognising patterns and triggers even when you weren't aware you were still working with them. But don't worry, that's a good thing!

We all have a habit of getting ourselves into cycles and bad patterns. Once we uncover and recognise what it is we have been caught up in, we can look at it with a different perspective and break the chain or change the direction.

I know all of the above sounds straightforward in theory, and I also know that it won't all be easy. But if you truly want to work through the dark bits, there will be a pot of gold waiting for you at the end of the rainbow. Well, maybe not gold, but at least a slice of cake.

Releasing

You really have got to wrap your head around letting go of things. Hanging on to negative emotions, thoughts, and issues is really damaging, and it can fester if left unresolved. Then it grows until there is such a huge elephant in the room you can't move because of it. Let it go. Release it. Yup, I know it is easy to sit here and tell you to let go. I know it isn't easy—trust me, I do! It is part of the process, and unless you start clearing out the junk, you won't be able to move forward and make way for the good stuff. I have included lots of ideas to help you release within this book, but the first step is to go into it knowing and accepting that you must get rid of stuff.

Note: Please remember, when you release stuff, you create a void. Unless you refill that void with positive vibes and intentions, the space will automatically fill itself with negative energy again. When you work with releasing spells or rituals, always includes some positive intentions to replace that which you let go of.

The Everyday Practical Stuff

Before we move onto the magical and, quite frankly, far more interesting stuff, I do want to cover some of the mundane options that might help you feel like your best self.

Sometimes stress is caused by taking on too much or your hectic workload. Planning ahead, knowing what you are doing and when you need to be doing it, and also where you need to be on any given date is a must for not getting stressed.

Practical changes are a good place to start. For example:

+ Make time for yourself. However busy your week is, make sure there is some time set aside for you. Do what makes you happy.

+ Get outside.

+ Set aside movie time. This one isn't always easy if you have a house full of teenagers like I do. But if you can schedule in at least a couple of hours a week, or even a month, to sit and watch your favourite movie with a cup of tea or glass of wine and a bowl of popcorn, it will really help.

+ Don't forget about date nights. If you are in a relationship, making time for each other is seriously important.

+ Get crafty. Knit, crochet, sew, paint, or write. Make sure you slot in some time to do the craft things that you enjoy.

The following are some other ideas to get you started.

It's Good to Talk

Getting support is very helpful. If you are in a relationship, please do talk to your partner. Communication goes a whole heap of a way to getting them to understand what is going on with you and being able to support you with it all. If you don't have a partner, what about a parent or sibling? Teacher, mentor, or friend? And if you really feel completely alone, then reach out—the world has provided support telephone helplines and networks for people that are struggling. Do a Google search for a national hotline or a centre in your area where you can just talk to someone. Alternatively, reach out on social media. There are support groups set up on some of the social sites, and there are always people happy to listen and lend support when you post that you are struggling. You don't have to deal with anything on your own—reach out.

Take Control of Your Health

When your health is not good, your moods and emotions find themselves in sync with it. It can be a cycle that you get pulled into, and it may even feel never-ending. But any cycle can be broken. The first step is self-care. Seeking out professional medical advice is paramount. If you have ailments, get them diagnosed properly. Then work out a course of medication. I would never advocate self-diagnosis. (Seriously, if you Google your symptoms, most of us would have already died from the black death.) Also, never self-medicate, even with herbal remedies. Herbal remedies can be extremely potent; some are toxic, and others can react with prescription or over-the-counter medications in adverse ways.

Do what you can to look after yourself in whatever way is needed. Rest when needed. Exercise as much as you can. I don't mean you have to join a gym and build up a six-pack, because you can count me out of that, but just taking a gentle stroll on a regular basis will help in all kinds of ways. Watch what you eat. I don't uphold the detox idea and I don't really believe in diets (many of them seem too extreme), but I do recommend a balanced diet. Eat sensibly; make sure you're eating plenty of fruits and vegetables. Try and cook from scratch regularly and be mindful of the sources of your ingredients. But have a treat for goodness' sake! Life is way too short to cut out all the good stuff.

In an ideal world our bodies would function perfectly, they would not suffer from any ailments or disabilities, and we could lie on the sofa stuffing our faces with chocolate cake with no ill effects. Sadly, life can be cruel. You will have to make the best with what you have ended up with (trust me, I know this sucks). But we can also do things to make it a bit easier. It is about finding a balance; everything in moderation. If, like me, you have a disease that can be triggered by certain foods, you need to pinpoint what they are. And that isn't always easy.

Onto the dreaded "E" word: exercise. I am not one for running around the park—my knees and lungs wouldn't take it, and I would collapse before I got past my garden gate. But I do like to walk in the fresh air; just around the block is good. It gets you outside and gets your limbs moving. Stretches are so very underrated too.

If you love to have a bath, then creating your own blend of bath salts is lovely. Scrubs work well if you like to shower. Body lotions can be easily made and imbued with your favourite scent and a bit of magic as well. (Some suggestions are included within this book.) Taking a bath or a shower can sometimes be the only time you get to yourself. Make the most of it by pampering yourself with lovely toiletries. Care of the body is a whole project.

Start Journaling

Yep, I know…journaling can be quite a challenge. But keeping a personal diary on how you feel each day, or even each week, can really help with releasing emotions and frustrations. Sometimes just writing things down can be the release that you need. Writing in a journal can help in a similar way.

A journal can also be useful to look back upon to track any cycles or patterns. Try jotting down the moon phase when you journal. Connecting with the energy of the day, the week, the month, or the season can be useful when journaling as well. How does the energy around you feel today?

It can also be beneficial to keep a notepad and pen handy when you meditate. Often things crop up in a meditation that you might like to jot down afterwards to remember or to research later. You can buy yourself a sparkly, bound paper journal and use funky-coloured pens, or you can type it up on your laptop or phone.

Clean House

It is seriously boring thinking about housework, and it's even more tedious to actually do it. But for me, when the house is untidy I can't focus. I have found that energy gets stuck when the house is in chaos as well; it has nowhere to flow. I don't advise getting your "Snow White" on, because let's face it—those woodland creatures are, in reality, pretty rubbish at cleaning. You will have to do the work yourself.

I am always busy, so to be honest, housework isn't at the top of my to-do list. When you have a considerable number of things going on, you must prioritise. Just take a few moments to tidy up every day; put things away and straighten it all up. The bathroom, kitchen, and toilet really need to be cleaned regularly, because otherwise, ewwwww. The dusting, however, is another matter. Dust will not kill you. As long as you do it occasionally so that you aren't left with layers that can be written in, keep it at a lower priority.

I have teenagers in the house, and they all need money on a regular basis. So to earn their allowance we have a washing up rotation. They take turns each day. They all do their own laundry, and they are each responsible for tidying and cleaning their own bedrooms. (I never go in their rooms—way too scary.)

What about the wardrobe? Have you got items lurking in there that don't fit any longer? Or that you loved in the shop but got home and hated? Clear stuff out. The bonus is that you will also be able to "pay it forward" by donating the unwanted clothes to charity. Be ruthless.

It is all about making life easier on yourself. Little things all add up.

Remember That Nature Heals

The phrase is used endlessly: "Get outside and enjoy nature; it heals." They say it frequently because it is true. If you can get to a forest, a river, a field, or an ocean, then fabulous. As a Witch I am supposed to love being in a forest, and whilst I do love trees, being dropped into the centre of a forest isn't my favourite spot. I am actually much happier in the middle of a field with lots of wide-open space around me. On the moors is perfect. Standing on the rocks beside the ocean, listening to the seagulls and the ocean waves, is bliss for me. But it isn't always possible to walk around the corner to your local forest or field. This is where we must make the best of it.

I love my garden. It isn't large; in fact, it is relatively small. But it is my sanctuary. I get out there as much as I can, even if it is just to stand outside and breathe the air for a few minutes. It allows me to reconnect with Mother Nature. Most cities will have, at the very least, a small park with grass and trees. Get to know your local area and find a spot that allows you to escape from everything and connect with nature. Failing that, even a window box with a few plants in it or a pot of herbs on a windowsill can be used in a pinch.

Find Your Sound

Noise of any kind can be enjoyable, uplifting, evocative, or even annoying, depending on what type of noise it is. The absence of sound can elicit the same reactions. Sound—or lack thereof—can be inspiring for your magic and can raise energy for spell or ritual work.

Any kind of sound or noise can be used to create energy for spell work or rituals. The choice of track can also be worked into your intent. Pick a particular band or song that makes you feel witchy. Choose a song that ties in with your theme to add to the layers of magic. If you like heavy rock or thrash metal, then use it! If you prefer something classical, go with that.

One of my favourite sounds is the drum. It has so many uses: it can clear negative energy around the house, cleanse your body, or create a meditative state. If you don't have a drum, you can create a similar sound by hitting an old biscuit tin or clapping your hands.

Singing bowls, crystal bowls, or gongs create an amazing sound as well. Each one has a unique and individual tone.

Singing is another sound that creates excellent energy, and it doesn't matter if you can't hold a note (which is of great relief to me). Just get a chant going or sing your favourite tune to raise the energy.

I love turning to nature for refreshing sounds. When I need to cleanse and soothe my soul, I think of the ocean. The sound of waves crashing on the shore and seagulls calling overhead restores me. I also find the sound of rain or birds singing to be very peaceful. If you can't get out into nature, YouTube videos and phone apps can provide all kinds of different soundtracks.

If silence is more your thing, be mindful that it is difficult to achieve complete silence. There will always be something in the background, even if it is very faint. It might be birds chirping or people outside chatting or the sound of the heating system in your house firing up. This is the sound of life happening all around you.

Remember: It is your ritual, your spell, your space—use what works for you, whether it is a song, nature sounds, drums, or even just silence.

Enjoy the Sweet Smell of Success

Another one of our senses is smell. Scent can evoke all kinds of memories, thoughts, and feelings. I recommend stocking up on scents that make you feel happy: the ones that remind you of loved ones, specific outings, places, or times of year. Whether it is in the form of scented candles, wax melts, incense, or essential oils, a whiff of happiness can go a long way to making you feel much better.

Just Say No

Setting boundaries for friends, work, and even family members can be extremely difficult. You don't have to say yes to everything that you are asked to do. You will end up exhausted and stressed because you haven't done anything for yourself. This is an important lesson to learn (and one that took me many years to learn myself). Don't allow others to take advantage of your good nature. Sadly, there are some people who will leech all of your energy without a care or a second thought. You need to make sure you only take on what you can deal with.

Know and understand your own limits. It really is OK to say no. Those that care about you will understand. Those that get offended by it probably aren't worth dealing with anyway. I am not saying never help a friend in need, of course. Just set boundaries so that you don't end up suffering because you are giving too much.

The same goes for family. Decide what you can deal with, what time you have, and what your energy levels are like, and make your own boundaries. Never feel guilty for saying you don't have the time or energy to do something for another person.

Give Thanks

Sometimes it can be incredibly difficult to see the positive. Life can really feel as if it is just throwing lemons at you with no ending in sight. However, if you can focus on the positive even in small ways, it really helps. Even in the darkest situations there are—hopefully—at least one or two good things.

Take some time to sit and give thanks for what you have. Wheedle out the good stuff, no matter how small it might seem, and work from there as a starting point. It might be something out in nature: the first daffodil in spring or the first bee of summer. These are small but gorgeous signs in a world that really can be beautiful. A roof over your head, a meal on the table, shoes on your feet—all these things are positive.

And yes, I do absolutely acknowledge that it can be difficult to come from a very dark place and be happy about having a pair of shoes on your feet. I am just giving this example as a starting point. Eventually life will stop throwing lemons, but until then, you might as well try to make some lemonade.

Become a Bookworm

One of my favourite pastimes is reading. I read different authors, but I always come back to Terry Pratchett. I can easily and very quickly lose myself in one of his books, despite having read all of them numerous times. I have to schedule reading time into my diary, otherwise it is very easy to just skip over it and do other things that are far less beneficial for my heart and soul. Make the time—it is important.

Choose Music for the Soul

Music has a big effect on our emotions and can change our mood entirely. Popping something you love on the music system and lying down with your eyes closed to chill out works beautifully. If you want to boost your energy and cheer yourself up, put on something that makes you dance and sing—something you know all the words to.

Enjoy Your Hobbies

Do you have any hobbies that you love? I must admit, cooking (more precisely, baking) is a hobby that I love. Writing is one of the things I love too; I can get totally lost in the words. Do what works for you. Whether it is crafting of some kind—knitting, crocheting, painting, drawing (you don't have to be any good at it), or building model aircraft—if it takes your mind away from everything and focuses your spirit, then do it.

Unleash the Waterworks

Never underestimate the cleansing power of having a good cry: a real tears-streaming, let-it-all-out bawl. There is no shame in crying. There is no embarrassment in giving in to it all and letting the floodgates open. It can be extremely cathartic and helps to cleanse and wash away some of the frustration. Have tissues on standby though, because it can get messy...

Set Some Goals

Before we start, what do you really want to achieve? It seems a bit pointless to throw yourself into everything without having some idea of where you want to end up. It's a lot of work to do with no real direction. Make a cuppa, grab a pen and paper, and sit down for a quiet moment.

Write a list with two columns. In the first column write things you want to change. What do you want to get rid of? It might be practical things, such as changing your job or how you run the list of chores in your home. It could be emotional feelings and their physical manifestations, like panic attacks.

In the second column write things that make you happy. What do you want to do that makes your heart sing? It could be a profession you have always wanted to do, moving to another place, or new (or old) hobbies such as reading, knitting, or writing. This column should include things that make you feel content, unstressed, and at peace.

Once you have your list, take another look at it. Do any of the items in the first column affect anything in the second column? A long commute to work might affect time spent doing hobbies or being tired. Having children that are lazy and untidy might affect how you feel. I have found it quite interesting to compare the two columns. There are often obvious links that can be changed quite easily.

Some things will take time. If you have "Marry a prince" in your second column, that one might be a bit unachievable. Make sure you keep the list as real as possible. But don't leave out any dreams or desires, such as a new profession or moving to a place you love. Not everything is impossible. This will give you something to aim for.

Don't forget to pat yourself on the back for any achievement. Some days just getting out of bed and putting on clothes can feel worthy of an award. This is a journey; it won't all happen in an instant. Give yourself credit for each and every step. Even if you take a step backwards and then forward again, remember to be proud that you turned it around. Celebrate and give yourself the credit you deserve for each and every achievement, no matter how big or small.

Start each day with a plan. It doesn't matter if you don't stick to it. Sometimes it might go out the window before you have even finished breakfast. The universe has a bizarre sense of humour.

However, making a plan can help ease you into the day and give you a guide and something to aim for. Start with self-care: shower, bathe, wash with lotions and potions that you love.

Have breakfast and a drink. (By a drink, I mean a soft one; if you start your day with a vodka, then we have real problems.) Your breakfast doesn't have to be fancy; it could just be a bowl of cereal or porridge. This gives you an excuse to sit still for a few minutes before your day begins.

Take note of the energy of the day. Step outside and breathe in the fresh air. What does the energy of the day feel like? You might get some inspiration or words of wisdom from Mother Nature whilst you are filling your lungs.

Then make a plan. What do you need to do? Like, *really* need to do? Prioritise. You don't need to schedule in every detail; just have a rough idea of how you will lay out your jobs and chores for the day. Take a look and see if you can combine some or make the list easier to handle. Try and fit in a bit of time to do something for you, even if it is just a lunch break in the garden. Finish off by telling yourself, "You can do this."

If you stick to the plan all day, then fabulous! You rocked it. If the plan went haywire, don't worry. You did what you could, and tomorrow is a new day.

Working with This Book

There is no straightforward answer for any of the situations presented in this book, and each person will deal with things in a different way. However, I hope I have provided some potential solutions within the pages of this book. You don't have to work with it all (although you can if you like). Have a read through and select bits that resonate with you.

You also don't have to use all the herbs, plants, or crystals that I have suggested. They are exactly that... suggestions. Trust your intuition along with what you have in your cupboards or garden. Work with items that feel right for you.

If you don't like the chant or words I have used in a ritual or spell, tweak them or rewrite them to suit you. It has to be personal and feel right for you. YOU are the important one in this scenario! Allow your mind to take you where it needs to go.

CHAPTER TWO

❦

The Spiritual You

We all lose connection with our spirituality at some point along the way, sometimes more than once. I myself have been there on more than one occasion. Life gets hectic and busy and your spirituality gets lost. Remember … you don't have to be a Super Witch; you also don't need to be perfect.

I think some people believe Witches get up at dawn each day to collect dew from the plants and venture out at midnight to pick herbs in the correct moon phase. The rest of the day is spent in meditation or creating spells and potions, followed by a naked ritual under the stars … And there may well be some that follow that regime, but I bet they are very few and far between.

Real life involves going to work, housework, chores, running errands, sorting children and spouses out, and all the other mundane stuff that needs to be done. I just don't have time to summon demons before breakfast! Your pathway is very personal to you, and you need to make it work alongside everything else. Don't beat yourself up if you missed a full moon or a sabbat; the fiery pits of Hades will not open up and swallow you. Do what you can, do what feels right to you, and work it into your schedule. Definitely don't let yourself get stressed out because you feel that you "aren't doing things properly." Your spirituality is within YOU, and it doesn't matter if life gets in the way from time to time. It will still be there when you are ready to pick it up again.

Stand outside and give thanks to nature. Feed the birds and breathe in the sunshine or the moonlight. You can even connect with nature whilst hanging out the washing or taking out the trash. It only takes a moment. Don't complicate things. This is your journey, your rules, and your pathway. Give yourself a break, do what you can, and make it work for you.

If you have lost your connection completely, there are ways to slowly and gently bring it back. You don't need to rush headlong into it. My recommendation is to ask yourself why you lost the connection in the first place. Is there a reason why it happened? Do you need to tweak or change your pathway a bit? Did you just need some time out? Did life just get too darn busy? It may be one, all, or none of these, but whatever it was, it can be sorted.

Often, I have realised my connection was broken for a reason. My solution was to sort out whatever it was, take some time away, and then slowly tiptoe back in. Baby steps.

My first step is usually to clean and clear out my altar. Take everything down, freshen it up, and re-dress it completely. Here are some other steps you can take to strengthen your connection:

+ Start meditating for a short while each day, perhaps in front of your newly dressed altar.
+ Read a new book about a spiritual pathway or reread one that you love.
+ Do some research on a deity, spirit animal, plant, or crystal you haven't studied before. Be guided by your intuition.
+ Do some drumming, singing, or dancing.
+ Craft some magic such as an incense blend, witch bottle, or a poppet.
+ Get outside and enjoy nature.
+ Turn off your phone and step away from your computer for a set amount of time each day. Start with fifteen or twenty minutes and work your way up. Set aside that time to do something you love.
+ Write a ritual, a chant, a spell, or a poem.

Losing your connection to spirituality honestly does happen to all of us at some point or other; know that you aren't the only one.

Visualisation

Working with visualisation can be key to creating the reality that you want. Having good visualisation skills helps with working magic, spells, healing, ritual, and meditation. But don't worry if you struggle with it. There are some simple exercises you can work with to hone your skills. And don't be scared off by the term "visualisation"—really, it is just a bit of daydreaming. You don't have to see clear and sharp images. Just getting the feel of what you are aiming for is perfect. It probably won't play like a high-definition plasma TV.

Try sitting quietly with a piece of fruit or a flower in front of you. Spend a few moments taking in all the details, the colour, the texture, the shape. Then close your eyes and try to recreate the item in your mind. Build it up bit by bit or fade it into focus. Once you have the image, try to imagine the scent or the taste.

You can practise the visualisation exercise with any item: a candle or piece of jewellery, perhaps.

The more you practise, the better your visualisation skills should become.

Grounding and Centring

Grounding and centring yourself are essential skills for a Witch to have in her kit bag, particularly if you are working with energy within spells or ritual. They also help to calm you down if you have found yourself in the middle of a situation.

You don't need to set aside a huge amount of time. In fact, in a sticky situation you can ground and centre within a minute. All it requires is some visualisation.

There are different techniques and styles, but the tree exercise below seems to work the best for me.

> Take a few deep breaths in and out. Place your feet flat on the floor and visualise roots beginning to grow from the soles of your feet ... the roots reaching out and pushing their way into the rich, dark soil of the earth. See the roots feeling their way, spreading out, and heading down. When the roots reach the centre of the earth, breathe in as you allow the energy from the centre of the planet to make its way back up through the roots and into the centre of your being. It may be your

solar plexus (tummy), but it might be your heart or somewhere else. Feel it radiating into your body and filling you with positive energy. When you have had enough, allow the excess to drain back down into the soil. Then slowly and gently start pulling your roots back up, finding their way through the soil and back into your feet.

If you are really tight on time, you can just clap your hands and stamp your feet.

Some other ideas for grounding and centring yourself:

+ Place your hands on the soil and visualise any excess or chaotic energy draining from your body into the ground.
+ Carry a pebble with you. When you feel airy or lightheaded, grab hold of the pebble and feel the connection to the earth.
+ Some crystals are really good at grounding. Carry one with you and when you need it, hold the crystal and connect with the grounding energy. Stones such as smoky quartz and hematite work well for grounding.
+ Eat something! Chocolate is very good for grounding, just saying…

Breathing

Focusing on your breathing is a good way to begin meditation. It can also help when you are facing a panic attack or when you are feeling anxious or stressed. By concentrating on how you breathe, you can calm yourself down.

There are several different breathing exercises that can be used. Find one that suits you.

Three Relaxing Breaths

Sit with your mouth closed and your tongue gently resting on your upper palate.

Take a slow, deep breath in through your nose. Breathe right down into your abdomen; feel it expand and your lungs fill completely.

As you breathe in, visualise your mind becoming clear and alert.

Hold that breath for a moment.

Then exhale slowly through your nose. As you exhale visualise stress flowing out of your body.

Hold your lungs empty for a moment.

Then repeat again twice.

Bellows Breath

Inhale and exhale rapidly through your nose, keeping your mouth closed (but relaxed). Your breaths in and out should be equal in duration, but as short as possible. This is a noisy exercise!

Aim for three in-and-out breath cycles per second if you can. It may take practice.

Breathe normally after each cycle.

Only do this exercise for ten to fifteen seconds on your first try. Each time you try it, see if you can last longer, eventually up to a minute in total.

Relaxing

Place the tip of your tongue against the ridge just behind your upper front teeth and keep it there for this entire exercise.

Exhale completely through your mouth, making a whooshing sound.

Close your mouth and inhale quietly through your nose to a count of four. (Count silently in your head.)

Hold your breath for a count of seven.

Exhale completely through your mouth, making a whooshing sound, for a count of eight.

Now inhale again and repeat the cycle three more times.

A Safe Place

By "safe place" I don't mean a physical room or spot (although it could be), but one inside your head. A sacred place that you can take your mind to when things get to be too much. Somewhere you feel safe and comfortable; a place that you can use to visualise and "bring yourself back."

Make yourself comfortable, somewhere you won't be disturbed, and close your eyes. To create your safe place:

Take a moment to feel the need for a visual representation of your safe place.

As your world around you dissipates, you find yourself… where?

Where are you? What type of place? Are you inside or outside? Is it warm or cold? Are you in a house, a castle, a hotel? Are you in a field, a forest, or by the sea? Take a long look around you, turning in a full circle to take in all your surroundings. What can you hear? What can you smell? Is there somewhere to sit or lie down?

This is your place.

Take some real time to explore everything. Walk around the boundary. Open boxes; look behind bushes. See all.

When you are ready, slowly and gently come back to this reality.

Know that this visualisation is YOUR place. You can visit whenever you want. You can also add fixtures and fittings if you want, or redecorate! Make it exactly how you want it and need it to be. Each time you visit, you may notice that something else has been added. It can be useful to add something such as a small pool or a mirror. This helps as a way of using the meditation space to gain clarity or answers. I ask a question and look into the pool for answers. When things get to be too much, you can take your mind to your place and spend a few moments—or longer—relaxing and releasing.

Meditations

Short meditations are good to start with, partly because most of us rarely get a huge amount of quiet time on our own, and partly because the mind doesn't like focusing for long periods of time. You can find moments for meditation in your everyday life. For example:

- Meditation can be done as you walk to work; count your steps and allow your mind to wander. (Do pay attention to traffic and crossing the road, though!)
- Sit quietly sipping a cup of tea, letting each sip take you further into a meditative state.

+ Spend a few minutes sitting quietly, focusing on your breathing. Let negative energy release on the out breath and take in positive energy on the in breath.

+ If you are a crafter, knitting and crocheting are excellent meditation tools.

Find a time of day and a method that suits you. Jot down any thoughts or images that came to mind during your meditation. It can be useful to refer back to them later.

If you're interested in trying a guided meditation, make yourself comfortable and find a place where you won't be disturbed. You don't have to bend like a pretzel. Just sit in a comfortable chair or lie on your bed. Perhaps throw a blanket over you, because when you sit still for a while your body temperature drops. You don't want your meditation interrupted by shivers! Read through the meditation a couple of times so that you have it straight in your mind. You could even record yourself reading it on your mobile or laptop and play it back to yourself. However you work with it, don't feel you are restricted to follow it exactly. And honestly, if the mind monkeys keep jumping in, just acknowledge the thoughts and release them as best you can. Two minutes of random daydreaming is better than no meditation at all.

Tea Meditation

Make your favourite hot tea (or coffee) and sit comfortably in a chair. Close your eyes if you prefer. Holding the cup in both hands, lift it up to your face and inhale deeply, taking in the scent of the drink, and exhale through your mouth.

Keep breathing in and out slowly. Let the scent and warm steam from the drink flow through your nose and down into your body.

Feel the heat of the cup on the inside of your hands. Allow that heat to permeate your skin and fill your body with warmth.

Then slowly take a sip of the beverage. Savour the taste in your mouth.

As you swallow, visualise the liquid bringing positive energy with it as it travels into your body.

Repeat the visualisation each time you sip your drink. Allow the liquid to fill you with positive and radiating energy.

When you have finished your drink, slowly and gently come back to this reality. Pop the cup down safely and wriggle your fingers and toes.

Affirmations

Affirmations are simply statements that we make—hopefully positive, but more often than not we find ourselves making negative ones instead. They can be made on purpose with the intent of wanting to change some aspect of our lives or way of thinking. They are often made automatically without even thinking about it. How many times have you said or heard someone say "Oh, I am no good at that"? Words have power and what we say, whether it is negative or positive, affects our moods and behaviour.

We can use affirmations or chants to change our way of thinking. We can choose to bombard our subconscious mind with positive thoughts and ideas rather than negative ones.

These sentences are positive affirmations:

- "I am worthy."
- "I am strong, confident, and courageous."
- "My life is full of happiness."
- "I deserve to be happy."
- "I am in control of my life."

They all sound good, don't they?

Now take a moment to think about the things you say automatically such as:

- "I can't do that."
- "I am too scared to do that."
- "I am not worthy."

I bet you make the negative statements all the time without being aware that you are. See if you can catch yourself doing it. Pay attention when you are speaking or even thinking. Stop yourself before you say it and see if you can turn a negative into a positive.

Don't beat yourself up if you slip; it happens. Just correct yourself. You are allowed to make mistakes in life. You can make bad decisions; we all do.

Allow yourself to recognise it and release it. Make an affirmation to cover it, something like, "Mistakes are OK. I release it and move forward." Work with positive affirmations every day if you can; it will really have an effect. You are in control. You have the power to make the change.

CHAPTER THREE

The Magical You

Your Craft and spirituality can be worked into your daily routine. When you do the housework, chant as you go along. Visualise negative energy being swept out of the door or sucked up into the vacuum cleaner. Think about all the magical properties of the ingredients you use in making dinner. Take two minutes out before you go to bed, step outside, and look up at the moon. Send her a wish or just a smile. It doesn't need to be more complicated than that. You cannot be all things to everyone, all of the time. Ultimately someone will lose out, and it will usually be you.

You don't need to have all the fancy tools or flouncy robes to be spiritual or magical. Keep things practical and affordable. Deity, Mother Nature, or the Divine really don't mind if you address them whilst wearing your pyjamas. They understand.

Rituals don't need to be long complicated affairs. Although it is good to go full-out on occasion, on a regular and more practical basis, keep it simple.

Make the magic work for you and fit into your schedule.

Spells

What is a spell? Essentially it is a series of words and/or actions, a wish, or a desire that contains the magical intent to make changes. The most important part, in my opinion, is that you believe in what you are doing. Spells do have a habit of following their own course. Often they are unpredictable and can have unexpected results. It is definitely a case of "Be careful what you wish for."

There is a very big difference between what you *want* and what the universe believes you *need*. Focus your intent, be true and strong in what you desire, and trust that the universe knows best. I also find that visualisation is key when working spells. You need to really "see" what it is you want to achieve.

There are many types of spells that you can work with: simple candle and petition spells, witch bottles, poppets, pouches, and more. How simple or complicated it is is up to you. I err on the side of keeping things simple and straightforward; I find there is less confusion. But go with what works for you.

I have presented some spell options in this book but, as always, trust your intuition and tweak or change the spell wording or ingredients to suit you.

All-Purpose Candle Spell

A very simple and straightforward spell. You will need a small candle (white is a good colour for all purpose), a lighter, and a candle holder. Make sure you put the candle on a flat, safe surface. Hold the candle in both hands and visualise your requirement. It might be a goal or a wish: healing or prosperity, for example. See the final result in your mind's eye and send that energy into the candle.

Set the candle in a holder and light the flame. State your requirement out loud. Be specific.

Sit quietly and watch the flame of the candle, still visualising your intent.

Allow the candle to burn out completely, then throw any remaining stub in the trash.

Never leave a burning candle unattended.

Rituals

The term "ritual" can sound a bit scary. Really it is just a set of actions that come together to make a whole. Rituals can be anything from a daily action, such as brushing your teeth, right up to a full-on ceremonial circle. Make it work for you. But relax…this is your party! You bring to it whatever you want to.

A basic ritual might involve: casting a circle, calling in the quarters (elements/four compass directions), inviting deity, working your magic, feasting (cake…). Then do it all in reverse: thanking deity, releasing the quarters, and closing the circle. Simple.

You can set up an altar and use all the tools such as a wand, but you can also perform a ritual with nothing but yourself. Casting a circle keeps the energy within your space but also acts as a barrier to protect against any negative energy coming in. You can draw the energy for your circle from the air, the sun, the moon, the earth, or any of the elements around you. Visualise a circle being created, then draw it up over you and then down below you, so you are in a bubble. It isn't a circle as such; more of a globe. When you call in the quarters you are inviting the energy from each of the four elements and compass directions to join your ritual: north—earth, east—air, south—fire, and west—water. Each one will bring a unique energy. Earth is very grounding and provides stability. Air is for intellect. Fire is for passion and energy, and water deals with emotions and releasing. They obviously have more correspondences than that; see what you feel connects them.

Cleansing

If you use any tools in ritual, or for working with crystals in particular, you may want to cleanse them first. Objects pick up energy from other people, and crystals will need cleansing after use to clear them from anything they have picked up during the magic worked. It is really simple to do. You can visualise a bright white or gold light surrounding the item and clearing out any negative vibes. Items can be placed in the moonlight or sunlight. Sprinkle with salt, sand, soil, or water. Pass the item through incense smoke or a candle flame. A word of caution: be careful with crystals and tools as some can be damaged by sunlight, water, or salt.

Here are some suggestions for cleansing:

+ **Visualisation:** This is the cheapest and simplest option. Visualise a white light coming from the sun, the moon, or the sky and direct it into the item. See it cleansing and purifying any negative energy away.

+ **Water:** Run your item under the tap or drop it into a bowl of water. Allow the water to wash away any negative energy.

+ **Incense:** Light an incense of your choice and waft it over the item or, holding it in your hand, move it through the smoke.

+ **Sun:** Leave your item in the sunlight, either outside (if it is safe) or on a windowsill for an hour or two—until you feel it is cleansed.

+ **Moon:** Leave your item in the moonlight, either outside (if it is safe) or on a windowsill for an hour or two—until you feel it is cleansed. This is best done under a full moon, when it is at its strongest.

+ **Earth:** Bury your item in the soil for a few hours. This is probably best done in a flowerpot, otherwise you might forget where you buried it…

+ **Air:** Hold the item in your hand and, using your breath, blow on it, turning the item around until you have literally blown away all the negative energy.

+ **Sound:** Place your item down and drum around it using your hands, or use a drum, singing bowl, cymbals, or a musical instrument of your choice.

+ **Rice:** Bury the item in a bowl of uncooked rice and leave for a few hours.

+ **Fire:** You need to be careful with this one. Light a candle and pass the item just above the flame to cleanse, then snuff out the candle.

+ **Crystals:** Some crystals are natural cleansers. Lay your item that needs clearing on top of a large quartz or amethyst cluster.

+ **Herbs:** Sprinkle a blend of herbs and/or petals over the item or pop them in a pouch or jar that is filled with herbs and plant matter.

Colour Magic

I love to work with colour magic. Colour has such a big impact on our emotions and moods. Each colour can evoke a feeling, brighten our day, or bring about calm. I like to include colour magic when I use candles for spell work, cloths for my altars, and even when I am deciding what to wear. Picking the right colour clothing can really change your mood. Working with colour in magic can boost the energy of the spell or ritual. It may be different for each person, but I have included my personal suggestions for colour magic in the following chapters.

Deity

Some people like to work with specific deities or pantheons all the time. My matron deity is an ancient goddess, the Cailleach. She has been walking beside me for many years now, but other deities have come and gone when I have needed their specific energy. For the last few years I have worked with the Indian god Ganesha alongside the Cailleach. Yep, it sounds like an odd mix, but they seem to tolerate each other. This past year the Celtic god Belenus has found me and I have been working with him; he seems to bring balance to the Cailleach. Others will work with whatever deity they feel is right for what they are working with.

Each deity has a unique and individual character. They have correspondences and energies that are quite specific. I would recommend that before you invite a deity into your ritual or spell work, you research them first. You don't want to call a war god into a spell to calm you down—the results could be disastrous! I am always guided by my intuition as to whom I work with. Again, trust your intuition, but also do your homework.

Always be respectful and polite. Ask, don't demand, and remember to give thanks and leave an offering. You don't get something for nothing. Be mindful that each deity has its own culture. Deities are sacred. Please be respectful to both the deity and the culture. Make this part of your research. Each one has a backstory, and a lot of them have specific rituals and associations. Respect is key here.

In this book I suggest deities to work with, but be guided by whoever comes to you. Some deities will shout and jump about to get your attention— listen to them.

Call to the Cailleach

This is a call that I wrote and use when I want to connect with the Cailleach, sometimes in ritual but often just standing at my altar.

My crone, you are the ancient one
You are the landscape beneath my feet
You are the mountains and the hills
My crone, you are the rock and stone that leads down to the shore
You are wisdom, you are knowledge

You are the keeper of mysteries, you are the old hag
The Cailleach, I welcome you

A Bundle of Magic

You could refer to this as a magic bundle, meditation bundle, or a medicine bundle. I like to work with it as a witch's bundle. Use a square of fabric (if you are handy with a needle you can sew a lining) and then just a piece of cord to tie it up. Lay the fabric out flat and add items that you feel need to go inside. Then you can fold or roll it up and secure it with the cord.

I have a bundle for when I meditate. It holds some herbs to help with meditation, a couple of crystals, and items that represent my spirit guides. I also have a bundle for working with the god and goddess. It includes representations of the deities I am working with at the time. I open the bundle up and lay out the contents when I am working magic.

Altars

An altar is basically a flat surface where you lay out your magical tools, offerings, and connections to deity and the elements. It also provides a focal point where you can connect with the Divine, work magic, and meditate. An altar is a reflection of you as a person. Keep it as simple or as full of items as you feel is right. It is your personal space. Nothing is right or wrong.

Now, as we are going to be working with you, inside and out, I believe it helps to make an altar to yourself. Not a "worship my ego" kind of altar but a place that represents you and honours your inner and outer being. It will also help to have a focal point to work with. Find a little space. It doesn't have to be huge or grand; just a small shelf or corner of a unit is enough. If you are "in the closet" with your pathway, then a tray that you can take out or put away in a cupboard works well.

Take some time to think about what you want to place on your altar. You don't have to chuck seventy-three different items at it on the first day; start simply. I would suggest placing a photograph of yourself in the centre, one that you like (or hate the least). You could add a vase of flowers, pieces of jewellery that you like, or personal items that have meaning for you. Add in photos or images of places you have visited that you enjoyed or have special memories in. Include items that you find comforting—maybe even your favourite bar of chocolate. This is your central point to work from. Items can be added or taken away when you want to. Keep it fluid: it doesn't have to be set out in a particular way, and it isn't set permanently in one layout.

Keep all the items positive; use things that you love and that make you smile. Write yourself a love letter. Tell yourself how wonderful you are and what makes you smile about yourself. What do you like about yourself? What do you think others like about you? Be a show-off and be proud of who you are. Keep your love letter on your "me" altar as a reminder that you are wonderful.

Your personal altar is also a good place to stand each day and say your affirmations or make petitions to deity. You could create altars for any deities you work with or animal spirit guides. If you don't have space for lots of altars, just use one and add in representations of what you are working with.

Don't forget to keep it spick-and-span. Dust stops the energy from flowing. If your altar is unloved, it can block your own energy. I always feel much better after clearing off, cleaning, and relaying my altar.

CHAPTER FOUR

❧

Getting Crafty

You can make magic with everyday items. Using your creative energy to fashion something, whether it is a loaf of bread or incense blend, not only gives you an end product but also helps focus your mind. Cooking, crafting, or meditating with a crystal can really help with all kinds of emotional and mental issues.

Take time out to channel your creative energy. It doesn't have to be fancy or complicated. Get outside and check out your local area. Get to know the local stores, find a supplier of local produce, seek out interesting and independent food stores. Visit local parks and gardens and get to know the flora and fauna.

Experiment with cooking, making incense blends, or herbal teas. Find out what flavours and scents you prefer and what emotions or feelings they bring to you. Make it personal!

Food

Kitchen Witchcraft is my pathway, and baking is my passion. I work magic into my food every day. When I cook, I charge the ingredients with intent. I stir clockwise to bring in positive energy, and I wash away negative energy when I clean and peel vegetables. Every single ingredient has magical energy, and these properties can be utilised when eaten or in spell work. For instance, cinnamon and lemon balm are both good to use in spells for success. And adding lemon to a recipe brings the magical energy of happiness.

In the following chapters, I have included some recipes for you to try. If you don't like an ingredient, experiment and see what else you can use. The recipes can be used just for you, your family, your friends, or in ritual. Some food ingredients also lend themselves easily to spell work, such as dried herbs and spices. Others, such as fruit, get a bit mouldy when left in spell pouches. Best to eat those to gain the magic!

Herbal Tea

Herbal tea is so versatile. You can use bought herbal tea bags or you can make your own. Herbal tea can be drunk hot or left to cool and served over ice. Tea bags can also be dropped into a bucket of water and used to wash your floors and surfaces, bringing the magic of the herbs with it. Work with fresh or dried herbs or mix and match herbal tea bags. As a general rule use one or two teaspoons of the dried herb mix, pour on hot water, brew for at least five minutes, then strain. If you are using fresh herbs, you may need to add a larger quantity. It can also be used as a mouth wash, gargle or hair rinse, or dropped into your bathwater.

Note: Please be careful and make sure you have identified the herb correctly. Never ingest herbs that you aren't sure about. Always check with a qualified practitioner if you are on medication, have health problems, or are pregnant.

Crystals

Within the pages of this book, I have suggested crystals that you may be drawn to work with. The recommendations given are just ideas—crystals that I feel will help with each situation, emotion, or issue. You may find others that work better for you personally. Don't go out and spend lots of money; work with what you have. Crystals are unique, and each one will have a specific energy. Some will work beautifully with you, others won't. They are all individual characters with personalities. Get to know them. However, there are certain crystals that lend themselves to our purpose, so I have included suggestions of those.

You don't have to rush out and purchase a huge stock of crystals. A simple pebble from the ground holds a huge powerhouse of magic. If you want to buy a crystal but can only afford one, go with clear quartz as it is a good all-rounder. Cleansing any crystals that you purchase before you work with them is advisable (see the cleansing suggestions in chapter 3).

Before you work with any crystal, I recommend connecting with the energy it contains. Sit quietly and hold the crystal in your hands. Open your mind and reach out with your "spidey senses" and connect with the aura/energy field of the crystal. Ask it what it can help you with. Carry the crystal with you and/or sleep with it under your pillow—this will help you connect to the crystal and it will also help make the link with your energy.

I also recommend meditating with any new crystal you acquire. Sit quietly and put the crystal down in front of you. Clear your mind and allow your focus to be directed at the crystal. See it, *really* see it, in great detail. What colours do you see? What inclusions, cracks, lines, or spots do you see on the surface? What about under the surface? Really delve deep into the stone. Explore…

Holding the crystal in your hand or creating a meditation journey pouch that holds crystals works well, but you can also lie or sit with crystals placed on your body. If you are lying down, place a crystal on your third eye. It will help you reach a meditative state and amplify your insight.

When you want to work with a crystal, you will need to charge it with the energy of your intent. Basically, you need to tell it what you would like it to do. Do be polite and ask it nicely, but make sure you really push that energy. The strength of your will and commitment to the outcome is paramount in any spell work. That crystal needs to be very, very clear about what you expect from it and what you would like it to do.

You can add to the programming by doing one, some, or all of the following:

+ Visualise your intent and send that image into the stone.

+ Set up a candle in a corresponding colour. Maybe even inscribe a symbol into the candle or sprinkle it with herbs and oils. Place the crystal in front of the lit candle and allow the energy to be soaked up into the stone.

+ Place the crystal in a pouch for a while and add dried herbs that correspond to your intent. Let the crystal fill up with the energy from the herbs.

- Light some incense and pass the crystal through the smoke whilst telling the crystal what you need from it.
- Create a gemstone altar and place the crystal on it to charge.

Once you have finished working magic with a crystal you can reuse it, but I would suggest cleansing it first (using one of the methods in chapter 3). If you don't, it will carry the energy from the last spell and could confuse the issue if you use it next time for another purpose.

Crystals can be carried with you, popped into your pocket or purse. Wear them in jewellery settings. Keep them on your altar or beside your bed. Place them around the house. Use them in spell pouches and witch bottles. Work with them in meditation and candle magic spells. They have a whole host of uses.

Herbs, Plants, and Flowers

Herbal magic is a passion of mine. This isn't medical or medicinal: you are tapping into the magical energy that each natural item holds. Once you connect with the spirit of the plant or flower you can ask for guidance or assistance. This connection can be made directly with the plant, flower, herb, or tree when it is still growing outside (or inside, if it is a potted plant).

You can also work with dried plant material or essential oils. These herbs, plants, and flowers can be added to incense blends, sachet powders, spell pouches, witch bottles, body lotions and potions, candle magic, or any kind of spell work. Each plant has a different energy, a spiritual character, or personality. For example, knotweed is an excellent plant to use in spells to dispel worry, and holly can bring about balance.

Incense

Incense can be a loose mixture burnt on charcoal or by lighting incense cones and sticks. Incense is used to clear negative energy, create sacred space, complement spell work, or add energy to a ritual. If you can't use incense for health reasons, you could try using essential oil on a burner or scented candles. I often pop loose incense onto the top of an oil burner with a tea light underneath. The heat warms the blend and disperses the scent but doesn't give off any smoke.

Incense is used frequently to cleanse, whether it is by passing the item through the smoke of the incense itself or by using incense to smudge something—your home, your body, or an item. The power of the smoke cleanses and purifies. I start with a tree resin base such as frankincense or copal. Add in something woody to help it burn longer, then dried herbs and spices. To boost the scent, you can add a few drops of essential oil to the mixture.

Essential Oils

An essential oil is a concentrated essence of the plant. The oil is extracted from either the seeds, peel, resin, leaves, roots, bark, or flowers. Oils will trigger our senses and will work holistically on the mind, body, and spirit. Essential oils have been used for thousands of years in religious ceremonies, for anointing, for filling a room with fragrance, in foods and perfumes, and for healing and well-being.

When purchasing essential oils, do make sure they are pure and not mixed with chemicals or "watered down." Some of the oils can be expensive, but remember that you only use a few drops at a time so they will last.

You may wish to make an oil blend. They are easy to make; all you have to do to create a blend is mix essential oils. If you are experimenting with blends, I would suggest testing them first. Put a drop of each essential oil on a small slip of paper (or paper towel), add the next oil, sniff to see if you like it, then add the next drop, etc. Once you've decided on your blend, you can mix the essential oils with your chosen base oil (if needed). This way you won't end up ruining a whole bottle of base oil by adding in random essential oils.

Never put essential oil straight onto your skin. Always mix it into a base oil first. You can use any type of base oil such as almond oil, jojoba oil, apricot kernel oil, coconut oil, or even olive oil. Any blend you are intending to use on your skin for anointing or massage *must* be diluted with a base oil. As a general rule of thumb, I would use ten millilitres of base oil to twenty or twenty-five drops of essential oil. Please test a drop or two on a small area of your skin before you go slapping on loads of oil, just in case you are allergic to it.

For a blend to use in an oil burner, bath, or diffuser, you can create a blend without using a base oil.

There are many simple ways to incorporate essential oils into your everyday life:

- Use essential oils to anoint yourself before ritual. Make sure to use a base oil.

- Add essential oils to your own bathwater for a ritual bath.

- Use essential oils for aromatherapy. A useful method for breathing in essential oils is to create your oil blend, then add it to a jar containing a couple of tablespoons of coarse sea salt. Mix together and pop a lid on the jar. Then, when you feel the need, open the jar and take a couple of deep breaths.

- Add your oil blend to an oil burner. I pop a piece of wax into the top first, then add the oil. Adding wax stops the oil from burning.

- Oil blends are also useful for dressing candles for spell work. Pick a corresponding oil to your intent and rub the candle with oil.

I have included some blend ideas in the following chapters; you can experiment and make your own.

Personal Wheel of Fabulousness

Crystal grids and what I call "wheels of magic" are a fabulous way to work magic. I use the principle of a crystal grid and usually start with a central stone. Then I work out from there, creating a pattern using small crystals and tumbled stones. I also work other items into the design: feathers, candles, leaves, flower heads, dried herbs, fresh herbs, fruit, seeds, dried pulses, shells, beads, and even tarot or oracle cards. The pattern is different each time, and I work intuitively. The design may be a star shape, a swirl, a spiral, or a random shape. If you trust your intuition, it will end up exactly how it needs to be.

I add whatever I feel needs to go into the design to make the magic work. Start with an intent in mind and select items that you feel need to go into the grid. If it is working magic for you, then you could place a photo of yourself in the centre (or a business card if you have one). Placing personal items of jewellery in the centre can also be done to charge them with magic.

Once you have all your items laid out, you need to activate the grid. Activation can be done with a crystal point, a wand, or just your finger. Start from the centre and tap each item in turn, visualising a thread or beam connecting them all together. Maybe add in a chant as you do this. Once you tap the last item, the grid is ready to make magic. Leave it in place for as long as you think and feel is necessary.

Items can be carried with you from the grid once you are finished with them, charged with the intent. Remember to cleanse any crystals used afterwards. Add any natural items to the compost bin or bury in the soil.

CHAPTER FIVE

Introduction to Shadow Work

What is shadow work? Think of it as working with those parts of your personality that you don't much like. With shadow work, you try to get to the bottom of why you do things and why you repeat behavioural patterns, then work with them to improve, dismiss, or incorporate those parts of you into a whole.

We all have dark sides. We all have shadow sides. We need this darkness—it creates the balance in our inner selves. What we need to do is to seek out and acknowledge those darker sides and work with them to keep ourselves in perfect harmony.

This can mean dealing with difficulties in facing sadness, sorrow, and anger, as well as any issues you may have with self-worth, self-esteem, and feeling that you deserve to be happy. It also covers all those feelings, emotions, and issues that you keep hidden from public view.

It is hard, it is difficult, it takes courage, there will probably be tears ... but it will be so worth the effort.

The "shadow aspect" is the part of your unconscious that represses all the negative aspects of your persona. These shadows are the parts of you that are instinctive and often irrational. They can be projected—taking one of your own personal issues or complexes and turning it so that you see that same issue as a deficiency in someone else.

Not acknowledging your shadow side can cause huge problems to your mental and emotional state and, in the worst-case scenario, can be crippling.

Your shadow can take on a human form in your dreams. Connecting with this form and interacting with it can help shed light on your state of mind. This can also be achieved by connecting and identifying your shadow in meditation or journeying.

The shadow also has many layers. The top outer layer is made up from direct personal experiences. The layers below that are made up from archetypes which form our psyche.

Your shadow personifies everything about you that you do not wish to acknowledge. When you start the journey into shadow work you will become aware of, and sometimes embarrassed or ashamed of, those qualities that you ignore in yourself. But you will notice that you always see them in others.

Sometimes the shadow self can completely overtake a person. Especially when that person is confused, in shock, or paralysed by indecision.

It can be a long process to work with your shadow, and at first you may hit a kind of balance, a sort of standstill. With courage, strength, and support, you can overcome anything. The effort will be worth it. Once you have done the downhill slide, things can only go up!

Shadow work is essentially a healing process. Once you start on the upward spiral, you will be aware of your shadow side and how it works. Understanding your shadow side will help you immensely when you need to deal with situations, emotions, and feelings that you experience. You will know why you feel that way and how to deal with it.

The goal is to be aware and to acknowledge your shadow. This will help you become a better, stronger person and to be at peace with yourself and others. It is, however, an ongoing process. Once started it will continue for your lifetime, but it should get easier.

Where do you start? I am going to include some exercises and meditations here; you don't need to work through them in order, but read through them and see which feels best for you to work with. If you can work with them all, then excellent. If you feel uncomfortable with any of them, then don't do them yet—come back to them later. This journey isn't going to be easy, so prepare for the work to begin…

Work with these tasks in conjunction with the magical exercises provided in this book.

Exercises

Reflection Exercise

The reflection exercise is about looking past your outer shell and seeing who you really are.

Find a pretty cup that you like and a drink to put into it—dark liquids work best. (Think a dark fruit juice or an herbal fruit tea.)

Make yourself comfortable.

Fill your cup half full of the liquid and hold the cup in your hands so that you can see the reflection of your face in the surface.

Once you can see your face, really focus on it—what do you see? Allow your subconscious to make comments.

If you get negative comments at first about wrinkles or bags under your eyes, just acknowledge them and let them go … You need to get past the judgmental stage.

It may take several attempts at this exercise, but you will eventually get to the stage of starting to see the "real" you in that reflection.

When you do get a glimpse of the inner you, acknowledge it and say out loud, "I see someone who …" Then drink from the cup. You are drinking in that positive affirmation; that real part of your "self" is then made whole.

Mirror Exercise

Once you have mastered the Reflection Exercise, try looking at yourself in the mirror. This exercise may take a few tries. I struggle with this one, but it is worth it.

Find a space where you can be alone and undisturbed. You could light a candle, but make sure you have plenty of light to be able to see yourself clearly.

Sit comfortably in front of a mirror large enough to see your whole head, face, and shoulders—or even better, a full-length mirror.

Look past the outer shell and see the real you inside.

Say hello to yourself, talk to yourself, acknowledge those areas of yourself that you aren't so happy with, and release them. Find those areas of your inner self that you are happy with or proud of and give thanks out loud for them.

Meditations

Meditation is a very good "foot in the door" for shadow work.

In the Shadows

This is a simple meditation to see what shadows your mind and soul is hiding. It may reveal all kinds of things you don't want to face right now. Know that you can walk away from the shadows at any time. You don't have to unearth everything all in one go. Take it a step at a time. I would recommend on your first visit you just look around and take note of what is there. Then, when you feel ready, go back in and deal with one item at a time.

Make yourself comfortable, close your eyes, and focus on your breathing... deep breaths in, deep breaths out...

You find yourself outside an old, run-down wood house. Notice what it looks like. Take in all the details: the door, the windows, what they are made of, what colour they are.

Make your way around to the side of the house and then around to the back door. Open it and walk into the kitchen.

Look around you. Take note of everything you see. Tiny things may be important; they may have meaning.

To one side of the kitchen is another door, the door to the cellar, to the basement. You walk toward it and turn the handle...

It opens to reveal a wooden staircase leading down into the dark...

On a shelf just inside the door is a torch. Pick up the torch and use its shining light to guide you as you descend.

Slowly and carefully, you take each step down, one step after another...

You reach the bottom and enter the dark basement. This room holds the aspects of your shadow. Take some time here and see what you can hear, feel, sense, and see. Only look at the parts that you feel ready to take on—you can come back later for the rest.

If you can't see anything, ask what is there for you...

When you have finished, and you are ready to return, slowly make your way back up the staircase, through the kitchen, and out of the back door.

Take some time to come back to this reality...

Open your eyes and wriggle your fingers and toes.

Eat and drink something.

Jot down any thoughts or images that came to mind during your meditation. It can be useful to refer back to them later.

The Rainbow Garden

The rainbow garden meditation will take you down through your layers. As you move through each colour of flower, you will go further. It works with the colours of the rainbow, which are also the colours of our chakras. As you work through each colour, it should lead you down through each layer of your subconscious. The idea is to take you to your inner self. It is a journey. See what you find there!

Make yourself comfortable, close your eyes, and focus on your breathing… deep breaths in, deep breaths out…

As your world around you dissipates, you find yourself in a beautiful landscape on a sunny day with blue skies. You are standing in the middle of a field surrounded by the most glorious grasses and flowers.

You are drawn to a patch of flowers to one side of you. They are casting a brilliant red wave of colour. Take in the red energy, run your hands through the red flowers, pick one, and breathe in the scent. Do you recognise what flowers they are? Look, listen, and allow yourself to be immersed in the passion, strength, and energy of the red flowers. Sit down, lie down, run around—allow yourself to be however you want to be within the red haze.

The flowers are starting to change… slowly at first, then a gush of orange flowers fill the area you are in. A wonderful orange wave of colour. Take in the orange energy, run your hands through the orange flowers, pick one, and breathe in the scent. Do you recognise what flowers they are? Look, listen, and allow yourself to be immersed in the passion, strength, and energy of the orange flowers. Sit down, lie down, run around—allow yourself to be however you want to be within the orange haze.

The flowers are starting to change… slowly at first, then a gush of yellow flowers fill the area you are in. A wonderful yellow wave of colour. Take in the yellow energy, run your hands through the yellow flowers, pick one, and breathe in the scent. Do you recognise what flowers they are? Look, listen, and allow yourself to be immersed in the passion, strength, and energy of the yellow flowers. Sit down, lie down, run around—allow yourself to be however you want to be within the yellow haze.

The flowers are starting to change . . . slowly at first, then a gush of green flowers fill the area you are in. A wonderful green wave of colour. Take in the green energy, run your hands through the green flowers, pick one, and breathe in the scent. Do you recognise what flowers they are? Look, listen, and allow yourself to be immersed in the passion, strength, and energy of the green flowers. Sit down, lie down, run around—allow yourself to be however you want to be within the green haze.

The flowers are starting to change . . . slowly at first, then a gush of blue flowers fill the area you are in. A wonderful blue wave of colour. Take in the blue energy, run your hands through the blue flowers, pick one, and breathe in the scent. Do you recognise what flowers they are? Look, listen, and allow yourself to be immersed in the passion, strength, and energy of the blue flowers. Sit down, lie down, run around—allow yourself to be however you want to be within the blue haze.

The flowers are starting to change . . . slowly at first, then a gush of indigo flowers fill the area you are in. A wonderful indigo wave of colour. Take in the indigo energy, run your hands through the indigo flowers, pick one, and breathe in the scent. Do you recognise what flowers they are? Look, listen, and allow yourself to be immersed in the passion, strength, and energy of the indigo flowers. Sit down, lie down, run around—allow yourself to be however you want to be within the indigo haze.

The flowers are starting to change . . . slowly at first, then a gush of violet flowers fill the area you are in. A wonderful violet wave of colour. Take in the violet energy, run your hands through the violet flowers, pick one, and breathe in the scent. Do you recognise what flowers they are? Look, listen, and allow yourself to be immersed in the passion, strength, and energy of the violet flowers. Sit down, lie down, run around—allow yourself to be however you want to be within the violet haze.

You have finally reached your inner self. See where the flowers lead you now. Do you see any pathways or a guide of any kind? Be guided to where you need to go. Ask any questions you have and listen carefully to the answers. Make note of any gifts you are given.

When you are ready, thank any guides you have met, hold your arms up to the sun, and feel the warmth on your face, then bend and place your hands on the earth and give thanks. Remember you can always return to this place.

Now work your way back through the rainbow of flowers…

Walk through the violet sea of flowers. Allow the colour and energy to wash over you. Breathe in their scent as you move on to the next colour…

Walk through the indigo sea of flowers. Allow the colour and energy to wash over you. Breathe in their scent as you move on to the next colour…

Walk through the blue sea of flowers. Allow the colour and energy to wash over you. Breathe in their scent as you move on to the next colour…

Walk through the green sea of flowers. Allow the colour and energy to wash over you. Breathe in their scent as you move on to the next colour…

Walk through the yellow sea of flowers. Allow the colour and energy to wash over you. Breathe in their scent as you move on to the next colour…

Walk through the orange sea of flowers. Allow the colour and energy to wash over you. Breathe in their scent as you move on to the next colour…

And finally, walk through the red sea of flowers. Allow the colour and energy to wash over you. Breathe in their scent.

Slowly and gently come back to this reality, feeling fresh and energised. Open your eyes and wriggle your fingers and toes.

Eat and drink something.

Jot down any thoughts or images that came to mind during your meditation. It can be useful to refer back to them later.

In the Library

The library meditation helps to deal with specific issues, particularly if they are from the past. You will need to focus on one incident that you feel uncomfortable or emotional about; something that you want to heal to help you move forward.

Make yourself comfortable in a place where you won't be disturbed Close your eyes and focus on your breathing... deep breaths in, deep breaths out...

As your world around you dissipates, you find yourself in the doorway of an old library. It is huge, and the walls are covered from floor to ceiling with wooden shelves packed with books of all shapes, sizes, and colours.

You spend a moment looking around in awe, taking in the sights, sounds, and smells.

Suddenly you feel drawn to explore. See where your intuition takes you.

You reach a bookshelf that is drawing your attention. You stop and scan the shelves until your eye fixes on one of the books. What colour is it? What size? What wording (if any) is on the spine? You take the book down from the shelf. Look at the cover detail. Taking the book with you, you find yourself a chair and sit down.

Open the book. It contains one of the memories or events from your past that you want to deal with. The book tells your story. You don't need to relive the event, just acknowledge that it happened. As you are looking at the book you notice someone walking toward you across the library floor. You look up and realise it is your younger self, the age you were at when the event happened. They walk up and sit down opposite you.

Talk to them. Reassure them that you are now older and wiser and can help and support them to work through the issue. Talk about what happened, why it happened, and release it. Let them know that it is finished with and that they don't need to carry the burden with them any longer. Sit and talk with them.

Once the conversation is done give your younger self a hug and tell them that you love them. As you hug them tightly, the image disappears and you are left feeling full of love and comfort.

Give yourself a moment to absorb what has happened. Then take the book back and place it on the shelf.

You can come back to this library any time you need, to just sit and be or to deal with other issues.

When you feel ready, make your way back to the doorway.

Slowly and gently bring yourself back to this reality. Wriggle your fingers and stamp your toes.

Eat and drink something.

Jot down any thoughts or images that came to mind during your meditation. It can be useful to refer back to them later.

Pull Up a Chair

This meditation is intended to confront (although I dislike the use of that word as it sounds harsh) someone that you have either fallen out with or who you feel has wronged you in some way. It could also be used to deal with your own demons by using the other person as a mirror. You won't actually be summoning the person physical or spiritually. This is purely a representation of how you see them. It helps open your subconscious thoughts about your relationship with them. This is about taking a look at a situation from another angle and getting a different viewpoint. You will be using your subconscious to get the "other side of the story." It will—hopefully—be enlightening.

Make yourself comfortable in a place where you won't be disturbed. Close your eyes and focus on your breathing … deep breaths in, deep breaths out …

As your world around you dissipates, you find yourself sitting in a comfortable armchair beside a large, wooden kitchen table. You look around to find your bearings and see that you are in an old cottage with beams over your head and a warm fire burning in a large fireplace.

In front of you on the table is a large pot of freshly brewed tea with steam coming from the spout. Two teacups and saucers are also laid out, and a tin of homemade cookies is beside them. You pour yourself a cup of tea from the pot. As you stir it, someone enters the room.

You look up and see who it is. It might be a family member, a work colleague, or a friend. It may even be a version of your younger self. It might be a stranger. Whomever it is, you feel safe and comfortable with their presence. They take a seat at the table opposite you and pour themselves a cup of tea.

Talk to them.

If you have a grievance with them personally, get it off your chest. Spill the beans—don't hold back. Tell them everything that you feel. Perhaps they are just there to bounce your own fears back. They may be with you to be used as a sounding board. Whatever it might be, be guided by your intuition and tell them what you feel needs to be said.

Now allow them to respond. They may tell you some hard truths, or they might show you another side of the situation. Let them finish talking.

If you have questions after they have spoken, ask them. Keep talking until you feel done.

Thank them for joining you as they get up and leave.

Take a moment, sip your tea, and eat a cookie (virtual cookies are calorie free). Take on board what they have said and give yourself time to process it.

When you are ready, come back to this reality. Wriggle your fingers and stamp your feet.

Eat and drink something.

Jot down any thoughts or images that came to mind during your meditation. It can be useful to refer back to them later.

PART TWO

MAGICAL
SELF-CARE FOR
SPECIFIC
CONDITIONS

CHAPTER SIX

Anxiety

Having anxiety issues on occasion is quite normal. I offer some magical assistance here. But if it really has started to take over your life, please do go and see your doctor about it. There are psychological therapies available as well as medication options. However, hopefully some of the magic within this book will really help you.

Let's look at what anxiety actually is from a medical viewpoint:[1]

- A feeling of worry, nervousness, or unease about something with an uncertain outcome
- A strong desire or concern to do something or for something to happen
- Feelings of tension and worried thoughts

Symptoms of anxiety can include trouble sleeping or concentrating. Anxiety can bring on bouts of dizziness, sweating, or heart palpitations. It can also make you feel very on edge or irritable. Anxiety can be for a specific reason such as an upcoming exam or interview. But it can also be a constant feeling that takes over your everyday life.

Anxiety is one of those leftover reactions from when humans were chased by animals; it is a fight-or-flight response. Thankfully, we don't often get chased

---

1. Note: Medical descriptions for all the emotional and mental issues were taken from the National Health Service guideline website.

by large animals nowadays, but other modern-day concerns such as work, money, or health can trigger anxiety.

In this chapter you will find magical suggestions to help ease your anxiety. Work with as many of them as you like. Follow your intuition and be guided by it as to what you choose to work with.

Affirmations. Regular positive statements can change the way we think about ourselves and our situations.

Colour Magic. Colour plays an important part in how we feel and can affect our emotions; work with it to boost positive energy.

Herbs. This section will contain my suggestions of herbs to work with in magical spell workings. Pick from my ideas or use your own—be guided by your intuition.

Foods. All foods have magical properties. I have given you some suggestions that can be eaten or used in spell work. I've also included a recipe in each chapter.

Herbal Teas. These can be created with herbs and spices that help alleviate negative issues. Work with my suggestions or use your own.

Incense and Oils. Scents can bring up strong emotions. Work with my suggestions to create incense blends or oil blends to use in ritual or spell work. You can also create these blends just because the scent will lift your mood!

Everyday Exercise. In this section you will find easy daily or regular routines to help get your positive energy flowing and get rid of the negative vibes.

Crystals. They hold such power in tiny, easy-to-handle form. Crystals can be worked with in all sorts of ways to help with all kinds of issues.

Meditation. Read through the script or even record it on your phone. Take some time out and work with the meditation for help and guidance.

Spell. You will find spells to help with any issue. Keep it simple and straightforward. If you don't have the items I have suggested, substitute them with whatever you feel is right. Personalise it; make the spell your own.

Ritual. The rituals included will not be too fancy or complicated. Often, the rituals connect with a deity and the elements to work some magic.

Magic Bundle. In this section you'll find my suggestions for creating a magic bundle to help you through your situation.

Affirmations for Anxiety

I am calm.
I am in control.
I am confident.
I can do this.

Colour Magic for Anxiety

If you saw anxiety as a colour, what colour would you see? This will vary from person to person. For any negative emotion or issue that I want to release, I see black as a good colour to work with. White is also good because it is neutral.

Anxiety seems to me to be more of a mixture of colours, much like a child's messy scribble of dark squiggly lines. Dark purple or very dark blue would also symbolise anxiety for me. Colour can be brought in with pens; used in spell work, flowers, or altar cloths for ritual; or introduced via candle colours in magic—all to rid anxiety.

Herbs to Combat Anxiety

These are for magical use, NOT consumption.

+ Agrimony
+ Cramp bark
+ Hypericum
+ Passionflower
+ Rose
+ Rue
+ Valerian

Foods to Combat Anxiety

These can be used magically and/or eaten.

+ Celery
+ Chamomile
+ Chives
+ Cinnamon
+ Cloves
+ Grapes
+ Green tea
+ Hops
+ Lavender
+ Lemon balm
+ Plums
+ Turmeric

Recipe: Cloves, Cinnamon & Chocolate Cookies

If anything can make you feel better, it is a freshly baked cookie. This recipe contains the magical ingredients cinnamon, cloves, and sultanas—all of which are good for combating anxiety. Oh, and of course they are delicious too, which always helps.

Magic of the Ingredients

+ Butter—antidepression, nurturing, love
+ Chocolate—positive energy, happiness, love
+ Cinnamon—success, healing, power, protection, changes, focus
+ Cloves—love, clarity, protection, repels negativity, stress relief
+ Sugar—to make life sweet!
+ Sultanas—love, happiness

You can charge or bless the ingredients as you add them to the mix or do so once the cookies are made. Hold your hands over them and say:

Chocolate magic, food for me
Help to clear and cleanse my anxiety

Cloves, Cinnamon & Chocolate Cookies
 175 g (6 oz) unsalted butter, softened
 200 g (7 oz) dark muscovado sugar
 75 g (2¾ oz) caster sugar
 ½ teaspoon ground cinnamon
 ¼ teaspoon ground cloves
 1 large egg
 1 egg yolk
 250 g (9 oz) self-rising flour
 175 g (6 oz) chocolate chips
 175 g (6 oz) sultanas

Preheat the oven to 180°C (350°F).

Line two baking trays with baking parchment.

Cream the butter, sugars, and spices together until light and creamy.

Mix in the whole egg and yolk.

Add the flour, chocolate chips, and sultanas and mix to bring the dough together.

Take tablespoonfuls of the mixture and shape into balls. (You should get about 30 from this mixture.) Place the balls on a lined baking tray, leaving enough space between them for the cookies to spread during cooking.

Bake for 12–15 minutes or until the cookies start to colour but are still chewy in the middle.

Transfer to a wire rack to cool.

The cookies will keep in an airtight container for up to a week.

Herbal Teas for Anxiety

These are some herbal teas that can be drunk on their own to help ease anxiety:

 • Chamomile
 • Cinnamon

+ Cloves

+ Green tea

+ Lavender

+ Lemon balm

+ Passionflower

+ Rose

+ Turmeric

Try creating your own blends. Here are some of my favourite combinations.

+ Chamomile can be drunk on its own, but it tastes lovely if you add half a teaspoon of vanilla extract (which also lends its magic)

+ One teaspoon ground cinnamon, three cloves, and one crushed cardamom pod per mug of hot water

+ Lavender tea (two teaspoons of lavender flowers per mug of hot water) can be drunk on its own but also works well if you mix it with chamomile. One teaspoon of each per mug of hot water

+ Pop four cups of water into a saucepan, add one teaspoon of ground turmeric and a pinch of ground black pepper, and simmer for ten minutes. Strain the tea into a cup and add a dash of honey or lemon

+ One teaspoon chamomile, one teaspoon fennel seeds, one teaspoon mint leaves, and half a teaspoon lemon balm per mug of hot water

+ Pop one teaspoon black tea, three cardamom pods, three cloves, half a teaspoon cinnamon, and half a teaspoon ground ginger into a pan with two cups water and simmer for eight to ten minutes. Add a dash of milk (any kind) to serve

+ Simmer two or three slices of root ginger, one stick of cinnamon, one teaspoon honey or agave, and two cups milk (any kind) in a saucepan for eight to ten minutes

Incense and Oil Blends for Anxiety

Any of these can be used in spells, rituals, body care, anointing, cleansing, and more to help ease anxiety. Each one can be used on its own or mixed with others in a blend.

- Agrimony
- Chamomile
- Cinnamon
- Cloves
- Hops
- Lavender
- Lemon balm
- Passionflower
- Rose

Incense Blends

To create this blend, add one part of each of the following: sandalwood, jasmine, pine, chamomile, frankincense resin, frankincense, cloves, and cinnamon.

Essential Oil Blends

- Combine six drops lemon balm, three drops lemon, three drops pine, and two drops bergamot or orange. Use in your bath or on an oil burner/diffuser or mix with a base oil to use on the body.
- Combine three drops frankincense, three drops rose, and two drops geranium. Use in your bath or on an oil burner/diffuser or mix with a base oil to use on the body.

Everyday Exercise for Anxiety

This method works when you don't want to work with a full ritual. Wake early (if it is still dark, even better!) or work this in the evening when the sun has set. Make yourself a hot drink and then sit down in a quiet place. Light some candles around the room and turn the electric lights off. Sit down with your cuppa and just enjoy the candlelight and silence. Quietly and peacefully, sip your drink and focus on breathing deeply and slowly. Inhale calm air and exhale any worries. Sit for as long as you want to. Make sure to snuff out the candle once you're finished.

Crystals for Anxiety

Carry crystals with you, use them in magical spells, or meditate with them. Remember to charge the crystal with your intent before use and cleanse it afterwards. Cleansing suggestions can be found in chapter 3 of this book.

+ **Amber** helps stimulate the brain and nervous system to bring clarity and help release anxiety.

+ **Aventurine** in any colour brings calm energy and helps to release anxiety.

+ **Chrysoprase** opens your heart to positive energy, bringing happy emotions.

+ Use **clear quartz** in meditation to bring about calm, clarity, and balance of emotions.

+ **Green calcite** balances and transforms with the aid of good communication.

+ **Hematite** is grounding and can also bring balance and protection.

+ **Kunzite** bounces in with happy energy to bring emotional healing.

+ **Labradorite** heals, shields, and protects against negative energy.

+ Emotional balance and stability can be gained from working with **moonstone**.

+ **Pyrite** is excellent to help ease anxiety.

+ **Rhodonite** helps dispel the negative energy that causes anxiety.

+ Place a piece of **rose quartz** over your heart to release stress quickly.

+ **Rutilated quartz** heals, repairs, and restores energy.

+ **Tiger's eye** works to find balance and increase the flow of energy together with being very grounding.

+ All colours of **tourmaline** are useful. Black brings protection and grounding, blue is releasing and healing, and green deals with emotional issues.

Meditation for Anxiety

Make yourself comfortable in a place where you won't be disturbed. If you feel drawn to, put on some light music, drumming, or chanting. Light your incense or oil blend if you would like.

As your world around you dissipates, you find yourself on a riverbank. The sky above you is a clear blue and the sun is shining. The warm rays feel glorious on your skin. The air smells fresh and sweet. You can hear birds singing and bees buzzing.

To one side of you is a field with a crop growing happily, edged with wildflowers and plants. On your other side is a wide river that is gurgling and tripping along. The water tumbles lazily over rocks and laps at the side of the bank.

A pair of ducks swim by, quacking to each other, and over on the far side of the bank you see movement and watch as two otters slip quietly into the water. They swim and dive about, playing and having fun above and below the water line.

You sit down on the bank and watch the otters as they seem to perform their antics just for you. They have no worries and not a care in the world. They are playful, fun, and happy.

When you are ready you get up and turn to face the field. Watch as the bees buzz busily in and out of the wildflowers that grow on the edge and in amongst the hedgerow that forms a barrier between the riverbank pathway and the crops.

A tall plant moves slightly in the warm summer breeze. The yellow spikes of a flower catch your eye. You move closer and reach out your hand to touch the plant. The stems are covered with bright buttercup-yellow flowers, so pretty and bright. A butterfly flutters past and lands on your hand so you keep very still. It flaps its wings, showing off the beautiful rainbow colours. Within a moment it is gone, off into the air to the next plant.

You keep your connection with the plant, and you feel the energy it has. The plant wants to make a link with you so you open your mind. The plant tells you it is agrimony and it can help you with whatever you need.

You sit yourself down beside the agrimony flowers and know that it is listening to you. Spend some time telling it your reason for anxiety or anything else you feel drawn to open up about. It listens . . .

When you have finished talking, the plant responds. It gives you guidance and wisdom. Be open to what it tells you . . .

Finishing up, the plant reminds you that you are strong and confident, and you thank it for the advice given.

You stand up and take in your surroundings again. There are more ducks swimming past now, and a pair of swans majestically float by. The otters have moved farther down the river, but you can still hear them splashing about.

Know that you can always return to this place whenever you need to.

Slowly and gently come back to this reality. Wriggle your fingers and toes and open your eyes.

Have something to eat and drink.

Jot down any thoughts or images that came to mind during your meditation. It can be useful to refer back to them later.

Spell to Combat Anxiety

This spell has the purpose of focusing your mind on something relaxing and calming. Just the actions of sitting and focusing on your breathing and working on controlling those anxiety feelings should help. When you follow that with a creative activity, it gives your anxiety an escape route. Channel the anxiety out through creativity. The spell ends with the action of throwing away some of the spell ingredients, which should also aid in letting go.

You will need:

+ Flat dish or tray
+ Sand, soil, or small seeds (sesame work well) to fill the tray
+ Several crystals of your choice (or taken from the list in this book) or a selection of small pebbles or shells
+ Music
+ Incense (optional)

Gather together all your items and find a quiet space where you won't be disturbed. Put some of your favourite music on, preferably something positive and happy. If you have a favourite incense, you can light that too (or use a blend suggested in this book).

You will need to sit comfortably with space in front of you for your items. Place the tray down and fill it with the sand, soil, or seeds and level it out with your hand.

Place your feet flat on the floor and just close your eyes for a moment. Try and focus on your breathing. I appreciate this isn't always easy when you are anxious. Ground yourself using the exercise in this book or your own preferred method.

When you feel as calm as you can be, open your eyes.

Now allow the sound of the music to wash over you. Go past the lyrics and the main tune—delve deeper and find the base notes.

Then allow your intuition to take over and draw patterns in the tray of sand/soil/seeds using your finger(s). Swirls, lines, circles…it doesn't matter what you draw, and it does not need to be a work of art! Let your fingers do the drawing.

Take your crystals, shells, or stones and place them in the tray to add to your creative pattern.

If you feel the need, you can smooth the surface over and start drawing again. Do this as many times as you feel the need to.

Let your anxiety drain out of your body, through your fingers, and into the sand.

When you feel ready, remove the crystals, shells, or stones. (If you used crystals, they will need to be cleansed before being stored to use again.)

The sand, soil, or seeds need to be disposed of. If you have a compost bin, pop it in there. You could throw it on the earth (although be careful where you throw it if you used seeds) or it can be thrown into running water such as a river or ocean. Alternatively, dump it in the trash.

As you dispose of the spell ingredients, say:

Anxiety that overwhelms me is now gone
Anxiety you are not wanted, be done!

Floating Candle Ritual

This is a ritual designed to help alleviate anxiety. I have called upon the goddess Kuan Yin for this ritual as she embodies strength, transformation, and enlightenment. She is also a very compassionate goddess who is happy to help and always willing to listen.

The spell within this ritual incorporates the cleansing, purifying, and soothing element of water. It also combines that with the destructive (in a good way) element of fire, allowing it to burn your anxiety away.

This ritual can be done using the items listed below, or you can sit quietly in your space and just visualise the whole thing.

You will need:

+ Four candles, one for each quarter
+ One central candle
+ Dish big enough to hold your water and the floating candles
+ Jug of water (enough to fill half the bowl)
+ Three floating candles (tea lights)
+ Matches or a lighter
+ Something to eat and drink

Cast your circle. Walk around in a circle deosil (clockwise) or turn around on the spot if you are limited for space. Visualise a soft, glowing light forming a circle around you. When the circle is complete, visualise the light forming above you and below you to form a globe. As you cast the circle, say:

Circle of light
Circle of peace
Circle of protection
Circle this place

Call the quarters. Turn and face each compass direction, starting with the north and working deosil (clockwise). North is earth, east is air, south is fire, and west is water.

Light a candle at each point. As you light each one, say:

Element of earth, bringing stability and grounding
Please join me in this place
Blessings of earth
Element of air, bringing peace and clarity
Please join me in this place
Blessings of air
Element of fire, bringing energy and passion
Please join me in this place
Blessings of fire
Element of water, bringing emotion and calm
Please join me in this place
Blessings of water

As you light the central candle, say:

I call upon the beautiful and wise goddess Kuan Yin
Hear my prayer and bring your compassion
To assist me with this rite
Blessings to you

Set the dish down in front of you and slowly pour the water from the jug into the dish. As you pour, visualise your anxiety washing away. You are the jug and the water is your anxiety. Watch as it transfers from you to the dish.

Once the dish is full, set each tea light on the surface. As you light each one, say:

As the water flows, my anxiety wanes
As the water flows, my anxiety disappears
As the candle flame lights, my anxiety burns away
Make it so!

Once all three candles are lit, take some time to sit and watch. See the water ripples washing away your anxiety. Watch as the flames burn up your anxiety, literally burning it away. See yourself anxiety free, calm, and confident.

Take a sip of your drink, raising your glass to Kuan Yin.

Take a few bites of your food.

When you are ready, snuff out the floating candles.

Then close the ritual. As you snuff out the central candle, say:

My thanks to you, great goddess Kuan Yin
For your compassion and care
Please continue to guide and support me
With blessings and thanks

Snuffing out each quarter candle in turn, starting in the west, work widdershins (counterclockwise) and say:

Element of water
My thanks for lending your energy today
Blessings of water
Element of fire
My thanks for lending your energy today
Blessings of fire
Element of air
My thanks for lending your energy today
Blessings of air
Element of earth
My thanks for lending your energy today
Blessings of earth

Then walk the circle widdershins (counterclockwise) and say:

Circle of light
Circle of peace
Circle of protection
Circle this place
This circle is now open but never broken

Dispose of any candle stubs and pour the water onto the earth. Pour the rest of your drink and crumble some of your food onto the earth as an offering to Kuan Yin.

Bundle for Anxiety

To begin, choose a piece of fabric that makes you feel calm and grounded. You will need a cord or ribbon to tie it with, or you could use a drawstring pouch.

Your anxiety bundle can be filled with anything that you feel drawn to add—with the exception of fresh food or herbs because those would go mouldy! You could add crystals, dried herbs, seeds, dried leaves, twigs, dried flower petals, small tokens, beads, buttons, coins, small ornaments, etc. Trust your intuition.

Sit quietly or meditate to decide which things to add. Reach out to a deity such as Kuan Yin and ask what needs to go in. It might only be one or two items at first—you can add to it over time.

Each item is representative of your journey to remove your anxiety. Charge each item individually before you pop it in the pouch. Hold each one in your hand and visualise positive energy entering it, bringing calm, peace, and protection from anxiety.

Here are my suggestions:

+ Chamomile (this could be a tea bag)
+ Lavender
+ Rose petals (white ones for peace)
+ Cinnamon stick
+ Cloves
+ Piece of rose quartz
+ Piece of hematite
+ Pebble to keep you grounded
+ Small photo of yourself where you are happy and content

Keep the bundle on your altar or somewhere that you will see it. Use it when you meditate, either holding it on your lap or opening it up and handling each item in turn. You can also reach for it when you feel anxious. Draw upon the energy within to fill your mind and spirit with calming and peaceful energy.

The modern world is fast-paced and hectic. It can throw all kinds of challenges our way, ones that can easily set off anxiety.

Learn what your triggers are. Learn the best way for you personally to prevent anxiety from overtaking you, and learn how to deal with any fallout.

If you find yourself feeling more anxious than usual, refer back to this chapter for magical suggestions that might help.

CHAPTER SEVEN

Stress

Stress is described as a state of mental or emotional strain brought about by difficult circumstances. It is our body's response to life events or situations. It might be a result of an unexpected event, a threat, or a feeling that you are in a situation you cannot control. The feeling of being overwhelmed and under pressure takes over.

If spread over a long period of time, stress can be incredibly wearing and quite exhausting. It can affect your emotions, bringing on regular and uncontrollable feelings of anger, frustration, or sadness. Your behaviour may be affected, causing a lack of decision-making capabilities, a fuzzy memory, and withdrawing into yourself.

In extreme cases stress can affect your physical health too. It can cause headaches and nausea. You may also suffer from shortness of breath, aches, and palpitations. Extreme and prolonged stress has been linked to digestive disorders such as irritable bowel syndrome and stomach ulcers. Having been diagnosed with a bowel disease at sixteen, I lived with it for many years before I realised that an attack often occurred shortly after I had experienced a stressful situation.

In this chapter you will find magical suggestions to help ease stress. Work with as many of them as you like. Follow your intuition and be guided by it as to what you choose to work with.

Affirmations. Regular positive statements can change the way we think about ourselves and our situations.

Colour Magic. Colour plays an important part in how we feel and can affect our emotions; work with it to boost positive energy.

Herbs. This section will contain my suggestions of herbs to work with in magical spell workings. Pick from my ideas or use your own—be guided by your intuition.

Foods. All foods have magical properties. I have given you some suggestions that can be eaten or used in spell work. I've also included a recipe in each chapter.

Herbal Teas. These can be created with herbs and spices that help alleviate negative issues. Work with my suggestions or use your own.

Incense and Oils. Scents can bring up strong emotions. Work with my suggestions to create incense blends or oil blends to use in ritual or spell work. You can also create these blends just because the scent will lift your mood!

Everyday Exercise. In this section you will find easy daily or regular routines to help get your positive energy flowing and get rid of the negative vibes.

Crystals. They hold such power in tiny, easy-to-handle form. Crystals can be worked with in all sorts of ways to help with all kinds of issues.

Meditation. Read through the script or even record it on your phone. Take some time out and work with the meditation for help and guidance.

Spell. You will find spells to help with any issue. Keep it simple and straightforward. If you don't have the items I have suggested, substitute them with whatever you feel is right. Personalise it; make the spell your own.

Ritual. The rituals included will not be too fancy or complicated. Often, the rituals connect with a deity and the elements to work some magic.

Magic Bundle. In this section you'll find my suggestions for creating a magic bundle to help you through your situation.

Affirmations for Stress

I have the necessary tools to deal with any situation.
I will be calm and organised.
I can deal with this.
I am calm and focused.

Colour Magic for Stress

If you saw stress as a colour, what colour would you see? This will vary from person to person. For any negative emotion or issue that I want to release, I see black as a good colour to work with. White is also good because it is neutral.

For me, the colour of stress is loud and brash: lots of manic colours that make your head hurt and your eyes go funny. Fluorescent maybe? Busy, in your face, and hectic colours. I would counter them with gentle pastel shades—something that is calming and soothing.

Herbs to Combat Stress

These are for magical use, NOT consumption.

+ Alyssum
+ Betony
+ Cramp bark
+ Passionflower
+ Pulsatilla
+ Self-heal
+ Skull cap
+ Valerian

Foods to Combat Stress

These can be used magically and/or eaten.

+ Basil
+ Black tea
+ Blueberries
+ Chamomile
+ Chocolate (dark)

+ Cloves

+ Green tea

+ Lavender

+ Lemon balm

+ Milk

+ Mint

+ Rhubarb

· Salt

+ Yogurt

Recipe: Chocolate Bark

I love making chocolate bark. It is very simple and can be adapted with all sorts of flavours. Chocolate can really help to soothe your nerves, calm you down, and make you feel better. It is an edible hug.

Magic of the Ingredients

+ Chocolate—positive energy, happiness, love

You can charge or bless the ingredients as you add them to the mix or do so once the chocolate bark is made. Hold your hands over them and say:

With the magic love and energy of chocolate
May my stress become much less

Chocolate Bark

+ Chocolate (your favourite kind)

+ Toppings of your choosing, such as:

  + Chopped marshmallows

  + Pieces of fudge

  + Chocolate chips

  + Crushed-up mini chocolate eggs

  + Chopped nuts

  + Dried fruit

- Small pieces of fudge brownie
- Any kind of sweets or candy bars chopped up
- Shredded coconut
- Candied citrus peel
- Any kind of boiled sweet chopped up and sprinkled on top is good (albeit very crunchy)

To start with, you will need a tray lined with baking parchment.

Take your base chocolate and melt it either carefully in the microwave or in a bowl over a pan of simmering water. Your base chocolate can be dark, milk, or white, or even all of them swirled together! (I've included no weights here because you can make as much or as little as you like, but try a large bar.)

Pour the melted chocolate over the baking parchment, spreading it into an even layer. (It doesn't need to be perfectly square.)

Immediately sprinkle your toppings over the melted chocolate, giving them a little press so that they sink into the chocolate base. I like to drizzle some more melted chocolate over the top.

Pop in the fridge to set. Depending on your fridge settings, it shouldn't take long to set—an hour or so will be fine.

Peel off the baking parchment. Chop or break the chocolate into pieces. Enjoy!

Recipe: Fabulous Hot Chocolate

There isn't anything better to calm you down and give you that "ahhhh" moment than a big, steaming, hot mug of hot chocolate.

The simplest way to make hot chocolate is to take a mug of hot milk (any kind), drop a couple of squares of chocolate in, and stir until melted. Add a pinch of cinnamon to spice it up and you are set.

If you want to make a really sumptuous hot chocolate, this is the go-to recipe in our house. We make a big batch of the powder mix and keep it in an airtight jar so that it's all ready when we need it.

Magic of the Ingredients
- ✦ Chocolate—positive energy, happiness, love
- ✦ Malted milk powder—feminine power, goddess energy, moon magic, nurturing, love, spirituality
- ✦ Sugar—to make life sweet!

You can charge or bless the ingredients as you add them to the mix or do so once the hot chocolate is made. Hold your hands over them and say:

Magic chocolate, hot and sweet
Relax and calm me, head to feet

Fabulous Hot Chocolate
100 g (3½ oz) plain dark chocolate

100 g (3½ oz) cocoa powder

100 g (3½ oz) icing (confectioners) sugar

50 g (1¾ oz) cornflour

50 g (1¾ oz) malted milk drink powder (Horlicks, Ovaltine, etc.)

Pinch of salt

1 teaspoon ground cinnamon

Grate the chocolate and mix it together with all the other dry ingredients. This can then be stored in an airtight jar.

When you want to make a mug of hot chocolate, mix two teaspoons of the dry ingredient mix with a little milk to make a paste.

Add a mug of milk and pop it all into a saucepan.

Simmer for five minutes, whisking regularly, until it thickens a little. Then drink!

In my family, we like to add double the amount of powder to the milk (four teaspoons to one mug of milk) and eat it with a spoon like hot chocolate custard.

Herbal Teas for Stress

Part of drinking herbal tea for stress is to stop and take a moment to sit quietly and drink the tea slowly. Just the actual effect of sitting and drinking "frozen" in time will really help ease stressful emotions.

These are some herbal teas that can be drunk on their own to help ease stress:

- Basil
- Black tea
- Chamomile
- Cloves
- Green tea
- Lavender
- Lemon balm
- Milk
- Mint
- Passionflower

Try creating your own blends. Here are some of my favourite combinations:

- Two teaspoons of lavender flowers and two slices of fresh orange per mug of hot water
- Juice of half a lemon, a couple of lemon slices, a slice of root ginger, and one teaspoon of honey per mug of hot water
- One teaspoon chamomile, one teaspoon lemon balm, and a slice of root ginger to a mug of hot water
- Both green tea and chamomile work fine on their own to help de-stress, but you can change it up by adding slices of lemon or orange to perk up the flavour
- A twist on the classic chai latte is created by using chamomile tea rather than black tea leaves
- Pop one tablespoon chamomile tea leaves (or a chamomile tea bag), three cloves, one teaspoon vanilla extract, and one teaspoon ground

cinnamon into a pan with a mug of milk (any kind). Simmer gently for five to eight minutes. Strain and drink

Incense and Oil Blends for Stress

Any of these can be used in spells, rituals, body care, anointing, cleansing, and more to help you de-stress. Each one can be used on its own or mixed with others in a blend.

+ Bergamot
+ Chamomile
+ Lavender
+ Rose
+ Vetiver
+ Ylang ylang

Incense Blends

+ Equal parts lavender flowers, frankincense resin, and dried orange peel
+ Equal parts chamomile, lavender flowers, copal resin, and a few drops of ylang ylang oil
+ Equal parts sandalwood, pine, and lemongrass
+ Equal parts chamomile, jasmine, and pine
+ Equal parts lavender flowers, jasmine, and sandalwood

Essential Oil Blends

+ Combine five drops vetiver and seven drops sandalwood. Use in your bath or on an oil burner/diffuser or mix with base oil to use on the body.
+ Combine six drops ylang ylang and six drops chamomile. Use in your bath or on an oil burner/diffuser or mix with base oil to use on the body.
+ Combine six drops lavender and two drops peppermint. Use in your bath or on an oil burner/diffuser or mix with base oil to use on the body.

+ Combine six drops lavender and four drops chamomile. Use in your bath or on an oil burner/diffuser or mix with base oil to use on the body.

Everyday Exercise for Stress

Life is ridiculously busy most of the time, and rushing around just adds to the stress of the day. However, if you can fit a little morning ritual in before you start the day, it can really help to set you off on the right foot. I have been guilty of rushing out the door without having eaten breakfast or grabbing a cereal bar to eat as I rush to the car. Aside from not being very good or kind to your body, this sets the tone for the day: missing out on important things and being overwhelmed and rushed. If you can fit a ritual like this into your morning, do it.

Sit down at a table to eat your breakfast. Make yourself a nice pot of tea or a pot of coffee: not just a quick throw-a-tea-bag-into-a-cup kinda beverage but nice tea leaves in a pot or fresh coffee in a percolator. And eat something! Grab a slice of toast or make a bowl of porridge. (Also see the recipe for Porridge Any "Witch" Way in chapter 9. These oats are brilliant and easy to make.) Sit down, drink, and eat. Take a moment to breathe and to sort through your to-do list in your head before you race out the door. This is a quiet "prepare yourself for the day" moment. You may have to get up a teeny bit earlier to fit it in. Honestly, you will feel so much better for it.

Crystals for Stress

Carry crystals with you, use them in magical spells, or meditate with them. Remember to charge the crystal with your intent before use and cleanse it afterwards. Cleansing suggestions can be found in chapter 3 of this book.

+ **Amber** works as a generator of energy and can be useful to improve the nervous system, bringing clarity and focus.
+ **Amethyst** brings clarity, calm, and balance of the mind and emotions. It is also an excellent stone to meditate with.
+ **Aquamarine** has a cleansing energy to help release and clear out unwanted negative vibes.
+ Green **aventurine** is soothing and brings cleansing and releasing.

+ **Azurite** is a transformation stone and has the ability to release stress quickly.

+ **Carnelian** has the ability to encourage healing and helps to release stress and imbalance.

+ The happy yellow colour of **citrine** makes it perfect to work with to release stress and tension from the body. It is warm and comforting but also carries a strong energy to transform.

+ **Labradorite** works with negative energy, turning it around to positive energy.

+ **Lapis lazuli** works with balance and accessing really deep levels to remove stress.

+ Work with **moonstone** to bring emotional stability and calmness. It helps quickly release stress.

+ **Obsidian** works with emotions on a deep level, helping to release, transform, and change.

+ **Rhodonite** balances the heart, sorting out your emotions in the process. It also has stabilising and grounding properties.

+ **Rose quartz** soothes and understands, releasing stress quickly.

+ Use **selenite** to bring about relaxation and ease stress and tension in the body.

Meditation for Stress

Make yourself comfortable in a place where you won't be disturbed. If you feel drawn to, put on some light music, drumming, or chanting. Light your incense or oil blend if you would like.

As your world around you dissipates, you find yourself standing with your feet in soft, warm sand on the edge of ocean. The sky is blue and the sun is warm on your skin. The waves are crashing gently on the golden-yellow sandy shore. Above you seagulls fly, squawking messages loudly to each other.

You take several deep breaths in and out, relishing in the fresh, salty sea air. Listen to the sounds around you. What do you hear?

You turn around in a circle, looking at the scenery and taking in all that surrounds you.

To one side you notice a grass bank, so you make your way across the soft sand toward it. When you reach the green grass, you sit down and make yourself comfortable. As you sit a beautiful scent wafts up on the sea air. Looking at the grass beneath you, you notice that it isn't the usual grass you are familiar with. You run your hand over the foliage and the scent hits you again. Looking more closely you also see small, white, daisy-like flowers. You wonder what type of plant it is, and the name "chamomile" floats into your head.

You are drawn now to lie down on the chamomile grass. Resting your head gently, you breathe in the gorgeous scent and allow the magic of chamomile to permeate through your body. You can feel it soothing and calming every fibre of your being. Take some time and allow the scent of chamomile to wash over you.

As you lie still, listen carefully to the ocean waves as they lap and crash gently and calmly onto the beach. The sound combined with the scent of the chamomile creates a soothing and calming medicine for all your senses.

Questions might pop into your head. Allow them to and then listen carefully for the answers or any guidance that is forthcoming. Whether it is from the wisdom of the ocean or from the medicine of chamomile, pay attention to the words.

When you have the answers that you need (they might not necessarily be what you wanted to hear, but pay heed to them) you ease yourself up into a sitting position. It is then that you notice a large gull sitting in front of you, watching patiently.

He squawks at you and you realise he is asking if you have any need for his counsel. Talk to him and listen to what he has to say…

Once your conversation is finished, he spreads his wings wide and takes off into the air.

You stand yourself up and walk back down to the shoreline. As you do you notice something on the ground. Pick it up and take a look. This is a gift for you, and it has meaning.

Take a last look around at your surroundings. Know that you can come back to this place any time.

When you are ready, come back to this reality. Wriggle your fingers and toes and slowly open your eyes.

Eat and drink something and make notes of any guidance you were given. Think about what you've just experienced. Maybe do some research about the gift you were given.

Jot down any thoughts or images that came to mind during your meditation. It can be useful to refer back to them later.

Spell to Combat Stress

For any spell that works with de-stressing I like to start with the cause of the stress and remove that first. Then, because negative energy just loves a void, I make sure to bring in something positive as well. This spell brings balance into play a little bit. It also involves burning stuff, which is always very satisfying.

You will need:

- One black candle
- One white candle
- Two pieces of paper
- Fireproof dish/cauldron
- Matches or a lighter
- Pen
- Herb to signify banishing stress, such as cloves
- Herb to signify positive energy, such as lemon balm

First we must focus on getting rid of the stress in your life. Light your black candle and take a sheet of paper and write down everything that is causing you stress. Be specific and detailed.

Once you have finished writing, take a pinch of your banishing herbs (e.g., cloves) and pop them in the middle of your sheet of writing. Then fold the paper around the herbs. Make the folds away from you so that you send the energy away. Turn the paper counterclockwise each time so that you continue to fold away from your body. As you fold say a chant such as:

With each fold I banish stress
With each turn I get rid of this mess
Stress and worry now be gone
With this spell my stress is done

Once you have a little package of paper and herbs, light it from the black candle and drop it into your dish/cauldron to burn. It is easier to hold the package with a pair of tongs over the flame—just be careful not to burn yourself! Please also be mindful that smoke can set off fire alarms.

Leave the package in the dish to burn away whilst you turn your focus to the good stuff.

Now light the white candle and take your second sheet of paper. Write down all that is good in your life and include positive things that you would like to replace the stress with. Be specific and detailed.

When you are finished writing, sprinkle some of the positive-energy herbs (e.g., lemon balm) into the centre of your writing. Then fold the paper around the herbs. This time make sure you fold the paper toward you. Turn it clockwise each time so that you continue to fold toward you, bringing the good energy in. As you fold say a chant such as:

Positive energy come to me
Now from stress I am free
Good vibes and luck to come my way
Happiness will be with me from this day

Once you have your little package of herbs, light it from the white candle and drop it into your dish/cauldron to burn.

Leave the package in the dish to burn and take a few moments to visualise all the stress leaving your life and being replaced with positive and happy energy. See your life as you wish it to be.

Then snuff out both of the candles. Take the ashes from the dish and sprinkle them in the wind or dump them onto the soil.

Send thanks out to the universe or up to the moon or the sun.

Witch Bottle Ritual

This is a ritual to help you release any stress. I suggest calling upon the Celtic goddess Cerridwen for this ritual as she is excellent to work with for healing and transformation. Her cauldron is also representative of transformation and rebirth.

The spell within this ritual is to create your own "cauldron" of magic to help alleviate stress. It utilises witch bottle magic. Use whichever bottle or jar you have that you think suits your needs. I have given ideas for contents of your witch bottle, but it is yours and should be very personal to you. Trust your intuition about what needs to go inside.

This ritual can be done using the items listed below, or you can sit quietly in your space and just visualise the whole thing.

You will need:

+ Small dish of salt
+ Small dish of soil
+ Incense
+ Small dish of water
+ One central candle to represent the goddess Cerridwen
+ Matches or a lighter
+ Clean jam jar with a lid
+ Items to fill a witch bottle such as dried rice, flour, nails, pebbles from your garden, leaves, piece of string, or dried herbs (I like to use basil, chamomile, and lavender)
+ Something to eat and drink

During this ritual we will create a witch jar/bottle. A witch bottle provides protection and is essentially filled with ingredients that soak up any negative energy within your room or household. Use a base ingredient that soaks up liquid such as dried rice, split peas, oats, lentils, or flour. (I save any out-of-date ingredients found at the back of the kitchen cupboard for this.) Then add in a couple of nails to bring protection. Leaves and pebbles from your garden make it personal to your property. A cobweb from your house is also good to add because let's face it: we all have them! Add dried herbs of your choosing, making sure to include herbs that remove negative energy and others that bring in positive. Go with what you have in your kitchen cupboard and follow your intuition. A piece of string is also used to tie in the intent.

Before you start, place a small dish of soil in the north, place the incense in the east, light a candle in the south, and pop a small dish of water in the west.

Cast your circle. Walk around in a circle deosil (clockwise) or turn around on the spot if you are limited for space. Visualise a soft, glowing light forming a circle around you. When the circle is complete, visualise the light forming above you and below you to form a globe. As you cast the circle, say:

> Circle of light
> Circle of peace
> Circle of protection
> Circle this place

Call the quarters. Turn and face each compass direction, starting with the north and working deosil (clockwise). North is earth, east is air, south is fire, and west is water. As you face each one, say:

> Element of earth, bringing stability and grounding
> Please join me in this place
> Blessings of earth
> Element of air, bringing peace and clarity
> Please join me in this place
> Blessings of air
> Element of fire, bringing energy and passion
> Please join me in this place
> Blessings of fire
> Element of water, bringing emotion and calm
> Please join me in this place
> Blessings of water

Lighting the central candle, say:

> I call upon the strong and compassionate goddess Cerridwen
> And ask that you bring your strength, guidance, and courage

To assist me with this rite
Blessings to you

Now get your witch bottle items out in front of you. Take the jar and hold it up. Ask Cerridwen to give her blessing to your "cauldron."

Then take each ingredient and charge it with the intent of dispelling negative energy, de-stressing you and your household and bringing in protection. After charging, add each item to the jar. Take the piece of string and tie three knots in it, saying:

With this first knot I rid myself of stress
With this second knot I dispel stress from my life
With this third knot I seal the deal

Pop the string into the jar and top with other ingredients until the jar is full. Screw the lid on and hold the jar in both hands, saying:

With this witch jar held by me
I remove all stress and negativity
So mote it be!

Take a sip of your drink, raising your glass to Cerridwen.
Take a few bites of your food.
Then close the ritual. Face the centre and hold your arms wide, saying:

My thanks to you, great goddess Cerridwen
For your strength, courage, and wisdom
Please continue to guide and support me
With blessings and thanks

Face each direction in turn, starting with the west. Work widdershins (counterclockwise) and say:

Element of water
My thanks for lending your energy today
Blessings of water
Element of fire
My thanks for lending your energy today

Blessings of fire
Element of air
My thanks for lending your energy today
Blessings of air
Element of earth
My thanks for lending your energy today
Blessings of earth

Then walk the circle widdershins (counterclockwise) and say:

Circle of light
Circle of peace
Circle of protection
Circle this place
This circle is now open but never broken

Pour the water onto the earth. Pour the rest of your drink and crumble some of your food onto the earth as an offering to Cerridwen. Snuff out the central candle.

The witch bottle should be placed in the centre of your home (tucked away somewhere is fine). I have one in my kitchen and one behind the sofa in the living room.

The jar will need emptying and refilling on occasion. I tip the contents into the trash and wash the jar out. I then cleanse it with incense smoke and refill with fresh ingredients. You will know when it needs redoing; the energy in the room or house will change.

Bundle for Stress

To begin, choose a piece of fabric that makes you feel calm and grounded. You will need a cord or ribbon to tie it with, or you could use a drawstring pouch.

Your stress bundle can be filled with anything that you feel drawn to add—with the exception of fresh food or herbs because those would go mouldy! You could add crystals, dried herbs, seeds, dried leaves, twigs, dried flower petals, small tokens, beads, buttons, coins, small ornaments, etc. Trust your intuition.

Sit quietly or meditate to decide which things to add. Reach out to a deity such as Cerridwen and ask what needs to go in. It might only be one or two items at first—you can add to it over time.

Each item is representative of your journey to remove the stress from your life. Charge each item individually before you pop it in the pouch. Hold each one in your hand and visualise positive energy entering it, bringing calm, peace, and protection and relieving you from stress.

Here are my suggestions:

- A smooth pebble (this reminds you to stay grounded; find one that feels smooth and nice to the touch so that, if you need to, you can hold it in your hand to de-stress)
- Something from your childhood that makes you smile (perhaps a photo of yourself or a small piece of a cuddle cloth you had)
- Your favourite sweets (choose something that reminds you of your inner child)
- Piece of amethyst
- Some dried lavender flowers
- A few cloves

Keep the bundle on your altar or somewhere that you will see it. Use it when you meditate, either holding it on your lap or opening it up and handling each item in turn. You can also reach for it when you feel stressed. Draw upon the energy within to fill your mind and spirit with calming and peaceful energy.

I do believe stress is quite a modern issue. We have to deal with a huge amount of overwhelming pressure at work, at home, as parents, in relationships, basically just as human beings. Everyone has high expectations and standards.

Learn and understand that you can only be the best you can. Ignore others and their way of thinking.

If you find yourself feeling more stressed than usual, refer back to this chapter for magical suggestions that might help.

CHAPTER EIGHT

Depression

Living with depression is like living under your own little black rain cloud. Depression is described as being in severe despondency and dejection. When you think of depression, you may think of words like misery, unhappiness, sorry, gloom, despair, etc.

Like most emotional issues, depression can range from mild to severe and can come and go without warning. One of the most common symptoms of depression is fatigue, but symptoms are different for everyone. You might feel sad or not be interested in usual events and projects. You may lose your appetite or have trouble sleeping. You may experience lack of concentration or have difficulty making decisions. In very severe cases, depression may cause a person to think about taking their own life. Please do seek medical assistance if you think you are suffering from depression—help is out there. Medication and psychotherapy can be very effective treatments for depression.

In this chapter you will find magical suggestions to help ease depression. Work with as many of them as you like. Follow your intuition and be guided by it as to what you choose to work with.

Affirmations. Regular positive statements can change the way we think about ourselves and our situations.

Colour Magic. Colour plays an important part in how we feel and can affect our emotions; work with it to boost positive energy.

Herbs. This section will contain my suggestions of herbs to work with in magical spell workings. Pick from my ideas or use your own—be guided by your intuition.

Foods. All foods have magical properties. I have given you some suggestions that can be eaten or used in spell work. I've also included a recipe in each chapter.

Herbal Teas. These can be created with herbs and spices that help alleviate negative issues. Work with my suggestions or use your own.

Incense and Oils. Scents can bring up strong emotions. Work with my suggestions to create incense blends or oil blends to use in ritual or spell work. You can also create these blends just because the scent will lift your mood!

Everyday Exercise. In this section you will find easy daily or regular routines to help get your positive energy flowing and get rid of the negative vibes.

Crystals. They hold such power in tiny, easy-to-handle form. Crystals can be worked with in all sorts of ways to help with all kinds of issues.

Meditation. Read through the script or even record it on your phone. Take some time out and work with the meditation for help and guidance.

Spell. You will find spells to help with any issue. Keep it simple and straightforward. If you don't have the items I have suggested, substitute them with whatever you feel is right. Personalise it; make the spell your own.

Ritual. The rituals included will not be too fancy or complicated. Often, the rituals connect with a deity and the elements to work some magic.

Magic Bundle. In this section you'll find my suggestions for creating a magic bundle to help you through your situation.

Affirmations for Depression

Life is precious. I will make the most of every moment.
I am strong and confident.

I've got this!
My life is important. I am important.
I am in control of my life and I will make it count.

Colour Magic for Depression

If you saw depression as a colour, what colour would you see? This will vary from person to person. For any negative emotion or issue that I want to release, I see black as a good colour to work with. White is also good because it is neutral.

For me, depression is dark: blacks, browns, sludgy greens. Kind of deep, dark "into the forest" colours. It is also messy, scribbly harsh lines drawn in a haphazard manner. The colours of depression are definitely not bright, sun-shiny yellows.

Herbs to Combat Depression

These are for magical use, NOT consumption.

- Agrimony
- Bergamot
- Betony
- Celandine
- Cyclamen
- Hyacinth
- Hypericum
- Passionflower
- Rose
- Sweet pea
- Valerian
- Yarrow

Foods to Combat Depression

These can be used magically and/or eaten.

- Basil
- Cardamom

+ Chamomile

+ Garlic

+ Grapefruit

+ Lavender

+ Lemon

+ Lemon balm

+ Marjoram

+ Mustard

+ Orange

+ Rosemary

+ Saffron

+ Thyme

+ Turmeric

+ Yogurt

Recipe: Cheese and Rosemary Muffins

These are delicious and can really lift your spirits.

Magic of the Ingredients

+ Margarine, milk, and cheese—antidepression, nurturing, love

+ Mustard—clarity, protection, faith, success

+ Rosemary—protection, love, purification, healing

You can charge or bless the ingredients as you add them to the mix or do so once the muffins are made. Hold your hands over them and say:

Muffins of cheese and rosemary
Lift my spirits and set me free

Cheese and Rosemary Muffins

225 g (8 oz) margarine

250 g (9 oz) plain all-purpose flour

1 teaspoon salt

1 teaspoon chopped rosemary

1 teaspoon mustard

3 teaspoons baking powder

225 g (8 oz) grated cheese (strong cheddar works well)

2 eggs

230 mL (8 fl oz) milk

Extra grated cheese

Preheat the oven to 200°C (400°F).

In a large bowl, add the flour, salt, rosemary, mustard, and baking powder. Mix in the margarine, then add the cheese.

Beat eggs with milk. Mix into the flour mixture.

Grease a twelve-hole muffin tin and divide the mixture equally into the tin.

Sprinkle extra cheese on the top of the muffins. (Don't miss this step; it is what makes them extra yummy!)

Bake for 20 minutes.

Herbal Teas for Depression

These are some herbal teas that can be drunk on their own to help ease depression:

- Basil
- Cardamom
- Chamomile
- Grapefruit
- Lavender
- Lemon
- Lemon balm
- Marjoram
- Orange
- Passionflower

+ Rose
+ Rosemary
+ Thyme
+ Turmeric

Try creating your own blends. Here are some of my favourite combinations:

- One teaspoon dried passionflower, one teaspoon lavender, and a slice of lemon per mug of hot water
- Black tea with a slice of lemon
- Two cardamom pods, one teaspoon turmeric, and a spoonful of honey or agave per mug of hot water
- One teaspoon dried lemon balm, a slice of lemon, and a slice of orange per mug of hot water
- One teaspoon dried rosemary and a slice of orange per mug of hot water
- One teaspoon dried lavender, one teaspoon dried lemon balm, and a few rose petals per mug of hot water

Incense and Oil Blends for Depression

Any of these can be used in spells, rituals, body care, anointing, cleansing, and more to help with your depression. Each one can be used on its own or mixed with others in a blend.

+ Agrimony
+ Basil
+ Bergamot
+ Cardamom
+ Chamomile
+ Grapefruit
+ Hyacinth
+ Lavender
+ Lemon
+ Lemon balm

+ Marjoram

+ Orange

+ Passionflower

+ Rose

+ Rosemary

+ Sweet pea

+ Thyme

+ Valerian

+ Yarrow

Incense Blends

+ Equal parts frankincense, rosemary, and cardamom
+ Equal parts dried orange peel, lemon peel, grapefruit peel, and rose
+ One part frankincense, two parts orange, two parts rosemary
+ One part frankincense, two parts lemon, two parts lavender

Essential Oil Blends

+ Combine six drops of each: lavender, rose, and lemon. Use in your bath or on an oil burner/diffuser or mix with a base oil to use on the body.
+ Combine six drops lemon, six drops orange, and four drops rosemary. Use in your bath or on an oil burner/diffuser or mix with a base oil to use on the body.
+ Combine four drops basil, six drops grapefruit, and four drops orange. Use in your bath or on an oil burner/diffuser or mix with a base oil to use on the body.
+ Combine two drops cardamom, six drops bergamot, and six drops rose. Use in your bath or on an oil burner/diffuser or mix with a base oil to use on the body.

Everyday Exercise for Depression

The burning of herbs for psychic and spiritual cleansing is found in many religions. You may be most familiar with the term *smudging*, which refers to the

Native American practice. Generally, you smudge by burning herbs and waving the smoke through the aura to cleanse the energy field of a person, object, or room.

The theory behind this type of cleansing is that the smoke attaches itself to the negative energy and as it clears, it takes the negative energy with it. It is a good idea to perform this ritual on yourself on a regular basis as well as your home and workspace. Make it part of your weekly housework. After you've dusted and vacuumed, smudge your home and yourself with an incense of your choice.

Many indigenous peoples of the Americas used sage, sweetgrass, or cedar to make a smudge bundle, but you can use whatever you have on hand. (Please don't import dried herbs from across the globe. Use an herb or plant that grows locally to you. A local herb will have more personal energy and will also be more eco-friendly.) I use whatever I have in the garden, which is often sage, lavender, and rosemary. You can make your own bundle by cutting stems of the plants, tying them together with wool or twine, and leaving them to dry. Once dried, it is ready to use.

Light one end of the bundle and then blow out the flame so it is just smouldering. It is wise to hold the bundle over a bowl to catch any bits that may fall off—this may just save you from burning holes in the carpet. You can guide the smoke over yourself by using a feather or your hands (whichever you prefer). Bring the smoke up over your head, down your shoulders and your arms, around your torso and your back, down your legs, and end with your feet. Don't forget to do the soles of your feet to ensure that you walk on the right path. Visualise the smoke lifting away all the negative energies, thoughts, and emotions that have attached themselves to you.

When you are smudging your house, make sure the smoke gets in all the corners and around the windows and doors. If you want to be really thorough, you can waft smoke in all the cupboards and drawers too.

When you have finished, put out your herb bundle using a bowl of sand or earth. Make sure the herb stick is completely extinguished before leaving it unattended.

If you are like me, you will find the herb bundle a bit awkward to use sometimes. That's when you can use loose herbs on a charcoal block or, for even more convenience, a shop-bought incense stick. Both of these options will do the job just as well. It is your intention and the smoke that is important.

If you can't stand the smoke, try smudging with an oil burner or scented candles. You can also pop loose incense on an oil burner, allowing the burner to just warm the mix without the smoke. If you can't work with smoke or scent, perform the same ritual but use salt or saltwater.

Crystals for Depression

Carry crystals with you, use them in magical spells, or meditate with them. Remember to charge the crystal with your intent before use and cleanse it afterwards. Cleansing suggestions can be found in chapter 3 of this book.

- **Amber** is a good crystal to work with to help alleviate depression as it stimulates brain functions.
- Green **apatite** connects with the heart to bring balance to the emotions and helps overcome difficulties.
- **Carnelian** heals and warms while releasing energy to bring about a balance.
- **Hematite** can be used to bring you back to earth, to ground you, and to find a level of stability.
- **Kunzite** is full of positive, happy energy, allowing you to let down your barriers so the good stuff can flow in.
- **Lapis lazuli** is all about balance and can help remove old, deep layers of junk that can drag us down.
- **Lepidolite** stabilises your moods and emotions, bringing calming energy in.
- **Moss agate** balances emotions and energy. It also aligns with the heart to set you free.
- Work with **pyrite** to help ease depression as it brings about balance and helps release negative energy.
- The patterns within **rutilated quartz** help bring about repair for the body and spirit along with encouraging a positive flow of energy.
- **Smoky quartz** is grounding and calming and helps focus your energy.

+ **Sunstone** is packed full of emotional strength and stability.
+ **Tiger's eye** brings a balancing energy with a flow of happiness.

Meditation for Depression

Make yourself comfortable in a place where you won't be disturbed. If you feel drawn to, put on some light music, drumming, or chanting. Light your incense or oil blend if you would like.

As your world around you dissipates, you find yourself standing outside an old, red brick wall that stretches out in front of you. Just beside you is a large wooden door set into the wall. The door is slightly ajar. It is a beautiful summer day: the sky is blue and the sun is warm on your skin.

You decide to push the door open and walk through...

Spread out before you is an amazing kitchen garden packed full of plants, vegetables, fruits, herbs, and flowers of all kinds.

The air is filled with a gorgeous scent and the sound of bees busily going about their business. Butterflies of all colours are also flitting about between each plant.

You stand and take it all in: the sights, the sounds, and the smells.

There is a pathway that leads through the plant and flower beds, so you start to wander, investigating each flower or fruit and vegetable bed as you come to it. Smell the flowers and feel the leaves and plants.

Eventually you see a large wooden bench up against the back wall, so you make your way toward it. The bench has several comfy-looking cushions and a small table beside it. The table is set with a large teapot and a cup and saucer. You sit down, make yourself comfortable, and pour a cup. The tea is hot and sweet and has a sharp but refreshing lemon taste.

Looking at the ground in front of you, you notice that it is full of herbs of all different varieties. The scent that is permeating the air is quite heady.

One of the herbs catches your eye. It has deep green leaves that look a bit like peppermint, but when you reach out and rub the leaves you get the scent of lemon. Your connection with the herb sparks the name "lemon balm" in your mind.

As you hold the leaves a butterfly lands on the back of your hand, fluttering its colourful wings, and you sit quite still while it rests. It has a message for you ... listen carefully.

When the butterfly is ready, in the blink of the eye it is gone, off around the garden.

You realise you are still holding on to the lemon balm leaf and feel a strong connection to the plant. Talk to it, ask it any questions that you have, and listen for the answers.

When you are ready, you thank the plant and lean back against the bench. Take a look around the garden. If nothing else draws you for the moment, you make your way back across the pathway to the gateway that you entered through.

Turn and take a few deep breaths in, breathing in the beautiful scent, and then walk back through the gate. Know that this place is always here if you need or want to return at any time.

Slowly and gently come back to this reality. Open your eyes and wriggle your fingers and toes.

Eat and drink something.

Jot down any thoughts or images that came to mind during your meditation. It can be useful to refer back to them later.

Spell to Combat Depression

The word "fetish" is thought to originate from the Portuguese word *feitiço*, meaning charm or spell, so essentially it is an item filled with magic.[2] You will find versions of them in most cultures. Often they are created to represent the Divine or to house a spirit. Others are just natural items imbued with magical intent. The term fetish covers a wide variety of magical items such as bones, magic pouches, poppets, statues, and even jewellery. I like to use items nature provides me with: feathers, leaves, twigs, stones, etc.

Once your fetish is created, it will need activation. That means you will need to charge it with the energy of your magical intent. If you have made your fetish from natural items, it will already have a certain amount of energy

---

2. *Merriam-Webster Dictionary*, s.v. "fetish," accessed January 27, 2020, https://www.merriam-web ster.com/dictionary/fetish.

within it because natural items have their own spirit energy. Be mindful that once your fetish is created, it is essentially a living thing and will need attention.

For your depression fetish, I suggest using natural items such as:

- Pebbles (a hagstone is perfect, if you can get one)
- Shells
- Feathers
- Twigs
- Dried leaves
- Dried berries
- Animal bones

The items I have suggested all have the spirit of Mother Nature and can be activated to help relieve depression. But don't be afraid to get creative: use bones, paintings, images, spirit bottles, witch bottles, witches' ladders, statues, dolls, poppets, beaded cloths, pebbles, twigs, or feathers … the material choice is endless.

You can soak your item in oils or scented water, pass it through incense smoke, or add corresponding herbs. This will add an extra layer of magic and make it personal to you. If you are dedicating it to a specific deity, use items that are associated with them.

Take your items and, if you can, tie them together with natural twine, or pop them into a fabric pouch. The organza ones you get with wedding favours are perfect for this.

Each item will need to be charged with your intent. Hold it in your hand and visualise your depression lifting and the energy from the items cleansing and clearing away the darkness. Carry the fetish with you and hold it whenever you need an extra boost. As long as you pay your fetish attention and keep feeding it energy, it will keep working for you.

Creativity Ritual for Depression

This is a ritual designed to help lift your spirits and dispel the darkness. I have used the strong masculine energy of the Greek/Roman god Apollo for this ritual. He brings a powerful punch of healing but also adds wisdom and knowledge.

You will need representations of the four elements for this ritual in the form of soil (earth), incense (air), candle (fire), and water. The ritual also calls upon the expression of artistic creativity, but it doesn't matter if you have no artistic abilities. The point of the spell is to release your depression in a creative outlet.

This ritual can be done using the items listed below, or you can sit quietly in your space and just visualise the whole thing.

You will need:

+ Small dish of soil
+ Incense
+ One central candle to represent the god Apollo
+ Small dish of water
+ One black candle
+ One white candle
+ Matches or a lighter
+ Paper
+ Pens, crayons, coloured pencils, or other colouring items
+ Something to eat and drink

Before you start, place the dish of soil in the north, place the incense in the east, light your central candle in the south, and pop the dish of water in the west.

Cast your circle. Walk around in a circle deosil (clockwise) or turn around on the spot if you are limited for space. Visualise a soft, glowing light forming a circle around you. When the circle is complete, visualise the light forming above you and below you to form a globe. As you cast the circle, say:

Circle of light
Circle of peace
Circle of protection
Circle this place

Call the quarters. Turn and face each compass direction, starting with the north and working deosil (clockwise). North is earth, east is air, south is fire, and west is water. As you face each one, say:

> Element of earth, bringing stability and grounding
> Please join me in this place
> Blessings of earth
> Element of air, bringing peace and clarity
> Please join me in this place
> Blessings of air
> Element of fire, bringing energy and passion
> Please join me in this place
> Blessings of fire
> Element of water, bringing emotion and calm
> Please join me in this place
> Blessings of water

As you light the central candle, say:

> I call upon the strong and supportive god Apollo
> And ask that you bring your shining light of strength, guidance, and courage
> To assist me with this rite
> Blessings to you

Light your black candle and take your piece of a paper and colouring items.

Now draw! It doesn't matter what it is. Allow your depression to channel out of your body and through your hands, into the pens and pencils, and onto the paper. It can be an image of whatever you like; allow your intuition to guide you.

This image is your depression in art form. And no, it doesn't have to be beautiful or artistic. It doesn't matter if it looks like a two-year-old got hold of mum's makeup bag… it is your art.

Let it all out and onto the paper.

When you are done, carry the paper to each of the quarters in turn.

Sprinkle a pinch of soil from the north on the image and say:

May the power of the element of north bring stability to my life

Waft the paper through the incense smoke in the east and say:

May the power of the element of east bring clarity to my thoughts

Swish the paper above the candle flame in the south (make sure it is safely above it) and say:

May the power of the element of south bring passion and creativity to my life

Sprinkle a few drops of water from the west onto the paper and say:

May the power of the element of west calm and balance my emotions

Snuff out the black candle.

Light the white candle and place your picture in front of it. Sit quietly for a time and visualise peace filling the space that depression had previously taken up. See your life as peaceful, happy, and content.

When you are ready, scribble on the picture or tear it into pieces.

Take a sip of your drink, raising your glass to Apollo.

Take a few bites of your food.

Then close the ritual. As you face the centre and hold your arms wide, say:

My thanks to you, great god Apollo
For shining your light of true strength, courage, and wisdom
Please continue to guide and support me
With blessings and thanks

Facing each direction in turn, starting with the west, work widdershins (counterclockwise) and say:

Element of water
My thanks for lending your energy today
Blessings of water
Element of fire
My thanks for lending your energy today
Blessings of fire

Element of air
My thanks for lending your energy today
Blessings of air
Element of earth
My thanks for lending your energy today
Blessings of earth

Then walk the circle widdershins (counterclockwise) and say:

Circle of light
Circle of peace
Circle of protection
Circle this place
This circle is now open but never broken

Snuff out the candles and pour the water onto the earth. Pour the rest of your drink and crumble some of your food onto the earth as an offering to Apollo.

The paper pieces can now be disposed of by burying them in the soil, throwing them into running water, or putting them in the trash.

Bundle for Depression

To begin, choose a piece of fabric that makes you feel happy. You will need a cord or ribbon to tie it with, or you could use a drawstring pouch.

Your depression bundle can be filled with anything that you feel drawn to add—with the exception of fresh food or herbs because those would go mouldy! You could add crystals, dried herbs, seeds, dried leaves, twigs, dried flower petals, small tokens, beads, buttons, coins, small ornaments, etc. Trust your intuition.

Sit quietly or meditate to decide which things to add. Reach out to a deity such as Apollo and ask what needs to go in. It might only be one or two items at first—you can add to it over time.

Each item is representative of your journey to remove depression from your life. Charge each item individually before you pop it in the pouch. Hold each one in your hand and visualise positive energy entering it, bringing calm, peace, and happiness and relieving you from depression.

For me, a depression bundle has lots of happy colours and memories in it. Here are my suggestions for things to include in yours:

+ Photos of happy times are always useful as they inspire positive thoughts and emotions
+ Yellow crystals such as citrine or goldstone
+ Get some citrus energy in there by adding dried orange or lemon peel
+ Sun representations, sun key chains, or charms
+ Smiley emoji symbols
+ Hearts—get some love energy in your bundle!
+ Herbs such as lemon balm, lavender, or cinnamon

Keep the bundle on your altar or somewhere that you will see it. Use it when you meditate, either holding it on your lap or opening it up and handling each item in turn. You can also reach for it when you feel low. Draw upon the energy within to fill your mind and spirit with calming and happy energy.

Depression can be a very lonely and isolating emotional state to be in.

Remember that you are never alone.

Reach out. Help is available in many forms.

If you find yourself feeling depressed, refer back to this chapter for magical suggestions that might help.

CHAPTER NINE

Panic Attacks

A panic attack is an overwhelming feeling of total, disabling anxiety. Panic attacks come on suddenly with little or no warning. They can be very frightening, but thankfully they usually don't last more than a few minutes. In fact, most panic attacks don't last longer than twenty minutes and are typically not dangerous or harmful. However, if you experience a lengthy attack or if you are seriously worried, please do seek medical advice immediately.

The symptoms of a panic attack are terrifying. You may sweat and tremble. You may feel dizzy or nauseous. Most panic attacks cause difficulty breathing and a racing heartbeat. It can sometimes seem like you are having a heart attack.

Panic attacks are caused by that same pesky fight-or-flight response we discussed in chapter 6. During a panic attack, your body is trying to cope in the only way it knows how. Responding to the sudden spike in fear or anxiety, your body attempts to take in more oxygen (presumably to assist you in running away from a sabre-toothed tiger…). This causes your heart to beat faster and the muscles in your body to tense up.

I had a bout of panic attacks a few years back that included severe chest pains. It was incredibly frightening. After discussing the situation with my doctor, he believed I had been under a tremendous amount of stress and needed to adjust my work schedule. He was right.

One of the most powerful things you can do during a panic attack is focus on your breath. The breathing exercises within this book (and from other resources) that regulate your breathing can really help to bring a panic attack down quickly and easily.

In this chapter you will find magical suggestions to help with your panic attacks. Work with as many of them as you like. Follow your intuition and be guided by it as to what you choose to work with.

> **Affirmations.** Regular positive statements can change the way we think about ourselves and our situations.

> **Colour Magic.** Colour plays an important part in how we feel and can affect our emotions; work with it to boost positive energy.

> **Herbs.** This section will contain my suggestions of herbs to work with in magical spell workings. Pick from my ideas or use your own—be guided by your intuition.

> **Foods.** All foods have magical properties. I have given you some suggestions that can be eaten or used in spell work. I've also included a recipe in each chapter.

> **Herbal Teas.** These can be created with herbs and spices that help alleviate negative issues. Work with my suggestions or use your own.

> **Incense and Oils.** Scents can bring up strong emotions. Work with my suggestions to create incense blends or oil blends to use in ritual or spell work. You can also create these blends just because the scent will lift your mood!

> **Everyday Exercise.** In this section you will find easy daily or regular routines to help get your positive energy flowing and get rid of the negative vibes.

> **Crystals.** They hold such power in tiny, easy-to-handle form. Crystals can be worked with in all sorts of ways to help with all kinds of issues.

> **Meditation.** Read through the script or even record it on your phone. Take some time out and work with the meditation for help and guidance.

> **Spell.** You will find spells to help with any issue. Keep it simple and straightforward. If you don't have the items I have suggested, sub-

stitute them with whatever you feel is right. Personalise it; make the spell your own.

Ritual. The rituals included will not be too fancy or complicated. Often, the rituals connect with a deity and the elements to work some magic.

Magic Bundle. In this section you'll find my suggestions for creating a magic bundle to help you through your situation.

Affirmations for Panic Attacks

I am calm. I am at peace.
Slowly, gently, surely, I am one with myself.
Breathe.
I can focus and have clarity of mind.
There is no fear; there is no panic.

Colour Magic for Panic Attacks

If you saw a panic attack as a colour, what colour would you see? This will vary from person to person. For any negative emotion or issue that I want to release, I see black as a good colour to work with. White is also good because it is neutral.

For me, a panic attack would be represented by all sorts of chaotic colours with a dark centre. To counter panic attacks, I would use pastel colours—specifically those along the yellow spectrum—to bring light into the darkness.

Herbs to Combat Panic Attacks

These are for magical use, NOT consumption.

+ Aloe
+ Alyssum
+ Benzoin
+ Cowslip
+ Hypericum
+ Lungwort
+ Passionflower
+ Patchouli

+ Self-heal
+ Valerian

Foods to Combat Panic Attacks

These can be used magically and/or eaten.

+ Blueberry
+ Chamomile
+ Lavender
+ Lemon balm
+ Lettuce
+ Mint
+ Poppy seeds

Recipe: Porridge Any "Witch" Way

Porridge is comforting and can have any number of flavourings added to boost the flavour *and* the magic.

Magic of the Ingredients

+ Milk—antidepression, nurturing
+ Oats—passion, comfort

You can charge or bless the ingredients as you add them to the mix or do so once the muffins are made. Hold your hands over them and say:

Porridge oats all warm and snug
A comforting big bowl for me to hug

Porridge Any "Witch" Way

100 g (3½ oz) porridge oats

230 mL (8 fl oz) milk (this can be cow's milk, almond milk, or an alternative of your choice)

Place the oats and milk in a saucepan and simmer over low heat for a couple of minutes. This won't take long.

If you are using spices or flavourings, add them *before* you heat.

Variations

Banana, Blueberry & Coconut. After your porridge is cooked, add sliced banana, fresh blueberries, and a spoonful of shredded coconut.

Spiced Apple. Add half a teaspoon ground cinnamon, a pinch of ground cloves, and a dash of ground nutmeg to your porridge mix as you cook it. Once the porridge is cooked, grate an apple on top.

Spiced Trail Mix. Add half a teaspoon ground cinnamon and half a teaspoon vanilla extract to your porridge mix as it cooks. Top with a sprinkle of trail mix (a mixture of seeds, nuts, and dried fruit).

Banana & Honey. Add half a teaspoon vanilla extract to your porridge mix as it cooks. Top with sliced banana and a drizzle of honey or maple syrup.

Blackberry & Apple. Cook your porridge and top with a handful of blackberries and grated apple. If you are using frozen blackberries, add them as you cook the porridge mixture.

Cocoa Loco. Add half a tablespoon cocoa powder to your oats and cook with the milk. Top this with a spoonful of shredded coconut and/or sliced banana.

Herbal Teas for Panic Attacks

These are some herbal teas that can be drunk on their own to help ease a panic attack:

+ Chamomile
+ Green tea
+ Lavender
+ Lemon balm
+ Passionflower
+ Peppermint

Try creating your own blends. Here are some of my favourite combinations:

+ One teaspoon dried chamomile, one tablespoon lemon juice, a slice of root ginger, and one teaspoon honey per mug of hot water

+ One teaspoon chamomile and one teaspoon peppermint per mug of hot water

+ One teaspoon chamomile and one teaspoon lavender per mug of hot water

+ One teaspoon lavender, one teaspoon chamomile, and one teaspoon peppermint per mug of hot water

Incense and Oil Blends for Panic Attacks

Any of these can be used in spells, rituals, body care, anointing, cleansing, and more to help with your panic attacks. Each one can be used on its own or mixed with others in a blend.

+ Basil
+ Bergamot
+ Chamomile
+ Cinnamon
+ Frankincense
+ Jasmine
+ Lavender
+ Lemongrass
+ Patchouli
+ Peppermint
+ Pine
+ Rose
+ Sandalwood
+ Vanilla
+ Vetiver
+ Ylang ylang

Incense Blends

+ Equal parts lavender, sandalwood, and jasmine
+ Equal parts frankincense, pine, and cinnamon and a few drops of vanilla oil
+ Equal parts frankincense, sandalwood, and lemongrass
+ Equal parts pine, lemongrass, and lavender

Essential Oil Blends

+ Combine three drops of each: ylang ylang, vanilla, and jasmine. Use in your bath or on an oil burner/diffuser or mix with a base oil to use on the body.
+ Combine three drops patchouli, two drops cinnamon, and four drops bergamot. Use in your bath or on an oil burner/diffuser or mix with a base oil to use on the body.
+ Combine three drops rose, three drops lavender, and two drops jasmine. Use in your bath or on an oil burner/diffuser or mix with a base oil to use on the body.
+ Combine three drops bergamot, three drops chamomile, and two drops pine. Use in your bath or on an oil burner/diffuser or mix with a base oil to use on the body.

Everyday Exercise for Panic Attacks

This is a little ritual to help if you feel a panic attack coming on. I like to think of it as the "Let's Get Physical" ritual. Don't worry—it doesn't involve any running!

The space between your index finger and thumb on your left hand is an acupressure point that, when pinched, helps to calm your nerves. Place your thumb on top of your hand and your first finger underneath your hand. Pinch to relieve panic.

Next, tap your chest. Hold three fingers together and try tapping gently in the centre of your chest, just under your breastbone. Tap for a few seconds to help calm you down.

Finally, do some stretching. Stand with your feet slightly apart and make sure your knees are bent slightly. Stretch your arms up above your head and breathe in deeply, then bring your arms back down, shaking them to release any stress.

Repeat this exercise as needed.

Crystals for Panic Attacks

Carry crystals with you, use them in magical spells, or meditate with them. Remember to charge the crystal with your intent before use and cleanse it afterwards. Cleansing suggestions can be found in chapter 3 of this book.

- **Amazonite** soothes emotions and alleviates fear.
- **Chrysocolla** dispels negative energy and brings about calm and peace.
- **Dumortierite** is a laid-back stone that brings harmony and happiness.
- **Green tourmaline** heals the heart and channels the energy throughout your body, providing strength and courage.
- **Howlite** soothes the emotions and helps release.
- **Kunzite** is a pure, happy energy that deals with stressful emotions.
- **Larimar** soothes the emotions. It helps you feel calm and peaceful.
- **Smoky quartz** calms the mind and helps bring focus and clarity.
- **Snowflake obsidian** balances emotions and brings release.
- **Sodalite** brings balance to your emotions.
- **Turquoise** strengthens and protects. It is a very calming stone. It also has a strong psychic connection.

Meditation for Panic Attacks

If you can bring this meditation to mind during an attack, it will help. This meditation will give you something to focus on. Alternatively, it also helps to work with this meditation shortly after an attack to help bring you back to balance.

Make yourself comfortable in a place where you won't be disturbed. If you feel drawn to, put on some light music, drumming, or chanting. Light your incense or oil blend if you would like.

As your world around you dissipates, you find yourself sitting quietly in the semidarkness. You do not feel afraid; in fact, you feel incredibly safe and comfortable.

Looking around, you realise you are in a cave that is lit by candlelight. Candles are all around you, placed on rocks and set into holes in the cave wall. You notice that the candlelight is also glinting off the walls, which sparkle with crystals.

You look down and see that you are sitting on warm, soft blankets and cushions that circle the dying embers of a fire in the centre. Beside the fire is a small pile of logs and sticks. You throw a couple onto the fire and it catches, throwing out warmth and more light.

You sit quietly and watch the flames dancing around in front of you. You notice that there is a basket beside you that appears to have herbs and flowers in it. You pick up the basket and look inside. You recognise some of the plants: lavender, cinnamon, sandalwood, and pine. Others are unfamiliar to you but you pick them up and hold them, breathing in the scent.

You feel the need to throw a handful of the herbs onto the fire, which you do.

The flames spark and hiss as the herbs burn. Ask your questions and listen to the fire as it gives you answers, guidance, and wisdom…

If you need to, throw another handful of herbs into the flames…

When you are finished you realise it is now much lighter in the cave and you look up to see light in the distance, so you make your way toward it.

As you walk you realise you are heading toward the opening of the cave. Walking slowly, you run your hands along the cave walls, which are cool and soothing.

The cave mouth opens onto a sandy beach beside the shore. The sunlight greets you with warmth.

You walk across the sand and splash in the edges of the waves, the cool water washing over your feet.

Looking down, you see something on the ground and pick it up. This is a gift for you.

When you are ready, turn and head back to the mouth of the cave.
As you enter the darkness, slowly and gently come back to this reality.

Open your eyes and wriggle your fingers and toes.

Eat and drink something.

Note what your gift was. What does it mean to you?

Jot down any thoughts or images that came to mind during your meditation. It can be useful to refer back to them later.

Spell to Combat Panic Attacks

I regularly use poppets in my spell work. They are easy to make and work exceptionally well. Poppets have been used for thousands of years, going right back to Egyptian times. Originally, they were used for healing.

This section will walk you through how to make your own poppet. You don't need a lot of crafting skill or experience; this can easily be adapted. For example, I like to use felt to make the base poppet instead of fabric because I am lazy, I don't like sewing, and felt doesn't need hemming.

You will need:

- Fabric/felt in a calming colour
- Sewing needles and thread
- Stuffing
- Calming herbs like lavender
- Buttons (optional)
- Crystals (optional)
- Wool, cloth, or other soft textiles (optional)

To begin, think about how large you want your poppet to be—do you want it to be small enough to carry with you? Do you want it to be large enough that it won't get lost or misplaced? Once you've decided on the size, choose a simple shape for your poppet. I like to use a "gingerbread man" shape or sometimes just a "T" shape. Your poppet's shape depends on how artistic and creative you are. If you want to, you can even just tie a square of fabric up with an elastic band for your poppet's "shape." You don't have to choose a traditional poppet shape.

Sew a button on for one eye and embroider the other eye, or just embroider both eyes. Add a mouth and a heart, and the poppet starts to take shape. Remember, this is your poppet: it doesn't have to have any features at all if you don't want it to.

Fill the poppet with a little bit of stuffing to bulk it out and then fill the rest with an herb blend that corresponds with your intent, charging the herbs as you add them. For a panic attack poppet, I recommend using chamomile, lavender, and cinnamon. These herbs will work their magic while also releasing a pleasant scent that you can breathe in during an attack to help bring you back.

If you want, you can also pop a small crystal inside your poppet.

Once you're done stuffing the poppet, sew it up and charge it with your intent again.

If you'd like, you can add finishing touches to the exterior of your poppet. Sometimes I add wool for hair. Often I wrap small strips of cloth around the poppet's middle so that petitions can be written on slips of paper and tucked into the cloth bands.

The poppet can then be put on an altar to work its magic or carried with you. I recommend carrying it to help ease panic attacks.

Element Ritual for Panic Attacks

When you are mid-panic attack, you won't be in any frame of mind to work a full ritual. The ritual is intended to be worked to help prevent panic attacks from happening. The Greek goddess Artemis provides support in this ritual. She brings confidence, courage, and strength but also a big hit of independent energy.

For this ritual, you will need a small item that represents the four elements. Drawing upon the unique energy of each element will help provide you with the courage and confidence to prevent further panic attacks.

This ritual can be done using the items listed below, or you can sit quietly in your space and just visualise the whole thing.

You will need:

+ A pebble, feather, match, and shell
+ Matches or a lighter
+ Small fabric pouch

- One central candle to represent the goddess Artemis
- Mixture of herbs from the Herbs to Combat Panic Attacks list (or follow your intuition)
- Something to eat and drink

Before you start, place your pebble in the north, feather in the east, match in the south, and shell in the west.

Cast your circle. Walk around in a circle deosil (clockwise) or turn around on the spot if you are limited for space. Visualise a soft, glowing light forming a circle around you. When the circle is complete, visualise the light forming above you and below you to form a globe. As you cast the circle, say:

Circle of light
Circle of peace
Circle of protection
Circle this place

Call the quarters: Turn and face each compass direction, starting with the north and working deosil (clockwise). North is earth, east is air, south is fire, and west is water. As you face each one, say:

Element of earth, bringing stability and grounding
Please join me in this place
Blessings of earth
Element of air, bringing peace and clarity
Please join me in this place
Blessings of air
Element of fire, bringing energy and passion
Please join me in this place
Blessings of fire
Element of water, bringing emotion and calm
Please join me in this place
Blessings of water

As you light the central candle, say:

I call upon the strong and courageous goddess Artemis
And ask that you bring your healing powers, strength, guidance, and
courage
To assist me with this rite
Blessings to you

Sit quietly in the centre of your circle and visualise your safe place: a space in your subconscious that is just for you. It could be anywhere, any place, at any time. Take yourself there and just *be*. Draw on the landscape or any of the items in your safe place to bring you courage, strength, and peace. Spend as much time as you want in your safe place.

When you are ready, take your fabric pouch and turn to the north. Pick up the pebble and say:

Element of earth
I ask that you bless this pebble with your magic and energy
Allow it to impart to me stability and support

Pop the pebble into your pouch.
Turn to the east, pick up the feather, and say:

Element of air
I ask that you bless this feather with your magic and energy
Allow it to impart to me clarity and focus of mind

Pop the feather into your pouch.
Turn to the south, pick up the match, and say:

Element of fire
I ask that you bless this match with your magic and energy
Allow it to impart to me courage and strength

Pop the match into your pouch.
Turn to the west, pick up the shell, and say:

Element of water
I ask that you bless this shell with your magic and energy
Allow it to impart to me the ability to balance my emotions

Pop the shell into your pouch.

Now pick up your herb mixture and say:

> *Goddess Artemis*
> *I ask that you bless these herbs*
> *Allow their magic to impart to me the energy I need to stay calm, collected, and focused*

Pop the herbs into your pouch.

Take a sip of your drink, raising your glass to Artemis.

Take a few bites of your food.

Then close the ritual. Face the centre and hold your arms wide, saying:

> *My thanks to you, great goddess Artemis*
> *For your healing, strength, courage, and wisdom*
> *Please continue to guide and support me*
> *With blessings and thanks*

Face each direction in turn, starting with the west. Work widdershins (counterclockwise) and say:

> *Element of water*
> *My thanks for lending your energy today*
> *Blessings of water*
> *Element of fire*
> *My thanks for lending your energy today*
> *Blessings of fire*
> *Element of air*
> *My thanks for lending your energy today*
> *Blessings of air*
> *Element of earth*
> *My thanks for lending your energy today*
> *Blessings of earth*

Then walk the circle widdershins (counterclockwise) and say:

Circle of light
Circle of peace
Circle of protection
Circle this place
This circle is now open but never broken

Snuff out the candle.

Pour the water onto the earth. Pour the rest of your drink and crumble some of your food onto the earth as an offering to Artemis.

Carry the pouch with you. If you feel it needs recharging, ask Artemis to give her blessing and add another pinch of herbs.

Bundle for Panic Attacks

To begin, choose a piece of fabric that makes you feel calm and grounded. You will need a cord or ribbon to tie it with, or you could use a drawstring pouch.

Your panic attack bundle can be filled with anything that you feel drawn to add—with the exception of fresh food or herbs because those would go mouldy! You could add crystals, dried herbs, seeds, dried leaves, twigs, dried flower petals, small tokens, beads, buttons, coins, small ornaments, etc. Trust your intuition.

Sit quietly or meditate to decide which things to add. Reach out to a deity such as Artemis and ask what needs to go in. It might only be one or two items at first—you can add to it over time.

Each item is representative of your journey to remove panic attacks from your life. Charge each item individually before you pop it in the pouch. Hold each one in your hand and visualise positive energy entering it, bringing calm, peace, and protection from panic attacks.

This bundle needs to be all about balance and calm. Here are my suggestions:

+ Yin and yang symbols

+ Magnets

+ Something that makes you think of calm and peace—a picture of a dove or a Reiki symbol, perhaps

+ Coloured ribbons and tactile fabric pieces to run through your fingers to calm you down
+ Something that smells relaxing (a scented candle or a little jar filled with salt and a few drops of your favourite essential oils)
+ Herbs such as chamomile, mint, or lavender

Keep the bundle on your altar or somewhere that you will see it. Use it when you meditate, either holding it on your lap or opening it up and handling each item in turn. You can also reach for it when you feel a panic attack coming on. Draw upon the energy within to fill your mind and spirit with calming and peaceful energy.

Panic attacks can be scary but remember: *you* are in control.

Find out what triggers your panic attacks and the best way for you to deal with them on a personal level. Set up a recovery plan to help you get through them.

If you find yourself suffering from panic attacks, refer back to this chapter for magical suggestions that might help.

CHAPTER TEN

Fear

F ear is a negative emotion that is brought on by the threat of danger, harm, or pain. Symptoms include chills, hot flashes, difficulty breathing, fast heartbeat, tightness in the chest, sweating, and trembling. It can trigger nausea and upset your digestive system. It is also one of the situations that can cause the feeling of "butterflies in your tummy."

There may be things you are generally afraid of, like spiders or snakes, but fear can also be brought on in certain situations such as flying or being in a crowded place. Fear often goes hand in hand with anxiety.

In this chapter you will find magical suggestions to help when you feel afraid. Work with as many of them as you like. Follow your intuition and be guided by it as to what you choose to work with.

Affirmations. Regular positive statements can change the way we think about ourselves and our situations.

Colour Magic. Colour plays an important part in how we feel and can affect our emotions; work with it to boost positive energy.

Herbs. This section will contain my suggestions of herbs to work with in magical spell workings. Pick from my ideas or use your own—be guided by your intuition.

Foods. All foods have magical properties. I have given you some suggestions that can be eaten or used in spell work. I've also included a recipe in each chapter.

Herbal Teas. These can be created with herbs and spices that help alleviate negative issues. Work with my suggestions or use your own.

Incense and Oils. Scents can bring up strong emotions. Work with my suggestions to create incense blends or oil blends to use in ritual or spell work. You can also create these blends just because the scent will lift your mood!

Everyday Exercise. In this section you will find easy daily or regular routines to help get your positive energy flowing and get rid of the negative vibes.

Crystals. They hold such power in tiny, easy-to-handle form. Crystals can be worked with in all sorts of ways to help with all kinds of issues.

Meditation. Read through the script or even record it on your phone. Take some time out and work with the meditation for help and guidance.

Spell. You will find spells to help with any issue. Keep it simple and straightforward. If you don't have the items I have suggested, substitute them with whatever you feel is right. Personalise it; make the spell your own.

Ritual. The rituals included will not be too fancy or complicated. Often, the rituals connect with a deity and the elements to work some magic.

Magic Bundle. In this section you'll find my suggestions for creating a magic bundle to help you through your situation.

Affirmations for Fear

I have courage and strength.
I will overcome fear.
I am strong.
I fear nothing.

Colour Magic for Fear

If you saw fear as a colour, what colour would you see? This will vary from person to person. For any negative emotion or issue that I want to release, I see black as a good colour to work with. White is also good because it is neutral.

Fear for me would be a sludgy grey colour: dark but not quite black; kinda charcoal colour. The colour of fear can be counteracted by shining light on to it.

Herbs to Combat Fear

These are for magical use, NOT consumption.

+ Alyssum
+ Chamomile
+ Columbine (aquilegia)
+ Elm
+ Hypericum
+ Nettle
+ Passionflower
+ Rose
+ Self-heal
+ Yarrow

Foods to Combat Fear

These can be used magically and/or eaten.

+ Cumin
+ Fennel
+ Garlic
+ Ginger
+ Lavender
+ Lemon balm
+ Mint
+ Plum

+ Tea
+ Thyme
+ Turmeric
+ Vanilla

Recipe: Ginger Plum Cake

This recipe is just lush! This is a sumptuous, dive-right-in-headfirst kinda comfort cake, but it also brings the soothing magic of plums and the earthy, protective energy of ginger.

Magic of the Ingredients
+ Ginger—healing, power, love, success, protection
+ Milk and butter—antidepression, nurturing, love
+ Plums—love, relaxation, rebirth
+ Sugar—to make life sweet!

You can charge or bless the ingredients as you add them to the mix or do so once the cake is made. Hold your hands over them and say:

Fear be gone, fears allay
Plum and ginger keep fear at bay

Ginger Plum Cake
Butter, for greasing
2 tablespoons demerara sugar
500 g (17½ oz) plums
175 g (6 oz) butter
175 g (6 oz) dark muscovado sugar
140 g (5 oz) golden syrup
2 eggs
200 mL (7 fl oz) milk
300 g (10½ oz) self-rising flour
½ teaspoon sodium bicarbonate (baking soda)

1 tablespoon ground ginger

1 teaspoon mixed spice

Preheat your oven to 180°C (350°F).

Grease and line the base of a 23 cm (9 in) square cake tin with baking parchment. Butter the parchment as well, then sprinkle the inside of the tin with the demerara sugar.

Slice the plums in half (destone) and place the slices around the base of the tin in a single layer with the cut sides facing down.

Melt the butter, sugar, and syrup together in a pan over low heat. Stir until smooth and blended together.

Cool slightly, then stir in the eggs and milk.

Sift in the flour, sodium bicarbonate, and spices. Mix together until smooth.

Pour the batter into the tin, covering the top of the plums, and bake for 45–50 minutes or until firm to the touch.

Cool slightly in the tin, then turn out and leave to cool.

Herbal Teas for Fear

These are some herbal teas can be drunk on their own to help calm your fears:

- Chamomile
- Fennel
- Ginger
- Lavender
- Lemon balm
- Mint
- Nettle
- Passionflower
- Rose
- Tea
- Thyme
- Turmeric

Try creating your own blends. Here are some of my favourite combinations:

+ One teaspoon dried nettle, one teaspoon dried mint, and half a teaspoon fennel seeds per mug of hot water
+ One teaspoon lavender, one teaspoon lemon balm, and one tablespoon of rose petals per mug of hot water
+ Add a slice of lemon and a slice of root ginger to your usual black tea bag
+ A handful of rose petals and a dash of vanilla extract per mug of hot water

Incense and Oil Blends for Fear

Any of these can be used in spells, rituals, body care, anointing, cleansing, and more to help calm your fears. Each one can be used on its own or mixed with others in a blend.

+ Chamomile
+ Lavender
+ Lemon balm
+ Mint
+ Passionflower
+ Rose
+ Thyme
+ Vanilla
+ Yarrow
+ Ylang ylang

Incense Blends

+ Equal parts copal resin, lavender, rose, and thyme
+ Equal parts frankincense resin, ground ginger, lemon balm, and yarrow
+ Equal parts fennel seeds, nettle, mint, and frankincense resin

+ Equal parts thyme (including the stalks), copal resin, cumin seeds, and fennel seeds
+ Equal parts lavender flowers, chamomile, thyme, and dried lemon peel

Essential Oil Blends

+ Combine six drops ylang ylang, three drops lavender, three drops orange, and three drops pine. Use in your bath or on an oil burner/diffuser or mix with a base oil to use on the body.
+ Combine six drops frankincense, four drops pine, four drops mint, and three drops vanilla. Use in your bath or on an oil burner/diffuser or mix with a base oil to use on the body.
+ Combine eight drops chamomile, four drops lavender, four drops thyme, and two drops rose. Use in your bath or on an oil burner/diffuser or mix with a base oil to use on the body.
+ Combine six drops lavender, four drops rose, and four drops citrus (orange or lemon). Use in your bath or on an oil burner/diffuser or mix with a base oil to use on the body.

Everyday Exercise for Fear

The daily roar is a little ritual that can help you to start your day feeling fearless and full of courage. Pick an animal that you feel is strong and courageous, one that has little to no fear. The lion is a good example, but pick one that you feel a connection with. If you have the space for a little altar that you can dedicate to the animal, great! Otherwise just visualise the animal in your mind.

Then roar out loud. Yep, get vocal. Feel the energy of the sound coming up from the earth, through your feet, coursing through your veins, and out through your mouth. Give it some energy, a real grrrrrrrrrrrrrr!

Once you've roared yourself hoarse, shake your arms and legs, clap your hands a few times, and get your day started.

Crystals for Fear

Carry crystals with you, use them in magical spells, or meditate with them. Remember to charge the crystal with your intent before use and cleanse it afterwards. Cleansing suggestions can be found in chapter 3 of this book.

+ **Amethyst** works to soothe fears.

+ **Citrine** is balancing and relaxing and can increase your personal power.

+ **Fire agate** provides protection and helps allay fears.

+ **Garnet** helps protect and prevent any fears.

+ **Green calcite** helps to overcome fears.

+ **Hematite** uses its grounding energy to help alleviate your fears.

+ **Obsidian** deals with strong emotions, including deep-rooted or hidden ones. It helps bring healing, transformation, and change.

+ **Onyx** helps to alleviate fears and worries.

+ Fear is quickly released when using the healing energy of **rose quartz**.

+ **Rutilated quartz** deals with brain functions and the nervous system, helping to calm any fears.

+ **Smoky quartz** absorbs and stores energy, making it perfect to work with to create calm and dispel fears. It brings stability and protection.

Meditation for Fear

This meditation will hopefully give you peace of mind and help to alleviate your fears.

Make yourself comfortable in a place where you won't be disturbed. If you feel drawn to, put on some light music, drumming, or chanting. Light your incense or oil blend if you would like.

As your world around you dissipates, you find yourself standing outside a garden gate. Behind the gate a small pathway leads to the front door of a pretty thatched cottage. The garden behind the fence is beautiful, packed full of glorious summer flowers of all colours.

The sun is shining and the sky is blue. You can hear the bees buzzing around the flowers and the birds singing in the trees.

You stand for a moment and breathe in, just being in the moment. Enjoy the warmth of the sun on your face and the sound of nature around you.

As you stand there the front door opens slowly and a friendly face looks out at you. Who is it? You might recognise them; you may not.

Either way, you are pleased to see them and feel a sense of relief and comfort. You are invited in so you make your way through the gate, up the pathway, and into the cottage.

You are led into a comfortable sitting room with a large, overstuffed sofa and big farmhouse-style rocking chairs. There are two of them in front of the hearth, separated by a small table. You sit down in one of the rocking chairs. It is filled with comfortable, colourful cushions and you sink into it with ease.

Your host brings in a tray with a big pot of steaming coffee and slices of homemade cake. They sit in the rocking chair opposite you. They pour you a mug full of coffee and give you a slice of cake on a delicate tea plate.

You both drink and eat in silence. It is a comfortable, easy silence.

The windows to the cottage are open and you can hear the sounds of the countryside filtering through. The sunlight also tiptoes through the windows, casting pretty light patterns across the room.

A small dog wanders in, looks at you, and makes its way to your feet, where it promptly lays down, the warmth of its body lying right on your toes.

You notice a vase of flowers on the table next to you, tall stalks with roundels of tiny white flowers at the top. You lean in and smell the bouquet with its fresh but spicy scent. As you make the connection with the plant, the name "yarrow" jumps into your head. The plant has some wisdom, insight, and comfort to share with you. You listen carefully…

If you have questions, ask the plant and it will answer them for you…

When you are ready, you give thanks to the yarrow and the connection breaks. You sit back in your chair and notice that your host is looking across at you. They ask if you need any help or support.

Now is the time to talk to your host … tell them about your fears…

Your host listens and may give you some advice…

When you are finished, you thank your host for their kindness and stand up, ready to leave. The dog at your feet stirs and moves out of your way.

Your host reaches in their pocket and produces a gift for you. You thank them and take it.

Heading out of the cottage, you step through the front door into the garden and notice that yarrow plants are growing all around, weaving in and out of the other plants and flowers.

Know that you can always return to this place if you need to.

As you walk through the garden gate you slowly and gently come back to this reality.

Open your eyes and wriggle your fingers and toes.

Eat and drink something.

What gift were you given and what does it mean to you?

Jot down any thoughts or images that came to mind during your meditation. It can be useful to refer back to them later.

Spell to Combat Fear

This spell works with the powerful energy of animal magic. You will need to choose an animal that you feel embodies courage and confidence to be the foundation of this exercise. The lion is a good example, and the one I tend to use, but it could be a tiger, a whale, a wolf, or even a dinosaur. Once the spell is complete, hold that courageous energy in the back of your mind. You can draw upon your fearless animal energy whenever you need it.

You will need:

- Matchbox or small cardboard box that can be thrown away
- Photo of a lion (or another fearless animal)
- Slip of paper
- Pencil or pen

Sit quietly with the image of your fearless animal in front of you.

Take the slip of paper and write down your fear. (Whatever it is, try and keep it to one or two words.)

Now take the animal image and visualise it roaring or being loud, strong, and courageous. See it destroying your fear.

Place the animal image face-to-face with the slip of paper that contains your fear word(s). Then fold them up together, folding the paper away from you to dispel the fear. Fold this as small as possible.

Put the folded papers into the matchbox. If you have an open fire or a fire pit you can chuck the box into the flames to burn. Otherwise, throw the box in the trash.

Finish the spell by saying:

> My courage is loud
> My fear is gone

Transformation Ritual to Release Fear

This ritual's intention is to dispel your fears, whatever they might be. Kali is a fierce Hindu warrior goddess that can seriously kick some butt. She encapsulates a strong, feminine energy full of transformation and rebirth. She destroys in a cleansing and purifying way to allow transformation to take place.

The spell within this ritual draws upon binding magic to tie up your fears and the element of fire to release you from them.

This ritual can be done using the items listed below, or you can sit quietly in your space and just visualise the whole thing.

You will need:

- Four candles, one for each direction (white candles are fine, but you might like to have a colour that represents each quarter)
- One central candle to represent the goddess Kali
- Piece of paper
- Pen or pencil
- String or twine (make sure it is biodegradable)
- Essential oil (something that dispels fear—mint would be good)
- Matches or a lighter
- Something to eat and drink

Before you start, place a candle at each of the four compass points.

Cast your circle. Walk around in a circle deosil (clockwise) or turn around on the spot if you are limited for space. Visualise a soft, glowing light forming a circle around you. When the circle is complete, visualise the light forming above you and below you to form a globe. For this ritual, see the circle as dancing red and orange flames. As you cast the circle, say:

Circle of light
Circle of power
Circle of protection
Circle this place

Call the quarters. Turn and face each compass direction, starting with the north and working deosil (clockwise). North is earth, east is air, south is fire, and west is water. As you face each candle and light it, say:

Element of earth, bringing stability and grounding
Please join me in this place
Blessings of earth
Element of air, bringing peace and clarity
Please join me in this place
Blessings of air
Element of fire, bringing energy and passion
Please join me in this place
Blessings of fire
Element of water, bringing emotion and calm
Please join me in this place
Blessings of water

As you light the central candle, say:

I call upon the strong, courageous, and protective goddess Kali
And ask that you bring your protection, strength, guidance, and courage
To assist me with this rite
Blessings to you

Now take the sheet of paper and write down your fear (or more than one if you have them) on the left-hand side of the paper.

On the right-hand side of the paper, write down solutions or ways to combat those fears.

When you are finished, tear the sheet of paper in half down the centre. Take the "fear" side of the paper and roll it up. Dab it with the essential oil of your choice, then bind it tightly with string. As you wrap the twine around the paper, say:

My intent is with this twine
My fears I will tightly bind
Take my fears and keep at bay
Rid my fears and take them away

When you have bound the paper, tie a knot securely in the string.

Take the second half of the paper, the part with the solutions on it. Read through them and take a moment to focus on how you will bring them into reality.

Take a sip of your drink, raising your glass to Kali.

Take a few bites of your food.

Then close the ritual. Face the centre and hold your arms wide, saying:

My thanks to you, great goddess Kali
For your protection, strength, courage, and wisdom
Please continue to guide and support me
With blessings and thanks

Face each direction in turn, starting with the west. Work widdershins (counterclockwise) and say:

Element of water
My thanks for lending your energy today
Blessings of water
Element of fire
My thanks for lending your energy today
Blessings of fire
Element of air
My thanks for lending your energy today
Blessings of air
Element of earth
My thanks for lending your energy today
Blessings of earth

Then walk the circle widdershins (counterclockwise) and say:

Circle of light
Circle of power
Circle of protection
Circle this place
This circle is now open but never broken

Snuff out all the candles.

Pour the rest of your drink and crumble some of your food onto the earth as an offering to Kali.

The paper parcel of fear can be thrown into an open fire or firepit, buried in the garden, or thrown in the trash.

Fold the "solutions" paper and keep it in your bag, in your purse, or on your altar. If you feel fear rising, have a reread of it.

Bundle for Fear

To begin, choose a piece of fabric that makes you feel strong and courageous. You will need a cord or ribbon to tie it with, or you could use a drawstring pouch.

Your fear bundle can be filled with anything that you feel drawn to add— with the exception of fresh food or herbs because those would go mouldy! You could add crystals, dried herbs, seeds, dried leaves, twigs, dried flower petals, small tokens, beads, buttons, coins, small ornaments, etc. Trust your intuition.

Sit quietly or meditate to decide which things to add. Reach out to a deity such as Kali and ask what needs to go in. It might only be one or two items at first—you can add to it over time.

Each item is representative of your journey to dispel fear from your life and bring in courage. Charge each item individually before you pop it in the pouch. Hold each one in your hand and visualise positive energy entering it, bringing courage and protection and preventing fear from creeping in.

This bundle needs to be all about courage and protection. Here are my suggestions:

+ Iron nails to protect
+ Pebbles for strength and stability
+ Crystals that represent courage and protection
+ Relevant charms (I have a little silver athame charm from an old brace-let that works well for this)
+ Photo of your protective animal
+ Herbs that bring protection and courage (you might like to use ginger, mint, or thyme)

Keep the bundle on your altar or somewhere that you will see it. Use it when you meditate, either holding it on your lap or opening it up and han-dling each item in turn. You can also reach for it when you feel fear coming on. Draw upon the energy within to fill your mind and spirit with courage and protection.

We all experience fear on many occasions during our lives for different reasons.
Learning how to overcome your fears can help you move forward.
If you find yourself feeling more afraid than usual, refer back to this chapter for magical suggestions that might help.

CHAPTER ELEVEN

Guilt

Often the word "guilty" is used in the situation where a crime is committed. But we can carry guilt for all kinds of reasons. It all comes down to blame. Guilt is the feeling that you are responsible for causing a situation or upsetting a person. Guilt can make you feel worried, sad, depressed, irritable, agitated, or unable to concentrate. If you don't deal with it and let it go, you can get caught in a self-destructive cycle. Often we take on the feeling of guilt without having any grounds to do so. I am supreme at hanging on to guilt, usually for no apparent reason.

In this chapter you will find magical suggestions to help ease your guilt. Work with as many of them as you like. Follow your intuition and be guided by it as to what you choose to work with.

Affirmations. Regular positive statements can change the way we think about ourselves and our situations.

Colour Magic. Colour plays an important part in how we feel and can affect our emotions; work with it to boost positive energy.

Herbs. This section will contain my suggestions of herbs to work with in magical spell workings. Pick from my ideas or use your own—be guided by your intuition.

Foods. All foods have magical properties. I have given you some suggestions that can be eaten or used in spell work. I've also included a recipe in each chapter.

Herbal Teas. These can be created with herbs and spices that help alleviate negative issues. Work with my suggestions or use your own.

Incense and Oils. Scents can bring up strong emotions. Work with my suggestions to create incense blends or oil blends to use in ritual or spell work. You can also create these blends just because the scent will lift your mood!

Everyday Exercise. In this section you will find easy daily or regular routines to help get your positive energy flowing and get rid of the negative vibes.

Crystals. They hold such power in tiny, easy-to-handle form. Crystals can be worked with in all sorts of ways to help with all kinds of issues.

Meditation. Read through the script or even record it on your phone. Take some time out and work with the meditation for help and guidance.

Spell. You will find spells to help with any issue. Keep it simple and straightforward. If you don't have the items I have suggested, substitute them with whatever you feel is right. Personalise it; make the spell your own.

Ritual. The rituals included will not be too fancy or complicated. Often, the rituals connect with a deity and the elements to work some magic.

Magic Bundle. In this section you'll find my suggestions for creating a magic bundle to help you through your situation.

Affirmations for Guilt

The past is behind me.
I focus on the present and moving forward.
I live in the present.
I let go of old wounds and bad patterns.
I am whole.
I am worthy.

Colour Magic for Guilt

If you saw guilt as a colour, what colour would you see? This will vary from person to person. For any negative emotion or issue that I want to release, I see black as a good colour to work with. White is also good because it is neutral.

Guilt for me would be a fiery colour, red or orange, perhaps. The colour of embarrassment maybe? It needs to be counteracted with a soothing colour.

Herbs to Combat Guilt

These are for magical use, NOT consumption.

- Agrimony
- Alexanders
- Alyssum
- Benzoin
- Betony
- Birch
- Carnation
- Celandine
- Columbine (aquilegia)
- Cypress
- Lungwort
- Nettle
- Pine
- Rue
- Self-heal
- Valerian
- Vervain
- Witch hazel

Foods to Combat Guilt

These can be used magically and/or eaten.

+ Basil
+ Black pepper
+ Chamomile
+ Chives
+ Cloves
+ Coriander
+ Dill
+ Garlic
+ Ginger
+ Grapefruit
+ Green tea
+ Mint
+ Rhubarb
+ Rosemary
+ Salt
+ Star anise
+ Thyme
+ Turmeric

Recipe: Cheesy Garlic Bread

This is *the* best garlic bread...FACT. If you are feeling guilty, eating lots of cheese and garlic will definitely make you feel better.

Magic of the Ingredients
+ Butter and cheese—antidepression, nurturing, love
+ Garlic—healing, protection, dispelling negativity, strength, courage, antidepression
+ Pepper—dispelling negativity, strength, confidence
+ Salt—cleansing, purification, protection

You can charge or bless the ingredients as you add them to the mix or do so once the bread is made. Hold your hands over them and say:

Garlic, butter, and cheese
From the guilt, please set me free

Cheesy Garlic Bread

450 g (1 lb) cheese, grated (use all cheddar or a mixture of your favourites)

125 g (4½ oz) mayonnaise (real, not low fat)

Salt and black pepper

1 large baguette

30 g (1 oz) butter

4 cloves of garlic, crushed

Preheat the oven to 220°C (425°F).

Mix the cheese and mayonnaise together. Season with salt and black pepper and put to one side.

Cut the loaf in half lengthwise, then in half widthwise (so you have four loaves).

Melt a quarter of the butter in a frying pan/skillet and add a quarter of the crushed garlic.

Place one of the loaves face down in the pan. Swish it around so it soaks up the butter and garlicky goodness.

Toast for a couple of minutes until the bread starts to brown. Set aside.

Repeat with the rest of the butter and garlic and the remaining three loaves.

Once you've toasted all four loaves, spread the cheese mixture on top and pop them in the oven for 8–10 minutes.

Herbal Teas for Guilt

These are some herbal teas that can be drunk on their own to help ease the feeling of guilt:

+ Basil
+ Chamomile

- Coriander
- Ginger
- Grapefruit
- Green tea
- Mint
- Nettle
- Rosemary
- Thyme
- Turmeric

Try creating your own blends. Here are some of my favourite combinations:

- One teaspoon nettle, one teaspoon lemon balm, and a few rose petals per mug of hot water
- Green tea with a slice of root ginger
- Green tea mixed with one teaspoon mint
- Green tea with a dash of grapefruit juice
- One teaspoon nettle, one teaspoon mint, and a slice of root ginger per mug of hot water
- One teaspoon chamomile, one teaspoon rosemary, and a pinch of lavender buds per mug of hot water
- Half a teaspoon coriander seeds, one teaspoon mint, and a slice of root ginger per mug of hot water
- Half a teaspoon turmeric, a slice of root ginger, a pinch of black pepper, and a pinch of ground cinnamon (this blend can be steeped in hot water or simmered for five to eight minutes with milk)
- Half a teaspoon turmeric, a slice of root ginger, and a dash of lemon or grapefruit juice per mug of hot water

Incense and Oil Blends for Stress

Any of these can be used in spells, rituals, body care, anointing, cleansing, and more to help ease your sense of guilt. Each one can be used on its own or mixed with others in a blend.

+ Basil
+ Benzoin
+ Black pepper
+ Chamomile
+ Cloves
+ Coriander
+ Cypress
+ Ginger
+ Grapefruit
+ Mint
+ Pine
+ Rosemary
+ Star anise
+ Thyme

Incense Blends

+ Equal parts benzoin resin, carnation, and cypress
+ Equal parts benzoin resin, pine, and black peppercorns
+ Equal parts cloves, coriander seeds, and black pepper
+ Equal parts rosemary, pine, and dried grapefruit peel
+ Equal parts cloves, ginger, and star anise
+ Equal parts mint, pine, and carnation
+ Equal parts frankincense resin, pine, and cloves

Essential Oil Blends

+ Combine four drops frankincense, three drops ginger, and four drops grapefruit. Use in your bath or on an oil burner/diffuser or mix with a base oil to use on the body.
+ Combine four drops ginger, four drops grapefruit, and four drops pine. Use in your bath or on an oil burner/diffuser or mix with a base oil to use on the body.

+ Combine four drops mint, four drops grapefruit, and three drops basil. Use in your bath or on an oil burner/diffuser or mix with a base oil to use on the body.

+ Combine four drops chamomile, three drops pine, and five drops carnation. Use in your bath or on an oil burner/diffuser or mix with a base oil to use on the body.

Everyday Exercise for Guilt

Salt is a naturally cleansing and purifying ingredient. At the end of each day, grab a pinch of salt and put it in the palm of your hand. Add a little warm water and gently wash your hands with it. As you wash, visualise all the negative energy, bad habits, and old patterns being cleansed, released, and washed away. Say to yourself, "Guilt is not mine to hold on to. I release it." Then dry your hands and put on some moisturiser. As you rub it into your hands, visualise positive energy replacing the negative.

Crystals for Guilt

Carry crystals with you, use them in magical spells, or meditate with them. Remember to charge the crystal with your intent before use and cleanse it afterwards. Cleansing suggestions can be found in chapter 3 of this book.

+ **Aquamarine** soothes and helps you move past anger and old wounds.

+ **Chrysocolla** is a stone of communication and expression, dispelling negative energy and opening you up to truth and calm.

+ **Chrysoprase** heals a broken heart and helps reassure you.

+ **Citrine** helps you look forward, keeping you from getting stuck in the past.

+ **Fire opal** burns through old attachments and heals past wounds.

+ **Howlite** is calming. It helps release attachments and worries.

+ **Jasper** brings harmony, balanced energy, comfort, and security.

+ **Kunzite** helps you learn to love yourself.

+ **Larimar** is serene and relaxing, providing a worry-free energy.

+ **Lepidolite** helps you let go of the past and stay focused on the present.

+ **Peridot** is a stone of light that drives away darkness.

+ **Petrified wood** is calming, nurturing, and soothing and helps to heal past issues.

+ **Pink tourmaline** assists with self-love and acceptance.

+ **Rose quartz** brings clarity and dispels negative energy.

+ **Rutilated quartz** helps you let go.

+ **Serpentine** supports transformation and letting go of old patterns.

+ **Smoky quartz** removes old patterns and belief systems.

+ **Sodalite** brings understanding of your circumstances and focuses on the truth.

+ **Turquoise** brings awareness and aids in focusing on the truth.

Meditation for Guilt

This meditation will hopefully give you peace of mind and help you to release any guilt you have from past events.

Make yourself comfortable in a place where you won't be disturbed. If you feel drawn to, put on some light music, drumming, or chanting. Light your incense or oil blend if you would like.

As your world around you dissipates, you find yourself standing in the middle of a field. You are surrounded by tall grass waving gently in the breeze. The grass is interspersed with wildflowers of all types and colours. The sky above you is blue-grey and filled with streaks of white cloud.

You take in the sights, sounds, and scents around you. Breathe deeply…

You wander through the grass until you find a spot where the grass is much shorter. It is as if nature has created a clearing just for you. You sit down on the short grass and then lie down on your back, looking up at the sky.

You watch as the clouds move slowly above you. What shapes and images can you make out?

As you watch the clouds a large flock of birds comes into your line of sight. They wheel and turn across the sky, seemingly moving together as one. You watch their flying dance with fascination.

When the birds have moved on, you realise that some darker clouds have appeared and start to feel small spots of rain upon your skin. You decide to lie still where you are.

Think of all the guilt you are feeling. As the rain begins to fall faster and heavier, allow the water to release your negative emotions.

You stand up and throw your arms into the air and turn your face up to the sky. Shout and scream and really let go of all the guilt you have been holding on to as the rain purifies and cleanses you.

Just as soon as it started, the rain comes to an abrupt stop. The sun beams down from behind a cloud, helping you to dry out.

You walk further through the field toward a small woodland that stands next to the field. On the edge the branches of several pine trees dip down toward the grass of the field. You reach out your hand and touch the spiny needles from one of the branches. The scent of pine wafts up and you breathe in deeply.

As you make the connection to the pine tree, you feel the energy reach out to you. It asks you to talk, to release, to tell it what you are hanging on to. What old wounds need healing? So you talk…

When you are finished releasing, the pine responds with some wise advice. Listen carefully…

When you are ready, you thank the pine for the guidance and support.

Make your way back across the field, walking gently through the grasses and wildflowers, taking in the scents and sounds.

When you reach the clearing you see something on the ground: a gift that has been left for you. You pick it up.

Take a last look around you and know that you can come back to this place at any time.

Slowly and gently come back to this reality, wriggling your fingers and toes. Open your eyes.

Drink and eat something.

What gift were you given and what does it mean to you?

Jot down any thoughts or images that came to mind during your meditation. It can be useful to refer back to them later.

Spell to Let Go of Guilt

Guilt can really eat you up if you hold on to it. Work with this spell to release that negative vibe and allow yourself to move forward. A lot of guilty energy ties us to the moment we associate with it. Think about a situation that makes you feel guilty. Imagine a long, winding string connecting you to the person, event, or issue that keeps on tugging and reminding you of something you should let go of. Working with this spell will cut those ties and break the bad connection.

You will need:

+ Length of string, twine, or ribbon
+ Essential oil that corresponds to letting go of guilt (perhaps grapefruit or mint)
+ One black candle
+ One white candle
+ Matches or a lighter
+ Scissors

Light the black candle. Sit quietly and hold the string in your hands.

Think about the events, issues, or people that have caused you to feel guilt. For each one, tie a small knot in the string.

As you tie each knot visualise what happened (not in great detail, just get a general picture).

After you tie each knot move onto the next event/issue (if there is more than one).

When you are finished, dab each knot with some of the essential oil.

Snuff out the black candle and light the white one.

Go back to the first knot you tied and visualise the guilt caused by it being released as you untie the knot. Say:

The guilt with this is not mine
Release, let go, leave behind.

Then cut the string where you have untied it.

Visualise this action as a cutting of ties to that guilt, letting it go and moving forward. See your life being filled with positive energy. Then move on to the next knot and repeat the process.

Once you have untied all your knots, snuff out the white candle. Dispose of the pieces of string in the trash.

Ice Ritual to Release Guilt

This ritual is set with the intent of letting go of the past and any guilt that you have attached to events, issues, or people. In this ritual we are working with the energy of an orisha, Yemaya. She is associated with both the moon and the sea, so she brings a lot of control over emotions. She also heals and provides emotional support. The spell within this ritual works very simply with ice: as it melts it takes your guilt away with it.

This ritual can be done using the items listed below, or you can sit quietly in your space and just visualise the whole thing.

You will need:

+ Four candles, one for each direction (white candles are fine, but you might like to have a colour that represents each quarter)
+ One central candle to represent the goddess Yemaya
+ Dish of water
+ Essential oil to represent letting go of guilt (I suggest grapefruit, pine, or rosemary)
+ Ice cubes
+ Matches or a lighter
+ Something to eat and drink

Before you start, place a candle in each of the four compass directions.

Cast your circle. Walk around in a circle deosil (clockwise) or turn around on the spot if you are limited for space. Visualise a soft, glowing light forming a circle around you. When the circle is complete, visualise the light forming above you and below you to form a globe. As you cast the circle, say:

Circle of light
Circle of peace
Circle of protection
Circle this place

Call the quarters. Turn and face each compass direction, starting with the north and working deosil (clockwise). North is earth, east is air, south is fire, and west is water.

Light a candle at each point. As you light each one, say:

Element of earth, bringing stability and grounding
Please join me in this place
Blessings of earth
Element of air, bringing peace and clarity
Please join me in this place
Blessings of air
Element of fire, bringing energy and passion
Please join me in this place
Blessings of fire
Element of water, bringing emotion and calm
Please join me in this place
Blessings of water

As you light the central candle, say:

I call upon the strong, courageous, and compassionate goddess Yemaya
And ask that you bring your protection, strength, guidance, and love
To assist me with this rite
Blessings to you

Now take the dish of water and add nine drops of the essential oil to it. As you do so, say:

With this sacred oil
I bless this water and dedicate it to the goddess Yemaya

*May she help, guide, and assist me in releasing my negative emotions
of guilt*

The ice cubes represent each event, issue, or person that has caused your guilt. Take your first ice cube and drop it gently into the water. As you do so, state out loud what issue, person, or event it represents.

Repeat with as many ice cubes as you need to.

Once you are finished, say:

*As the ice melts into the pool of Yemaya
May she release me from the guilt*

Take a sip of your drink, raising your glass to Yemaya.

Take a few bites of your food.

Then close the ritual. Face the centre and hold your arms wide, saying:

*My thanks to you, great goddess Yemaya
For your protection, strength, compassion, and wisdom
Please continue to guide and support me
With blessings and thanks*

Face each direction in turn, starting with the west. Work widdershins (counterclockwise) and say:

*Element of water
My thanks for lending your energy today
Blessings of water
Element of fire
My thanks for lending your energy today
Blessings of fire
Element of air
My thanks for lending your energy today
Blessings of air
Element of earth
My thanks for lending your energy today
Blessings of earth*

Then walk the circle widdershins (counterclockwise), saying:

Circle of light
Circle of peace
Circle of protection
Circle this place
This circle is now open but never broken

Pour the rest of your drink and crumble some of your food onto the earth as an offering to Yemaya. Snuff out the lit candles.

Leave the water in a safe place until all the ice cubes have melted. Then you can tip the water into your garden or pour it onto the ground.

Bundle for Guilt

To begin, choose a piece of fabric that makes you feel calm, soothed, and guilt free. You will need a cord or ribbon to tie it with, or you could use a drawstring pouch.

Your guilt bundle can be filled with anything that you feel drawn to add—with the exception of fresh food or herbs because those would go mouldy! You could add crystals, dried herbs, seeds, dried leaves, twigs, dried flower petals, small tokens, beads, buttons, coins, small ornaments, etc. Trust your intuition.

Sit quietly or meditate to decide which things to add. Reach out to a deity such as Yemaya and ask what needs to go in. It might only be one or two items at first—you can add to it over time.

Each item is representative of your journey to dispel old guilt and past events that you are hanging on to. Charge each item individually before you pop it in the pouch. Hold each one in your hand and visualise positive energy entering it, bringing release, purification, and positivity.

Here are my suggestions:

+ Sea salt grains, perhaps in a little pouch
+ Something that represents the ocean or the sea
+ Shells, sea glass, and hagstone pebbles
+ A sprig of rosemary
+ A couple of pieces of star anise

Keep the bundle on your altar or somewhere that you will see it. Use it when you meditate, either holding it on your lap or opening it up and handling each item in turn. You can also reach for it when you feel the need to let go. Draw upon the energy within to fill your mind and spirit with positive energy.

Guilt can eat away at you and cause all sorts of issues. Don't let it!

Acknowledge, let go, and move forward.

Life is beautiful. Don't waste it stuck in the past.

If you find yourself feeling guilty, refer back to this chapter for magical suggestions that might help.

CHAPTER TWELVE

Worry

Worry is the feeling that causes anxiety. You can be concerned and anxious about a situation, problem, or person and even get into a panic about it. It can be very easy to take the small seed of worry and escalate it to totally unrealistic proportions. Worrying can cause sweating, headaches, and muscle tension. You might feel restless, ill at ease, and irritable. Worrying is a trait that I personally struggle with; I worry about everything!

In this chapter you will find magical suggestions to help ease your worries. Work with as many of them as you like. Follow your intuition and be guided by it as to what you choose to work with.

Affirmations. Regular positive statements can change the way we think about ourselves and our situations.

Colour Magic. Colour plays an important part in how we feel and can affect our emotions; work with it to boost positive energy.

Herbs. This section will contain my suggestions of herbs to work with in magical spell workings. Pick from my ideas or use your own—be guided by your intuition.

Foods. All foods have magical properties. I have given you some suggestions that can be eaten or used in spell work. I've also included a recipe in each chapter.

Herbal Teas. These can be created with herbs and spices that help alleviate negative issues. Work with my suggestions or use your own.

Incense and Oils. Scents can bring up strong emotions. Work with my suggestions to create incense blends or oil blends to use in ritual or spell work. You can also create these blends just because the scent will lift your mood!

Everyday Exercise. In this section you will find easy daily or regular routines to help get your positive energy flowing and get rid of the negative vibes.

Crystals. They hold such power in tiny, easy-to-handle form. Crystals can be worked with in all sorts of ways to help with all kinds of issues.

Meditation. Read through the script or even record it on your phone. Take some time out and work with the meditation for help and guidance.

Spell. You will find spells to help with any issue. Keep it simple and straightforward. If you don't have the items I have suggested, substitute them with whatever you feel is right. Personalise it; make the spell your own.

Ritual. The rituals included will not be too fancy or complicated. Often, the rituals connect with a deity and the elements to work some magic.

Magic Bundle. In this section you'll find my suggestions for creating a magic bundle to help you through your situation.

Affirmations for Worry

I let go of what I cannot control.
I focus on what I can deal with.
I am worry free.
I am carefree.
Life is good.

Colour Magic for Worry

If you saw worry as a colour, what colour would you see? This will vary from person to person. For any negative emotion or issue that I want to release, I see black as a good colour to work with. White is also good because it is neutral.

Worry for me would be a wishy-washy, pale green/blue colour. It'd be kinda insipid and not really any true, full-on colour. Counteract it with a bold, bright, happy colour.

Herbs to Combat Worry

These are for magical use, NOT consumption.

+ Alyssum
+ Benzoin
+ Dill
+ Holly
+ Hops
+ Knotweed
+ Passionflower
+ Rue
+ Skullcap
+ Valerian
+ Vervain
+ Witch hazel

Foods to Combat Worry

These can be used magically and/or eaten.

+ Basil
+ Blueberries
+ Chamomile
+ Fennel
+ Green tea
+ Lavender
+ Lemon balm
+ Mint
+ Poppy seeds

Recipe: Shortbread

Shortbread is simple but effective; it really helps soothe those worries. This is a basic recipe. You can add all kinds of flavourings, herbs, and spices to kick this shortbread up a notch. I've included some variation suggestions below.

Magic of the Ingredients

- Butter—antidepression, nurturing, love
- Sugar—to make life sweet!

You can charge or bless the ingredients as you add them to the mix or do so once the shortbread is made. Hold your hands over them and say:

Shortbread soothes, simply made
Keep my worries right away

Shortbread

125 g (4 oz) butter

55 g (2 oz) sugar

180 g (6 oz) plain flour

Caster sugar for decoration

Heat the oven to 190°C (375°F).

In a large bowl, beat butter and sugar together until smooth.

Add in the flour. If you are making a variation, add your extra flavourings as well. Stir until you have a smooth paste.

Transfer mixture onto a work surface and gently roll out until the paste is 1 cm (½ in) thick.

Cut into rounds or fingers and place on a baking tray. Sprinkle with caster sugar and chill in the fridge for 20 minutes.

Bake in the oven for 15–20 minutes or until pale golden-brown.

Set aside to cool on a wire rack.

Variations

+ Add one tablespoon of chopped basil leaves.

+ Add one teaspoon of fennel seeds.

+ Add the grated rind of one large orange.

+ Add the grated rind of two lemons or limes.

+ Add two teaspoons of dried chamomile.

+ Add two teaspoons of green tea leaves.

+ Add one tablespoon of chopped lemon balm leaves.

Herbal Teas for Worry

These are some herbal teas that can be drunk on their own to alleviate the feeling of worry:

+ Basil

+ Chamomile

+ Fennel

+ Green tea

+ Lavender

+ Lemon balm

+ Mint

+ Passionflower

Try creating your own blends. Here are some of my favourite combinations:

+ One teaspoon chamomile, one teaspoon passionflower, and a slice of lemon per mug of hot water

+ One teaspoon mint and one teaspoon basil per mug of hot water

+ One teaspoon fennel seeds and one teaspoon mint per mug of hot water

+ One teaspoon green tea and a slice of lemon per mug of hot water

+ One teaspoon green tea and one teaspoon mint per mug of hot water

+ One teaspoon lavender and one teaspoon passionflower per mug of hot water

Incense and Oil Blends for Worry

Any of these can be used in spells, rituals, body care, anointing, cleansing, and more to help ease your worries. Each one can be used on its own or mixed with others in a blend.

- Basil
- Benzoin
- Chamomile
- Fennel
- Lavender
- Lemon balm
- Mint
- Passionflower

Incense Blends

- One part frankincense resin, two parts lavender, and one part passionflower
- Equal parts benzoin resin, basil, and fennel seeds
- One part frankincense resin, two parts lemon balm, and two parts mint
- Equal parts lavender, chamomile, and lemon balm
- Equal parts mint, fennel seeds, and basil

Essential Oil Blends

- Combine six drops frankincense and ten drops lavender. Use in your bath or on an oil burner/diffuser or mix with a base oil to use on the body.
- Combine four drops lavender, four drops chamomile, and four drops lemon balm. Use in your bath or on an oil burner/diffuser or mix with a base oil to use on the body.
- Combine four drops lemon balm, four drops mint, and three drops fennel. Use in your bath or on an oil burner/diffuser or mix with a base oil to use on the body.

✦ Combine four drops frankincense, four drops fennel, and three drops basil. Use in your bath or on an oil burner/diffuser or mix with a base oil to use on the body.

Worry Beads

Beads are a brilliant tool for meditation and working through stressful emotions. Sometimes called worry beads, meditation beads, rosary beads, or mala beads, they act as a kind of anchor or a grounding point, giving you something to focus on.

Making your own set of worry beads is easy. Pick beads that you like and thread them onto a string. You can choose different beads for different purposes or you can have a string of plain beads that are all the same colour. It is your choice—use whatever works for you.

Be careful not to overload the string—you need to be able to slide the beads along. Leave plenty of space on the string to slide the beads along or tie a knot after each bead, leaving a small gap between the beads and knots.

If you aren't crafty or don't want to make your set of worry beads, sets of beads can be purchased from craft sites.

The beads can be used in several ways. A popular method is to hang the string between your thumb and your third finger, traditionally in your right hand. Using your middle finger, you rotate the beads toward yourself one at a time. Begin rotating the first bead and repeat the process with all the beads, continuing around the loop until you reach the start. Each time you rotate a bead, repeat a mantra or affirmation and take a breath.

A variation of this method is to hang the string on your middle finger and rotate the beads using your thumb. Rotate the beads one at a time in the same fashion.

I keep my set of worry beads on my altar. You will want to keep them somewhere safe; if not on your altar, perhaps in a drawer or box.

Your worry beads may need cleansing occasionally if you feel the energy is a bit off. Cleansing them with incense is perfect.

Everyday Exercise for Worry

I love a bit of drumming, and making noise can really help release negative emotion and raise your energy. If you have a drum, perfect! If not, you can improvise. Use a metal biscuit tin or a saucepan and wooden spoon. When you feel the need to release worry, fears, or tension, get your drum out and give it a good ol' bang! Walk around the house, stand in the yard, or take yourself out to the woods and make some noise. Really give it some gusto. With each bang of the drum, visualise your worries being crushed and destroyed. Let the sound take them away. And then possibly apologise to your neighbours…

Crystals for Worry

Carry crystals with you, use them in magical spells, or meditate with them. Remember to charge the crystal with your intent before use and cleanse it afterwards. Cleansing suggestions can be found in chapter 3 of this book.

+ **Amber** basically sorts your brain out, providing clarity of thought.
+ **Amethyst** clears the mind and brings clarity to any situation. It is calming and healing.
+ **Angelite** has a beautiful, peaceful energy to calm and soothe.
+ **Black tourmaline** is grounding and promotes self-confidence.
+ **Blue tourmaline** is a stone of peace.
+ **Blue lace agate** encourages a sense of calm and peace. It is a stone of communication so it can help you talk about your worries.
+ **Celestite** helps relieve worry, bringing balance and happy vibes.
+ **Citrine** is comforting and relaxing and brings security.
+ **Fluorite** helps the mind focus on what is important and helps bring balance.
+ **Hematite** has a grounding energy that brings things into perspective and helps alleviate worry.
+ **Larimar** is the perfect stone to take the burden of your worries.
+ **Lepidolite** is calm and tranquil, bringing balance to the spirit, mind, and soul.
+ You can depend on **red jasper** to keep you grounded and focused.
+ **Smoky quartz** uses a gentle energy to focus and clarify situations.

Meditation for Worry

Hopefully, this meditation will help you chill out and release your mind from worry.

Make yourself comfortable in a place where you won't be disturbed. If you feel drawn to, put on some light music, drumming, or chanting. Light your incense or oil blend if you would like.

As your world around you dissipates, you find yourself standing on the side of a grassy hill. Above you is the hilltop, and you have a view of other hills and mountaintops. The sun is shining, the sky is blue, and the air is fresh and sweet. It feels like late summer or early autumn.

The grass is lush beneath your feet, and stones and small boulders are scattered around. You take a look around you and see a small, chalky pathway leading toward the top of the hill so you begin to follow the path.

It is not steep—just a pleasant, comfortable climb. Take in the scenery, the sights, and the sounds around you as you walk and breathe in the fresh mountain air.

As the pathway rounds a bend, it opens out on to the top of the hill: a large, flat area of grass. You are surprised to see the ruins of what looks to be an old abbey or temple of some sort.

Walking over to the structure, you see that it is made from hand-carved stone. Some of the pillars are still standing along with a few low walls, but most of it has long since fallen. You put out your hand and feel the cold of the stone.

As you stand there quietly taking in the energy and feel of the place, you hear a noise and are drawn to the centre of the ruin. Walking over, you see an animal snuffling about looking for food. What animal is it? It looks up at you, and your eyes make a connection. You sit down quietly on a piece of broken wall and find yourself talking to the animal, telling it all about your worries and fears. The animal sits patiently, listening...

When you are finished, the animal responds to you...

Then, in a flash, the animal turns and is gone.

Your attention is drawn to what looks to be a purple blossom on a plant that is creeping and twisting its way up several of the pillars. You head on over and take a closer look.

The plant is indeed covered with purple flowers. They are strange-looking blossoms that have a wonderful scent, and you breathe in deeply. You feel the need to reach out and hold one of the flowers. A connection is made, and you feel the name "passionflower" pop into your mind.

This flower wants to listen too, so you talk…

Then it responds…

Once the message has been conveyed, you are given permission to pick the flower and take it away with you.

You feel the need to go to the edge of the hilltop, looking out over the scenery below. Shout… shout out loud… let all your worries out so that the breeze can carry them away…

Then take a final look around at the ruins and the scenery that surrounds the hill, taking it all in. Soak in every detail, knowing that you can always come back to this place if you need to.

You finally start to make your way back down the hillside pathway. Each step downwards feels like you are lightening your load, leaving your worries behind.

Slowly and gently come back to this reality, wriggling your fingers and toes. Open your eyes.

Drink and eat something.

Jot down any thoughts or images that came to mind during your meditation. It can be useful to refer back to them later.

Spell to Let Go of Worry

We are going to make mud pies with your worry! The magic of this spell is in the herbs and the soil. Each herb will help release the worry that is clinging to you, and the elements of nature will remove your worry. Let the earth and water clear and cleanse the negative emotions that you are carrying with you.

You will need:

+ Bowl of dried herbs of your choice (try to include herbs that corre-
spond to letting go of worry: basil, lemon balm, or mint)
+ Bowl of soil
+ Jug of water
+ Candle (optional)

Light your candle if you are using one. This is just to give you a sense of
focus.

Place the bowls and water in front of you.

Take a pinch of the dried herbs and visualise one of the things you worry
about. Drop it into the bowl of soil. Take another pinch of ingredients and
repeat, visualising the worry and then letting go of it as you drop it into the
soil. Repeat as many times as you feel necessary, transferring your worries
from your mind to the herbs, letting go of them as the herbs hit the soil.

When you are done, take the jug of water and pour a little into the soil.
Stir it with your fingers and make a sticky, muddy mess. Mix it up really well
so the herbs are totally covered by the mud. Say:

With the elements of earth and water
My worries are gone
With the elements of earth and water
My worries are done

The mud can then be tipped into the garden.
Snuff out your candle if you used one.

Candle and Herb Ritual to Release Worry

This ritual's intent is to help you let go of your worries. Here we work with
the power of the Hindu god Ganesha. He removes obstacles and blockages
and provides a pathway for new beginnings.

The spell within this ritual uses the magic of herbs, one for each element,
and candle wax to seal and remove. It also brings colour magic into play, using
black to dispel negative energy and white to bring in the positive.

This ritual can be done using the items listed below, or you can sit quietly
in your space and just visualise the whole thing.

You will need:

- Small dish of herbs or flowers to represent earth (honeysuckle, grass, or salt, for example)
- Small dish of herbs or flowers to represent air (alyssum, lavender, or mint, perhaps)
- Small dish of herbs or flowers to represent fire (I suggest basil, black pepper, or rosemary)
- Small dish of herbs or flowers to represent water (I recommend lemon balm, poppy seeds, or thyme)
- Fireproof dish or cauldron
- One central candle to represent the god Ganesha
- One black candle
- One white candle
- Matches or a lighter
- Something to eat and drink

Before you start, place a dish of herbs at each compass direction.

Cast your circle. Walk around in a circle deosil (clockwise) or turn around on the spot if you are limited for space. Visualise a soft, glowing light forming a circle around you. When the circle is complete, visualise the light forming above you and below you to form a globe. As you cast the circle, say:

Circle of light
Circle of peace
Circle of protection
Circle this place

Call the quarters. Turn and face each compass direction, starting with the north and working deosil (clockwise). North is earth, east is air, south is fire, and west is water. Running your fingers through each herb as you face each one, say:

Element of earth, bringing stability and grounding
Please join me in this place
Blessings of earth
Element of air, bringing peace and clarity

Please join me in this place
Blessings of air
Element of fire, bringing energy and passion
Please join me in this place
Blessings of fire
Element of water, bringing emotion and calm
Please join me in this place
Blessings of water

As you light the central candle, say:

I call upon the strong and wise god Ganesha
And ask that you bring your strength, guidance, and assistance to
remove blockages
To assist me with this rite
Blessings to you

Now light the black candle.

Take a pinch of herbs from the north/earth and visualise it containing one of your worries. Then sprinkle the herbs into your fireproof dish or cauldron.

Now take the black candle and drip a few drops of wax on top of the herbs, saying:

With the power of dark
I wipe out the worry

Next take a pinch of herbs from the east/air and repeat the process, dropping them into the cauldron, dripping them with wax, and saying the chant. Do this with a pinch of herbs from the south/fire and then with the west/water herbs. You should have a waxy, herby mess in the bottom of your cauldron now.

Snuff out the black candle.

Light the white candle. Drip some of the wax on top of the herb/wax mixture in your cauldron. Say:

With my worries gone
I let in the light

Drip as much white wax as you feel the need to, then snuff out the white candle.

Take a sip of your drink, raising your glass to Ganesha.

Take a few bites of your food.

Then close the ritual. Face the centre and hold your arms wide, saying:

> *My thanks to you, great god Ganesha*
> *For your strength, guidance, and wisdom*
> *Please continue to guide and support me*
> *With blessings and thanks*

Face each direction in turn, starting with the west. Work widdershins (counterclockwise) and say:

> *Element of water*
> *My thanks for lending your energy today*
> *Blessings of water*
> *Element of fire*
> *My thanks for lending your energy today*
> *Blessings of fire*
> *Element of air*
> *My thanks for lending your energy today*
> *Blessings of air*
> *Element of earth*
> *My thanks for lending your energy today*
> *Blessings of earth*

Then walk the circle widdershins (counterclockwise) and say:

> *Circle of light*
> *Circle of peace*
> *Circle of protection*
> *Circle this place*
> *This circle is now open but never broken*

Pour the rest of your drink and crumble some of your food onto the earth as an offering to Ganesha.

Unused herbs can be sprinkled into the garden or put away for use at a later date. The waxy herb blob will need to be scooped out of your cauldron and thrown in the trash.

Bundle for Worry

To begin, choose a piece of fabric that makes you feel calm, soothed, and worry free. You will need a cord or ribbon to tie it with, or you could use a drawstring pouch.

Your worry bundle can be filled with anything that you feel drawn to add—with the exception of fresh food or herbs because those would go mouldy! You could add crystals, dried herbs, seeds, dried leaves, twigs, dried flower petals, small tokens, beads, buttons, coins, small ornaments, etc. Trust your intuition.

Sit quietly or meditate to decide which things to add. Reach out to a deity such as Ganesha and ask what needs to go in. It might only be one or two items at first—you can add to it over time.

Each item is representative of your journey to dispel worry that you are hanging on to. Charge each item individually before you pop it in the pouch. Hold each one in your hand and visualise positive energy entering it, bringing release and positivity and preventing you from hanging on to worry.

Here are my suggestions:

- Anything that makes you feel calm, balanced, and focused
- Herbs that can help ease worries, such as fennel seeds, lemon balm, or poppy seeds
- Crystals that will alleviate worry, particularly ones that you can pick up and hold in your hand to release their energy to you
- A set of worry/meditation beads

Keep the bundle on your altar or somewhere that you will see it. Use it when you meditate, either holding it on your lap or opening it up and handling each item in turn. You can also reach for it when you feel the need to let go. Draw upon the energy within to fill your mind and spirit with positive energy.

Worry can eat away at you and send you into a downward spin.

Don't let it get the better of you: talk about it, research it, do something to clear it.

Change your thinking patterns for the better.

If you find yourself worrying more than usual, refer back to this chapter for magical suggestions that might help.

CHAPTER THIRTEEN

Grief

Grief is an overwhelming feeling of sadness and sorrow. It can be brought on by the loss or ending of many different things. Grief can lead to shock, anger, guilt, tiredness, and exhaustion, along with aches and pains. Severe grief can also spark anxiety.

Time is one of the best healers for grief, but it is important to remember that grief is not the same for everyone. How long someone grieves depends on the person and the situation. There is no time frame. Take your time and allow healing to happen at the pace it needs to.

Eventually, there will come a point when you want to move forward. Magic can help you learn to move past the grief. I would never suggest that you forget, just that you allow yourself to live and to step into the next part of your journey with hope and happy memories.

In this chapter you will find magical suggestions to help ease your grief. Work with as many of them as you like. Follow your intuition and be guided by it as to what you choose to work with.

Affirmations. Regular positive statements can change the way we think about ourselves and our situations.

Colour Magic. Colour plays an important part in how we feel and can affect our emotions; work with it to boost positive energy.

Herbs. This section will contain my suggestions of herbs to work with in magical spell workings. Pick from my ideas or use your own—be guided by your intuition.

Foods. All foods have magical properties. I have given you some suggestions that can be eaten or used in spell work. I've also included a recipe in each chapter.

Herbal Teas. These can be created with herbs and spices that help alleviate negative issues. Work with my suggestions or use your own.

Incense and Oils. Scents can bring up strong emotions. Work with my suggestions to create incense blends or oil blends to use in ritual or spell work. You can also create these blends just because the scent will lift your mood!

Everyday Exercise. In this section you will find easy daily or regular routines to help get your positive energy flowing and get rid of the negative vibes.

Crystals. They hold such power in tiny, easy-to-handle form. Crystals can be worked with in all sorts of ways to help with all kinds of issues.

Meditation. Read through the script or even record it on your phone. Take some time out and work with the meditation for help and guidance.

Spell. You will find spells to help with any issue. Keep it simple and straightforward. If you don't have the items I have suggested, substitute them with whatever you feel is right. Personalise it; make the spell your own.

Ritual. The rituals included will not be too fancy or complicated. Often, the rituals connect with a deity and the elements to work some magic.

Magic Bundle. In this section you'll find my suggestions for creating a magic bundle to help you through your situation.

Affirmations for Grief

I will remember that my life is for living.
I will live life to the fullest.
I am allowed to grieve.
My life is precious, and I am important.

Colour Magic for Grief

If you saw grief as a colour, what colour would you see? This will vary from person to person. For any negative emotion or issue that I want to release, I see black as a good colour to work with. White is also good because it is neutral.

Grief for me as a colour would be transparent, empty, and void. There would be no colour at all. To counteract this use all the colours of the rainbow.

Herbs to Combat Grief

These are for magical use, NOT consumption.

+ Bergamot
+ Carnation
+ Cypress
+ Hypericum
+ Poppy
+ Self-heal
+ Thyme
+ Witch hazel

Foods to Combat Grief

These can be used magically and/or eaten.

+ Black pepper
+ Cardamom
+ Cloves
+ Garlic
+ Lavender
+ Lemon
+ Marjoram
+ Orange
+ Poppy seeds
+ Rhubarb

Recipe: Lemon and Poppy Seed Cupcakes

This is a recipe for lemony, lush cupcakes that carry the magic of poppy seeds and lemon, both of which will add a bit of sunshine to your life.

Magic of the Ingredients

+ Butter and milk—antidepression, nurturing, love
+ Lemons—healing, antidepression, memory, antianxiety, love
+ Poppy seeds—calming, peace, protection
+ Sugar—to make life sweet!

You can charge or bless the ingredients as you add them to the mix or do so once the cupcakes are made. Hold your hands over them and say:

Cupcakes of lemon and poppy seed
Brighten my day and help me in need

Lemon and Poppy Seed Cupcakes

For the cupcakes:

250 g (9 oz) self-rising flour

250 g (9 oz) sugar

½ teaspoon sodium bicarbonate (baking soda)

1 tablespoon poppy seeds

270 g (9½ oz) butter, softened

4 large eggs

Zest from 4 lemons

1½ tablespoons lemon juice

1½ tablespoons milk

For the icing:

300 g (10½ oz) butter, softened

675 g (24 oz) icing sugar

4 tablespoons lemon juice

Preheat the oven to 190°C (375°F).

Pop all the dry cupcake ingredients into a bowl.

Add in the butter, eggs, lemon zest, and lemon juice and beat together for a minute.

Pour in the milk and beat again until combined.

Fill 18 muffin cases with the mixture and bake for 20 minutes.

Leave to cool on a wire rack.

To make the icing, beat the butter until pale and fluffy.

Sift the icing sugar in gradually and beat well.

Gradually add in the lemon juice and beat again.

Once the cupcakes are cool, ice them.

Herbal Teas for Grief

These are some herbal teas that can be drunk on their own to help soothe grief:

- Black tea
- Cardamom
- Cloves
- Lavender
- Lemon
- Marjoram
- Orange
- Thyme

Try creating your own blends. Here are some of my favourite combinations:

- Black tea bag with a slice of lemon
- Black tea bag with a slice of orange
- Black tea bag with a crushed cardamom and three cloves
- Two teaspoons lavender and a slice of lemon per mug of hot water
- One teaspoon marjoram, one teaspoon thyme, and a slice of lemon per mug of hot water
- Two crushed cardamoms and three cloves simmered in warm milk
- Two teaspoons thyme and a slice of lemon per mug of hot water

Incense and Oil Blends for Grief

Any of these can be used in spells, rituals, body care, anointing, cleansing, and more to help ease your grief. Each one can be used on its own or mixed with others in a blend.

- Bergamot
- Black pepper
- Cardamom
- Carnation
- Cloves
- Cypress
- Lavender
- Lemon
- Marjoram
- Orange
- Thyme

Incense Blends

- One part frankincense resin, two parts carnation, one part black pepper, and one part cypress
- Equal parts lavender, dried lemon peel, dried orange peel, and marjoram
- One part frankincense resin, one part cardamom, one part cloves, and one part black pepper
- One part dried orange peel, one part thyme, one part dried lemon peel, and a few drops bergamot oil
- Equal parts thyme, marjoram, and cloves
- Equal parts lavender, carnation, and dried lemon peel

Essential Oil Blends

- Combine six drops frankincense and ten drops lavender. Use in your bath or on an oil burner/diffuser or mix with a base oil to use on the body.
- Combine three drops lemon, three drops orange, and four drops cypress. Use in your bath or on an oil burner/diffuser or mix with a base oil to use on the body.
- Combine four drops lavender, three drops thyme, and three drops lemon. Use in your bath or on an oil burner/diffuser or mix with a base oil to use on the body.
- Combine four drops bergamot, three drops lemon, and three drops orange. Use in your bath or on an oil burner/diffuser or mix with a base oil to use on the body.

Everyday Exercise for Grief

Keep a nice, big, pretty jar or box somewhere visible. At the end of each day write something on a slip of paper that has made you happy. It doesn't have to be a big event: it could be finding your favourite cake at the bakery, seeing the first flower of spring, or even just being excited to crawl in bed.

If you have lost someone, write a favourite memory about them that popped into your head that day.

Remember to include positive thoughts about yourself too! Write down when you made someone else happy or did something you were proud of.

If you are having a bad day—or if you want to start the day on a positive note—take one of the memories out and read it, then refold and pop it back in the jar. Refer back to your jar of happiness whenever you need to.

Crystals for Grief

Carry crystals with you, use them in magical spells, or meditate with them. Remember to charge the crystal with your intent before use and cleanse it afterwards. Cleansing suggestions can be found in chapter 3 of this book.

- **Amethyst** dispels sadness and grief.
- **Ametrine** combines the soothing of amethyst and the happiness of citrine, helping you to move forward.

+ **Apache tear** gently cleanses grief and brings acceptance.

+ **Aquamarine** can help release grief.

+ **Azurite** heals, transforms, and brings understanding.

+ **Celestite** helps relieve sadness and brings a happy energy with it.

+ **Fire opal** helps heal grief, allowing you to move forward.

+ **Obsidian** is perfect for working through emotions and unpleasant experiences. It brings transformation.

+ **Lapis lazuli** works on a really deep level, helping to heal wounds.

+ **Larimar** brings peace and joy.

+ **Malachite** helps heal the heart and allows you to grieve fully.

+ **Mangano calcite** is all about self-love and acceptance.

+ **Moonstone** soothes and heals.

+ **Red jasper** brings a solid and down-to-earth energy, focusing on the practical things in life.

+ **Rhodochrosite** is a stone of unconditional love and inner peace.

+ **Rose quartz** heals emotions and helps open your heart again.

+ **Sugilite** brings support in times of grief and reminds you to be kind to yourself.

Meditation for Grief

This meditation will help you ease gently through the stages of grief.

Make yourself comfortable in a place where you won't be disturbed. If you feel drawn to, put on some light music, drumming, or chanting. Light your incense or oil blend if you would like.

As your world around you dissipates, you find yourself standing on the edge of a field. The sky above you is dark but the moon is full and shining above you, spreading a gentle light across the landscape. You stand quietly, soaking up the moonlight and breathing in the fresh, pleasantly warm air.

Taking in your surroundings, you see lush grass spreading out in front of you and what looks to be a circle of standing stones on the other side of the field.

You are drawn to the stones, so you start making your way across the grass toward them. There are a few sheep huddled up together at the edges of the field, and you can hear the bells tinkling that they have hanging around their necks.

As you reach the stone circle you feel an immense energy that is soothing, supporting, and comforting. You reach out a hand and touch the first stone. It is cold to the touch but tingles with energy. You feel encouraged to step between two of the stones and into the centre of the circle.

It is very quiet in the centre. You cannot hear any of the sounds of nature outside: not the sheep or the trees or the grasses swaying in the breeze. All is silent and peaceful.

There is a large, round, low stone in the centre. You walk over and sit down on it. In fact, it is large enough for you to lie down on. You lie on your back and look up at the moon.

She fills you with her soothing energy. Her moonlight rays comfort and support you, ease your raw emotions, and fill you with hope. Lie there until you are ready to get up...

As you start to sit up, you catch motion from the corner of your eye...

A large hare has hopped through the stones and is now staring at you. It does not appear frightened and sits up, cleaning its ears with its paws. All the while, it continues watching you...

It has a message... listen carefully...

The hare jumps quickly and is gone.

As you stand up, your leg brushes against a plant that is growing at the base of the centre stone. You are hit with a waft of delicious, spicy scent.

Bending down to touch the plant, you make a connection. The name "marjoram" enters your mind. The plant encourages you to talk, to release, to let go, and to let out your thoughts and emotions...

When you are finished, the plant gives you some comforting and supportive advice. You listen carefully.

Then the connection is gone and you stand up straight, taking a look around your surroundings again. You notice something small has appeared on the stone you were sitting on. You pick it up; it is a gift for you.

You make your way out between the stones and walk slowly back across the field. The sheep are still huddled up with their bells tinkling gently.

Taking a last look around, know that you can come back to this place at any time.

Slowly and gently come back to this reality, wriggling your fingers and toes. Open your eyes.

Drink and eat something.

What gift were you given, and what does it mean to you?

Jot down any thoughts or images that came to mind during your meditation. It can be useful to refer back to them later.

Spell to Let Go of Grief

Grieving is very personal, and it can only be done at your own pace. Each person is different and will need a varying amount of time to work through the grieving process. However, if you feel you have done what you need to do and want to release the emotion and move forward, this spell can help.

You will need:

+ Plant pot
+ A few seeds (flower seeds are lovely; pick something you like)
+ Soil
+ Water
+ Pebble

Take the pebble in your hands and send all your grief into it. Visualise the emotions draining from your body and entering the stone.

Place the pebble at the bottom of the plant pot and say:

My grief is released, I have now let go
The emotions are spent and will now help to grow

Fill the pot with soil.

Once the pot is almost full, sprinkle some seeds over the top of the soil. Cover them with a fine layer of more soil.

Pat the soil down gently and then water, saying:

From my grief, now buried and not shown
Positive flowers from these seeds are now grown

Place the pot in a warm, sunny spot and wait for your seeds to grow. Don't forget to water them!

Memory Tree Ritual to Release Grief

This ritual is set with the intent of releasing your grief, but it is also about remembrance. Memories are to be treasured.

I have called upon the Greek goddess Persephone for this ritual. She knows all about grief! Persephone understands the cycle of life and death, and she brings light and happiness to the darkest moments.

The spell within this ritual creates a memory tree. When you're finished with the spell, you can keep the memory tree in your home and add to it if you'd like.

This ritual can be done using the items listed below, or you can sit quietly in your space and just visualise the whole thing.

You will need:

+ A spindly branch or several large twigs
+ Plant pot or small bucket
+ Stones, pebbles, sand, or soil to fill the bucket
+ One central candle to represent the goddess Persephone
+ Small pieces of coloured ribbon or wool
+ Beads
+ Photos that hold good memories and include friends, family, and/or loved ones
+ Matches or a lighter
+ Something to eat and drink

Cast your circle. Walk around in a circle deosil (clockwise) or turn around on the spot if you are limited for space. Visualise a soft, glowing light forming a circle around you. When the circle is complete, visualise the light forming above you and below you to form a globe. As you cast the circle, say:

> *Circle of light*
> *Circle of peace*
> *Circle of protection*
> *Circle this place*

Call the quarters. Turn and face each compass direction, starting with the north and working deosil (clockwise). North is earth, east is air, south is fire, and west is water. As you face each compass direction, say:

> *Element of earth, bringing stability and grounding*
> *Please join me in this place*
> *Blessings of earth*
> *Element of air, bringing peace and clarity*
> *Please join me in this place*
> *Blessings of air*
> *Element of fire, bringing energy and passion*
> *Please join me in this place*
> *Blessings of fire*
> *Element of water, bringing emotion and calm*
> *Please join me in this place*
> *Blessings of water*

As you light the central candle, say:

> *I call upon the wise, understanding, and strong goddess Persephone*
> *And ask that you bring your strength, guidance, and support*
> *To assist me with this rite*
> *Blessings to you*

Now take your plant pot or bucket and fill it with sand, soil, or pebbles.

Then stick your branch or twigs into the pot so they stand up firmly and securely. This may take a bit of fiddling! This is your memory tree.

Now it's time for the fun part: decorating!

Take pieces of coloured ribbon or wool and tie them onto the branches. String a bead onto some of them if you want. For each ribbon you tie on, remember a good memory.

Tie some small photos of loved ones on the tree. This is about celebrating good memories and loved ones.

The tree should be full of happiness. Do not dwell on sad thoughts. Rejoice and celebrate life.

When you have finished decorating your tree, snuff out the candle.

Take a sip of your drink, raising your glass to Persephone.

Take a few bites of your food.

Then close the ritual. Face the centre and hold your arms wide, saying:

My thanks to you, great goddess Persephone
For your strength, guidance, and wisdom
Please continue to guide and support me
With blessings and thanks

Face each direction in turn, starting with the west. Work widdershins (counterclockwise) and say:

Element of water
My thanks for lending your energy today
Blessings of water
Element of fire
My thanks for lending your energy today
Blessings of fire
Element of air
My thanks for lending your energy today
Blessings of air
Element of earth
My thanks for lending your energy today
Blessings of earth

Then walk the circle widdershins (counterclockwise) and say:

Circle of light
Circle of peace
Circle of protection
Circle this place
This circle is now open but never broken

Pour the rest of your drink and crumble some of your food onto the earth as an offering to Persephone.

If you'd like to keep your tree, it can be placed somewhere in your home and added to whenever you'd like.

Bundle for Grief

To begin, choose a piece of fabric that makes you feel happy. You will need a cord or ribbon to tie it with, or you could use a drawstring pouch.

Your bundle can be filled with anything that you feel drawn to add—with the exception of fresh food or herbs because those would go mouldy! You could add crystals, dried herbs, seeds, dried leaves, twigs, dried flower petals, small tokens, beads, buttons, coins, small ornaments, etc. Trust your intuition.

Sit quietly or meditate to decide which things to add. Reach out to a deity such as Persephone and ask what needs to go in. It might only be one or two items at first—you can add to it over time.

Each item is representative of your journey to remember all of the good things in life. Charge each item individually before you pop it in the pouch. Hold each one in your hand and visualise positive energy entering it, bringing release and positivity and preventing you from hanging on to grief of any kind.

This bundle is all about memories—good ones. This bag should hold memories of the best moments of your life so far. Here are my suggestions:

- Photos, cinema tickets, or shells and pebbles from holidays
- Photos of loved ones
- Items that you have collected over time that remind you of outings, dates, and events
- Herbs and spices that help you alleviate grief (I would suggest poppy seeds, carnation, or thyme)

Keep the bundle on your altar or somewhere that you will see it. Use it when you meditate, either holding it on your lap or opening it up and handling each item in turn. You can also reach for it when you feel the need to let go. Draw upon the energy within to fill your mind and spirit with positive energy.

Mourning is a very personal journey.

Each person deals with grief in their own way and in their own time.

There is no "correct" way to deal with grief.

Take your time and work through things at your own pace.

If you find yourself grieving, refer back to this chapter for magical suggestions that might help.

CHAPTER FOURTEEN

Self-Esteem

Your self-esteem is a combination of a lot of things: your confidence in your abilities; what you think your worth is as a human being; and the faith and respect you have for yourself. If your self-esteem is low or has disappeared altogether, it can leave you feeling unconfident and unloved. You may feel bad about how you act, react, and look. You might ask yourself, *Am I attractive? Does my bum look big in this?* Low self-esteem leads to blame, guilt, and a desire to withdraw.

We all have moments of self-doubt that make us question if we are good enough. It is debilitating to keep questioning whether we are worthy or not. (Trust me, you are worthy just the way you are.) So let's turn things around—self-esteem really is just a state of mind. You are a wonderful human being and we need to celebrate that!

In this chapter you will find magical suggestions to help boost your self-esteem. Work with as many of them as you like. Follow your intuition and be guided by it as to what you choose to work with.

Affirmations. Regular positive statements can change the way we think about ourselves and our situations.

Colour Magic. Colour plays an important part in how we feel and can affect our emotions; work with it to boost positive energy.

Herbs. This section will contain my suggestions of herbs to work with in magical spell workings. Pick from my ideas or use your own—be guided by your intuition.

Foods. All foods have magical properties. I have given you some suggestions that can be eaten or used in spell work. I've also included a recipe in each chapter.

Herbal Teas. These can be created with herbs and spices that help alleviate negative issues. Work with my suggestions or use your own.

Incense and Oils. Scents can bring up strong emotions. Work with my suggestions to create incense blends or oil blends to use in ritual or spell work. You can also create these blends just because the scent will lift your mood!

Everyday Exercise. In this section you will find easy daily or regular routines to help get your positive energy flowing and get rid of the negative vibes.

Crystals. They hold such power in tiny, easy-to-handle form. Crystals can be worked with in all sorts of ways to help with all kinds of issues.

Meditation. Read through the script or even record it on your phone. Take some time out and work with the meditation for help and guidance.

Spell. You will find spells to help with any issue. Keep it simple and straightforward. If you don't have the items I have suggested, substitute them with whatever you feel is right. Personalise it; make the spell your own.

Ritual. The rituals included will not be too fancy or complicated. Often, the rituals connect with a deity and the elements to work some magic.

Magic Bundle. In this section you'll find my suggestions for creating a magic bundle to help you through your situation.

Affirmations for Self-Esteem

I am fabulous.
My beauty shines.
I radiate awesomeness.

I have the courage and confidence of a warrior.
I can do anything I put my mind to.

Colour Magic for Self-Esteem

If you saw self-esteem as a colour, what colour would you see? This will vary from person to person. For any negative emotion or issue that I want to release, I see black as a good colour to work with. White is also good because it is neutral.

When I think of self-esteem as a colour, I think of something loud and proud: perhaps a bright sunflower yellow or a sassy pink. It needs to shout confidence, love, and courage. But if you feel more confident in a darker colour, go for it!

Herbs to Boost Self-Esteem

These are for magical use, NOT consumption.

+ Agrimony
+ Alexanders
+ Betony
+ Carnation
+ Celandine
+ Columbine (aquilegia)
+ Cyclamen
+ Hyacinth
+ Hypericum
+ Rose
+ Sweet pea
+ Yarrow

Foods to Boost Self-Esteem

These can be used magically and/or eaten.

+ Basil
+ Black pepper

- Black tea
- Chocolate
- Cinnamon
- Cloves
- Coriander
- Fennel
- Ginger
- Lavender
- Lemon balm
- Marjoram
- Rhubarb
- Rosemary
- Thyme

Recipe: Fruit Tea Cake

There are many variations on this recipe, but essentially it is a cake packed with dried fruit, flavoured with tea, and baked in a loaf tin. You can use any kind of tea for this; I recommend breakfast tea, scented Earl Grey tea, or spiced chai tea (my personal favourite). Serve sliced on its own. It is also lovely lightly toasted and spread with butter or jam. This isn't a beautiful or extravagant-looking cake, but it tastes divine—a reminder that it is what is on the inside that counts!

Magic of the Ingredients

- Milk—feminine power, creativity, antidepression, nurturing, love
- Sugar—to make life sweet!
- Sultanas—love, happiness
- Tea—courage, strength

You can charge or bless the ingredients as you add them to the mix or do so once the cake is made. Hold your hands over them and say:

Self-esteem is brought to me
With love and sweet cake full of tea

Fruit Tea Cake

    50 g (2 oz) demerara sugar

    150 mL (5 fl oz) hot tea, any kind

    400 g (14 oz) dried fruit (I like to use sultanas, but you can mix them with raisins, currants, chopped dried apricots, or dried cranberries)

    50 g (2 oz) mixed nuts (pecan, walnut, cashew, hazelnut, etc.)

    1 large egg

    225 g (8 oz) self-rising flour

    1–2 tablespoons milk

Grease and line a 2-lb loaf tin.

Dissolve demerara sugar in the hot tea. Pour over the dried fruits.

Leave to soak. Soak overnight, if possible. If you only have a few minutes to soak, that works too! The fruit absorbs the tea, making them plumpscious (that's not a real word, but it describes it well).

Preheat the oven to 170°C (325°F).

Place the nuts on a baking sheet and pop them in the oven to toast for about 5 minutes. Keep an eye on them because they can burn easily. Remove to cool.

Once the nuts have cooled, roughly chop them.

Add an egg and the chopped nuts to the fruit mix. Sift in the flour. Stir well.

Add one tablespoon of milk. If the mixture is a bit stiff, add another one.

Spoon the mixture into the loaf tin.

Place in the oven on a low shelf and bake for about an hour or until the cake springs back in the centre.

Herbal Teas for Self-Esteem

These are some herbal teas that can be drunk on their own to help boost your self-esteem:

+ Basil

+ Black tea

+ Chocolate (cocoa nibs work best in tea blends)

+ Cinnamon

+ Cloves

+ Coriander

+ Fennel

+ Ginger

+ Lavender

+ Lemon balm

+ Marjoram

+ Rose

+ Rosemary

+ Thyme

Try creating your own blends. Here are some of my favourite combinations:

+ Black tea bag with a pinch of cinnamon and a couple of cloves

+ Black tea bag with one teaspoon of dried lemon balm

+ Black tea bag with a slice of root ginger

+ One teaspoon dried lavender flowers and a few rose petals per mug of hot water

+ A slice of root ginger and half a teaspoon of fennel seeds per mug of hot water

+ Black tea bag with a pinch of cocoa nibs

+ Half a teaspoon of coriander seeds, half a teaspoon of ground cinnamon, and a couple of cloves per mug of hot water

Incense and Oil Blends for Self-Esteem

Any of these can be used in spells, rituals, body care, anointing, cleansing, and more to help boost your self-esteem. Each one can be used on its own or mixed with others in a blend.

+ Basil
+ Black pepper
+ Black tea
+ Carnation
+ Chocolate (cocoa nibs)
+ Cinnamon
+ Cloves
+ Coriander
+ Fennel
+ Ginger
+ Hyacinth
+ Lavender
+ Lemon balm
+ Marjoram
+ Rose
+ Rosemary
+ Sweet pea
+ Thyme
+ Yarrow

Incense Blends
+ Equal parts cinnamon, cloves, and coriander
+ One part frankincense resin, two parts cinnamon, and one part ginger
+ Equal parts rosemary, thyme, rose, and lavender
+ Equal parts frankincense resin, fennel, and ginger
+ Equal parts cinnamon, rose, lavender, and lemon balm
+ One part black pepper, two parts cinnamon, and one part cloves

Essential Oil Blends

+ Combine six drops lavender, six drops rose, and six drops sweet pea. Use in your bath or on an oil burner/diffuser or mix with a base oil to use on the body.

+ Combine six drops lemon balm, six drops ginger, and six drops rosemary. Use in your bath or on an oil burner/diffuser or mix with a base oil to use on the body.

+ Combine eight drops coriander, five drops cinnamon, and five drops cloves. Use in your bath or on an oil burner/diffuser or mix with a base oil to use on the body.

+ Combine six drops cinnamon, eight drops ginger, and four drops black pepper. Use in your bath or on an oil burner/diffuser or mix with a base oil to use on the body.

Everyday Exercise for Self-Esteem

If you haven't already, make moisturiser a part of your daily routine. Apply in the morning and/or evening, and add in some affirmations as you do so. Use the affirmations suggested in this book, the ones taken from your self-esteem spell, or keep it simple and just repeat, "I love you. I love you. I love you," as you look at your reflection.

As you massage the moisturiser into your skin, look in the mirror and repeat your chosen affirmations. It might make you feel a bit silly at first, but honestly, you deserve to love yourself!

Crystals for Self-Esteem

Carry crystals with you, use them in magical spells, or meditate with them. Remember to charge the crystal with your intent before use and cleanse it afterwards. Cleansing suggestions can be found in chapter 3 of this book.

+ **Carnelian** brings a huge boost of confidence and harmony.

+ **Citrine** boosts self-confidence and your personal power.

+ **Fuchsite** is a stone of happiness and joy, allowing you to live life with a positive outlook.

+ **Hematite** is grounding and brings clarity and support.

* **Mangano calcite** is the self-love stone, bringing acceptance and a positive zing of self-worth.
* **Moonstone** helps reduce fears and brings you self-confidence.
* **Moss agate** works with the heart to open you up to confidence.
* **Opal** transforms your negative energies into positive energies, shining a light on the good traits.
* **Pyrite** eases frustration and also helps maintain the physical body.
* **Rhodochrosite** gives you a positive boost of self-love and helps you realise your full potential.
* **Rhodonite** brings balance to the heart and provides a big confidence boost.
* Self-confidence and self-esteem are both boosted with the use of **rose quartz.**
* **Sodalite** helps with the thought process, bringing clarity and the ability to see what is real.
* **Sunstone** will literally help you shine.

Meditation for Self-Esteem

This meditation will boost your self-esteem, helping you remember that you are amazing!

Make yourself comfortable in a place where you won't be disturbed. If you feel drawn to, put on some light music, drumming, or chanting. Light your incense or oil blend if you would like.

As your world around you dissipates, your ears are filled with the beautiful sounds of the jungle. Birds and animals call to each other all around you. The air is warm and filled with the scent of exotic plants. Surrounding you is the lush, brightly coloured foliage of a tropical jungle. Take a look around, listen carefully, and take a deep breath in and out.

Ahead of you there appears to be a winding pathway, so you start to make your way along it. Gorgeous weird and wonderful flowers line the side of the path. Creepers hang down from the trees on either side. The canopy above you is made up of huge green leaves from the trees, but there is enough space for light to come through.

As you walk through the tropical plants and trees you start to hear the faint sounds of water, quietly at first but getting louder. The pathway opens up to reveal a clearing. In front of you is an azure pool of water with a small waterfall cascading down into it. The scene is breathtaking.

Where the waterfall splashes onto the surface of the pool, it creates beautiful rainbows in the air. Birds with colourful plumage and huge, brightly painted butterflies flit in and out of the curtains of water.

You are drawn toward the pool and find somewhere comfortable to sit at the water's edge.

While sitting quietly, watching and drawing in all the wonderful energy, a small, colourful bird flies down to sit beside you. When you put your hand out it hops onto your fingers. You feel a connection has been made.

The bird begins to tell you that you are amazing and lists all the brilliant things about you … listen carefully.

When the bird has finished, it directs you to look into the pool of water. You can see your own reflection, a true reflection—one that shows just how fabulous you really are. Take a good look. Notice all the truly wonderful things about yourself. You radiate confidence, courage, and pure awesomeness.

Whilst you have been looking into the pool the bird has taken flight, but it has dropped a gift for you, which you pick up.

Your eye is drawn to a small plant at the edge of the water. You make your way over and reach out to touch the leaves. As your fingers brush the edge of the plant the name "cyclamen" jumps into your head.

The plant has a message for you. Listen very carefully …

If you have any questions, ask them now. Allow the cyclamen to share its wisdom and guidance with you …

When you are ready, thank the plant for sharing with you.

Take a long look around, then make your way back out of the clearing and along the pathway to where you started.

Know that you can return to this place whenever you need to.

Slowly and gently come back to this reality. Wriggle your fingers and toes. Have something to eat and drink.

What gift did the bird leave? What does it mean to you?

Jot down any thoughts or images that came to mind during your meditation. It can be useful to refer back to them later.

Spell to Boost Self-Esteem

Let's build up your self-esteem and make you realise just how amazing you really are. Take this spell slowly and work with baby steps. Start small; just one positive is a good starting point to build upon.

You will need:

+ A candle (purple or yellow both work well)
+ Happy, uplifting essential oil (any of the citrus scents would be good)
+ Base oil to dilute the essential oil of your choosing
+ Piece of paper
+ Pen
+ The largest mirror you have
+ Matches or a lighter

Sit in front of the mirror and light the candle. Make sure you set the candle on a safe, flat surface.

Take the paper and pen and start to write down all the good things about yourself. Think about what you like about your looks: you might like the colour of your eyes, your hair, or even the length of your fingernails. Also write down good deeds or nice things you have done for others; holding the door open for the person behind you in the coffee shop, for instance. Make note of the good qualities and skills you possess. Are you a good listener? Do you take care of pets? Can you cook a delicious pie or bake a nice cake? Your list doesn't need to be full of grand statements. Even the simplest positives are important.

Take your time with this and really focus on each one. If you struggle with this, maybe ask a trusted friend or family member to help you create your list. Your list doesn't have to be long; even one or two positives are good to start with.

Using your list as inspiration, write some affirmations to use later.

When you are ready, take the essential oil and anoint your pulse points (forehead, sides of neck, wrists) with it. Then look directly at your reflection in the mirror and say:

I came from the earth
Made by the Divine
I am beauty, I am love
I am confidence and courageous light

Allow the candle to burn out. Do not leave it unattended until the flame is extinguished.

Keep the paper with your positive thoughts and affirmations under your pillow. Read through at least one of them every day before you go to sleep. Read another when you wake up.

Add to the list when you think of more positives. If someone compliments you, add their comment too.

Ritual to Boost Self-Esteem

This ritual is set with the intent of knowing, recognising, and celebrating your own self-worth.

Aphrodite brings her energy to this ritual. As the Greek goddess of love, she also brings passion and focuses heavily on self-love.

You will need a photograph of yourself for this ritual. Put it in a nice frame. Be proud and pick a photo that you like. If you can't decide, ask a friend or family member to choose one for you.

You will also need a list of affirmations about yourself. Before you perform this ritual, read through the Spell to Boost Self-Esteem section. This way you can work with the list of affirmations you made.

This ritual can be done using the items listed below, or you can sit quietly in your space and just visualise the whole thing.

You will need:

+ A couple of handfuls of flower petals, such as rose
+ Photograph of yourself
+ Picture frame

+ One white, pink, or red central candle to represent the goddess Aphrodite
+ List of self-esteem affirmations
+ Essential oil that you love
+ Matches or a lighter
+ Dried herbs such as rosemary or thyme

Cast your circle. Walk around in a circle deosil (clockwise) or turn around on the spot if you are limited for space. Visualise a soft, glowing light forming a circle around you. As you walk the circle, sprinkle flower petals to create the boundary. When the circle is complete, visualise the light forming above you and below you to form a globe. As you cast the circle, say:

Circle of light
Circle of peace
Circle of protection
Circle this place

Call the quarters. Turn and face each compass direction, starting with the north and working deosil (clockwise). North is earth, east is air, south is fire, and west is water. As you face each compass direction in turn, say:

Element of earth, bringing stability and grounding
Please join me in this place
Blessings of earth
Element of air, bringing peace and clarity
Please join me in this place
Blessings of air
Element of fire, bringing energy and passion
Please join me in this place
Blessings of fire
Element of water, bringing emotion and calm
Please join me in this place
Blessings of water

As you light the central candle, say:

I call upon the beautiful goddess Aphrodite
And ask that you bring your love, guidance, and support
To assist me with this rite
Blessings to you

Pop the photograph of yourself inside the picture frame. Set it in front of the candle.

Take some of your chosen essential oil and anoint the picture frame with a dab in each corner. Say:

Aphrodite, the goddess of love
Bring me courage and confidence of self-worth
May I know and acknowledge my worth
That I am beautiful inside and out

Sprinkle some dried herbs over the photograph frame. Say:

With herbal magic and more
May it support my self-esteem and help it soar
Make it so!

Spend a few moments now connecting with the energy of Aphrodite. Allow her to come through and give you guidance.

Then hold the photograph of yourself in front of you. Talk to it. Repeat your self-esteem affirmations.

Take a sip of your drink, raising your glass to Aphrodite.

Take a few bites of your food.

Then close the ritual. Face the centre and hold your arms wide, saying:

My thanks to you, great goddess Aphrodite
For your love, guidance, and wisdom
Please continue to guide and support me
With blessings and thanks

Face each direction in turn, starting with the west. Work widdershins (counterclockwise) and say:

Element of water
My thanks for lending your energy today
Blessings of water
Element of fire
My thanks for lending your energy today
Blessings of fire
Element of air
My thanks for lending your energy today
Blessings of air
Element of earth
My thanks for lending your energy today
Blessings of earth

Then walk the circle widdershins (counterclockwise), sweep up the flower petals, and say:

Circle of light
Circle of peace
Circle of protection
Circle this place
This circle is now open but never broken

Snuff out the central candle.

Pour the rest of your drink and crumble some of your food onto the earth as an offering to Aphrodite.

The flower petals can be put in the compost or sprinkled on the garden. Place the photograph frame somewhere prominent, perhaps on your "honouring you" altar.

If you feel the need for another boost of self-esteem in the future, give the frame a dab of essential oil and/or a sprinkling of herbs.

Bundle for Self-Esteem

To begin, choose a piece of fabric that makes you feel confident; you will need a cord or ribbon to tie it with, or you could use a drawstring pouch.

Your self-esteem bundle can be filled with anything that you feel drawn to add—with the exception of fresh food or herbs because those would go mouldy! You could add crystals, dried herbs, seeds, dried leaves, twigs, dried flower petals, small tokens, beads, buttons, coins, small ornaments, etc. Trust your intuition.

Sit quietly or meditate to decide which things to add. Reach out to a deity such as Aphrodite and ask what needs to go in. It might only be one or two items at first—you can add to it over time.

Each item is representative of your journey to build your confidence and courage. Charge each item individually before you pop it in the pouch. Hold each one in your hand and visualise positive energy entering it, bringing confidence, self-love, and pride.

This bundle is really all about self-love. Its job is to remind you that you are amazing! This bag needs to contain things that lift your spirits and make you happy. Here are my suggestions:

+ Items that make you feel good about yourself (perhaps a badge for an achievement)
+ Photos of your loved ones or items that make you think of them
+ Brightly coloured items, even small things like buttons (this is a great way to incorporate colour magic)
+ Small mirror to remind you that you look and feel good
+ Dried flowers and herbs that bring a little sunshine and confidence

Keep the bundle on your altar or somewhere that you will see it. Use it when you meditate, either holding it on your lap or opening it up and handling each item in turn. You can also reach for it when you feel like you need a self-esteem boost. Draw upon the energy within to fill your mind and spirit with positive energy.

The process of boosting your self-esteem can take some time. Don't rush it.

Every tiny step, no matter how small, is still a step forward.

Remember that you are wonderful just the way you are!

If you find yourself struggling with low self-esteem, refer back to this chapter for magical suggestions that might help.

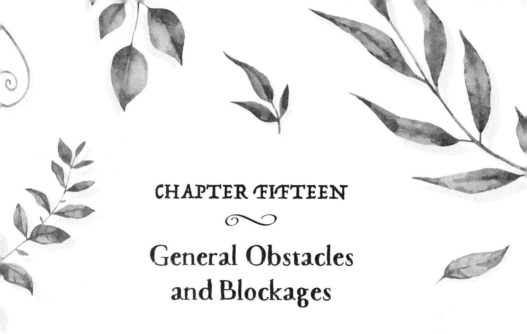

CHAPTER FIFTEEN

❧

General Obstacles and Blockages

People naturally hold on to a large amount of emotional baggage, whether in our minds, our hearts, or our physical bodies. When you hang on to things they can sit in your subconscious and fester, sometimes causing your emotions to spiral out of control. Honestly...let it all go! If you don't, you may suffer from blockages and emotional obstacles. Release the bad stuff in order to bring in the good stuff.

In this chapter you will find magical suggestions to help you overcome obstacles and break through blockages. Work with as many of them as you like. Follow your intuition and be guided by it as to what you choose to work with.

Affirmations. Regular positive statements can change the way we think about ourselves and our situations.

Colour Magic. Colour plays an important part in how we feel and can affect our emotions; work with it to boost positive energy.

Herbs. This section will contain my suggestions of herbs to work with in magical spell workings. Pick from my ideas or use your own—be guided by your intuition.

Foods. All foods have magical properties. I have given you some suggestions that can be eaten or used in spell work. I've also included a recipe in each chapter.

Herbal Teas. These can be created with herbs and spices that help alleviate negative issues. Work with my suggestions or use your own.

Incense and Oils. Scents can bring up strong emotions. Work with my suggestions to create incense blends or oil blends to use in ritual or spell work. You can also create these blends just because the scent will lift your mood!

Everyday Exercise. In this section you will find easy daily or regular routines to help get your positive energy flowing and get rid of the negative vibes.

Crystals. They hold such power in tiny, easy-to-handle form. Crystals can be worked with in all sorts of ways to help with all kinds of issues.

Meditation. Read through the script or even record it on your phone. Take some time out and work with the meditation for help and guidance.

Spell. You will find spells to help with any issue. Keep it simple and straightforward. If you don't have the items I have suggested, substitute them with whatever you feel is right. Personalise it; make the spell your own.

Ritual. The rituals included will not be too fancy or complicated. Often, the rituals connect with a deity and the elements to work some magic.

Magic Bundle. In this section you'll find my suggestions for creating a magic bundle to help you through your situation.

Affirmations for Obstacles and Blockages

I am ready to let go.
I am willing and able to move forward.
I release the past.
My life is ahead of me.

Colour Magic for Obstacles and Blockages

If you saw obstacles and blockages as a colour, what colour would you see? This will vary from person to person. For any negative emotion or issue that I want to release, I see black as a good colour to work with. White is also good because it is neutral.

I see blockages as the colour black, followed by the colour white. Initially, blockages are black as I deal with the issue and then white as I replace it.

Herbs to Combat Obstacles and Blockages

These are for magical use, NOT consumption.

- Agrimony
- Alexanders
- Bergamot
- Betony
- Birch
- Carnation
- Celandine
- Cypress
- Frankincense
- Lungwort
- Pine
- Rue
- Self-heal
- Valerian
- Vervain
- Willow

Foods to Combat Obstacles and Blockages

These can be used magically and/or eaten.

- Citrus (grapefruit, lemon, lime, and orange)
- Coriander

+ Fennel
+ Ginger
+ Lavender
+ Mint
+ Rosemary
+ Salt
+ Star anise
+ Thyme
+ Turmeric

Recipe: *Orange and Star Anise Yogurt Cake*

This is a lovely loaf cake filled with the flavours of bright orange and cleansing star anise. It is easy to make this a dairy-free recipe: simply use soy yogurt instead of Greek yogurt.

Magic of the Ingredients

+ Orange—love, happiness, uplifting, clarity, energy
+ Salt—cleansing, purification, protection
+ Star anise—purification, protection
+ Sugar—to make life sweet!
+ Yogurt—antidepression, nurturing, love

You can charge or bless the ingredients as you add them to the mix or do so once the cake is made. Hold your hands over them and say:

Release and remove the blockages stuck
Orange and star anise will bring me luck

Orange and Star Anise Yogurt Cake

200 g (7 oz) caster sugar

3 eggs, room temperature

200 g (7 oz) Greek yogurt

Zest of one orange

1 teaspoon vanilla extract

280 g (10 oz) self-rising flour

1 teaspoon baking powder

½ teaspoon salt

120 mL (4 fl oz) olive oil

Juice of two oranges

1 tablespoon sugar

1 star anise

Preheat your oven to 180°C (350°F).

Lightly grease a 2-lb loaf tin and line with baking parchment.

Whisk the sugar and eggs until well mixed.

Add in the yogurt, orange zest, and vanilla extract and mix together.

Sift in the flour, baking powder, and salt, then mix to combine.

Slowly pour in the olive oil and mix until combined.

Pour the mixture into the loaf tin and bake in the centre of the oven for 45–50 minutes or until a skewer inserted in the middle of the cake comes out clean.

Once cooked, take the loaf out of the oven and leave in the tin.

Gently heat the orange juice in a small pan with the star anise and sugar. Once the sugar is dissolved, discard the star anise and spoon the orange-sugar syrup over the warm cake.

Herbal Teas for Obstacles and Blockages

These are some herbal teas that can be drunk on their own to help overcome obstacles and break through blockages:

+ Citrus (grapefruit, lemon, lime, and orange)

+ Coriander

+ Fennel

+ Ginger

+ Lavender

+ Mint

- Rosemary
- Star anise
- Thyme
- Turmeric

Try creating your own blends. Here are some of my favourite combinations:

- Warm water with a slice of lemon
- Warm water with a slice of root ginger and a slice of lemon
- One teaspoon of fennel seeds, a piece of star anise, and a slice of lemon per mug of hot water
- A slice of root ginger, one teaspoon of dried mint, and half a teaspoon dried rosemary per mug of hot water
- One teaspoon of lavender flowers, a slice of root ginger, and a slice of lemon per mug of hot water
- Half a teaspoon of coriander seeds, a slice of orange, and a slice of root ginger per mug of hot water

Incense and Oil Blends for Obstacles and Blockages

Any of these can be used in spells, rituals, body care, anointing, cleansing, and more to help overcome obstacles and break through blockages. Each one can be used on its own or mixed with others in a blend.

- Agrimony
- Bergamot
- Birch
- Carnation
- Citrus (grapefruit, lemon, lime, and orange)
- Coriander
- Cypress
- Fennel
- Frankincense
- Ginger

+ Lavender
+ Mint
+ Pine
+ Rosemary
+ Rue
+ Star anise
+ Thyme
+ Turmeric
+ Valerian
+ Vervain
+ Willow

Incense Blends

+ One part frankincense resin, two parts lavender, and two parts pine
+ Equal parts pine, rosemary, and star anise
+ One part frankincense resin, one part fennel, one part star anise, and two parts mint
+ Equal parts coriander, dried orange peel, and ginger
+ Equal parts rosemary, thyme, and ginger
+ Two parts pine, one part coriander, and one part ginger

Essential Oil Blends

+ Combine six drops bergamot, six drops orange, and six drops grapefruit. Use in your bath or on an oil burner/diffuser or mix with a base oil to use on the body.
+ Combine six drops frankincense, four drops ginger, and four drops mint. Use in your bath or on an oil burner/diffuser or mix with a base oil to use on the body.
+ Combine four drops lavender, four drops pine, and six drops ginger. Use in your bath or on an oil burner/diffuser or mix with a base oil to use on the body.

+ Combine three drops fennel, three drops mint, three drops pine, and four drops lemon. Use in your bath or on an oil burner/diffuser or mix with a base oil to use on the body.

Everyday Exercise for Obstacles and Blockages

Next time you shower, bathe, or wash, use the water involved to help you release and let go. Water is a natural purifier.

In the shower, stand and let the water wash over you. It clears, cleanses, and takes all the negative energy down the drain. In the bath, let the water cleanse your body and soul. Even washing your face will cleanse negative energy. All you need to add is a dash of visualisation as you wash.

Crystals for Obstacles and Blockages

Carry crystals with you, use them in magical spells, or meditate with them. Remember to charge the crystal with your intent before use and cleanse it afterwards. Cleansing suggestions can be found in chapter 3 of this book.

+ **Amethyst** works with the mind. It is a "headology" stone to help you release the stuff that is clogging up your head.

+ **Aquamarine** brings everything to the surface, clearing negative energy and replacing it with hope and positive vibes.

+ **Citrine** releases, balances, and brings focus and clarity.

+ Emotional calm is brought about with **moonstone** after releasing negative energy.

+ **Peridot** removes blockages, allowing you to move forward and helping you recognise and attune to your life cycle.

+ **Petrified wood** has undergone a transformation, so it can help you do so too.

+ **Pink tourmaline** helps release all the bad stuff, leaving you open for the good things to fit right in.

+ **Rose quartz** mothers and nurtures, helping you to gently let go.

+ **Rutilated quartz** repairs, heals, and helps the flow of energy.

+ Use **selenite** to release negative energy from your body. It will also help remove blockages.

+ **Smoky quartz** can absorb negative energy and release it to Mother Earth to be transformed.

+ **Sodalite** brings about balance of emotions and clarity of thought.

Meditation for Obstacles and Blockages

This meditation will help you release, clear, cleanse, and purify all those negative vibes, emotions, obstacles, and issues that you are holding on to.

Make yourself comfortable in a place where you won't be disturbed. If you feel drawn to, put on some light music, drumming, or chanting. Light your incense or oil blend if you would like.

As your world around you dissipates, you find yourself on a grassy bank. The sky above you is grey and cloudy. In front of you is a dusty pathway that leads to an old bridge that appears to span across a large river.

The air around you is still and quiet, but you can hear the river as it meanders along. You make your way to the edge of the bridge.

The river is wide, but the bridge seems to traverse right across to the far side in the distance. Every so often along the bridge there are buckets, each one a different colour.

You walk to the first bucket. What colour is it? What does that represent to you? Painted on the side is the word "release." Look inside the bucket. What do you see?

You feel drawn to pick up the bucket and acknowledge the contents. What do the contents mean to you? This is something that you need to let go of. Get a picture in your mind of the situation, emotion, feeling, or issue that you need to release and then empty the contents of the bucket over the side of the bridge and into the flowing water of the river. As the contents spill out, release…

You put the empty bucket back onto the bridge, but as you do so you notice that it has refilled with beautiful flowers and foliage.

Feeling lighter and more positive in yourself, you move farther along the bridge toward the next bucket. What colour is it? What does that represent to you? Painted on the side is the word "release." Look inside the bucket. What do you see?

You feel drawn to pick up the bucket and acknowledge the contents. What do the contents mean to you? This is something that you need to let go of. Get a picture in your mind of the situation, emotion, feeling, or issue that you need to release and then empty the contents of the bucket over the side of the bridge and into the flowing water of the river. As the contents spill out, release...

You put the empty bucket back onto the bridge, but as you do so you notice that it has refilled with beautiful flowers and foliage.

You walk farther along the bridge to the next bucket. What colour is it? What does that represent to you? Painted on the side is the word "release." Look inside the bucket. What do you see?

You feel drawn to pick up the bucket and acknowledge the contents. What do the contents mean to you? This is something that you need to let go of. Get a picture in your mind of the situation, emotion, feeling, or issue that you need to release and then empty the contents of the bucket over the side of the bridge and into the flowing water of the river. As the contents spill out, release...

You put the empty bucket back onto the bridge, but as you do so you notice that it has refilled with beautiful flowers and foliage.

You can continue picking up buckets on the bridge for as long as you feel is necessary.

When you feel you have released everything, make your way to the far side of the bridge. Turn around and look back along the length of the bridge and all the buckets that you emptied. Take note of the beauty that now fills them. This is you. You have released that which no longer serves you.

There is one last bucket on the very end of the bridge. Move toward it. It is full of an herb. You brush you hand over the foliage and are greeted with the scent of thyme. Your hand has made a connection with the plant and it has some wisdom to share with you. Listen carefully...

When you are ready, thank the plant and take one last look back over the bridge. You won't be crossing back—now you are ready to move forward.

Step off the bridge and onto the grassy bank in front of you.

Gently come back to this reality. Open your eyes slowly. Wriggle your fingers and toes.

Eat and drink something.

Jot down any thoughts or images that came to mind during your meditation. It can be useful to refer back to them later.

Spell to Overcome Obstacles and Break Through Blockages

This is a very simple spell to release the negative energy that we hold on to. Part of being able to release issues and emotions is recognising them in the first place.

You will need:

+ Small glass jar or bottle
+ Small amount of sand or soil
+ Small feathers or seeds
+ One black candle
+ One white candle
+ Matches or a lighter
+ Envelope or piece of paper

Light the black candle and set the jar or bottle in front of you. Now take a moment to bring to the front of your mind anything that you want to let go of. It might be bad habits, negative emotions or issues, feelings, or even a connection to a person.

Now put a pinch of sand or soil in the empty jar. Each pinch represents one of the things you want to release. Say them out loud as you put each pinch into the jar.

When you have finished adding as many pinches as you need to, say:

This represents all that no longer serves me
All that I wish to release and leave behind

Light the white candle.

Tip the contents of the jar into the envelope. If you are using a piece of paper instead, tip the contents onto the paper and fold it up. Say:

I release you, I let go
I purify you from my mind, body, soul, and spirit

Throw away the envelope or piece of paper filled with soil/sand.

Take the now-empty jar and visualise positive feelings, emotions, people, and situations. Say them out loud as you put seeds or feathers into the jar.

When you have finished adding as many seeds or feathers as you want to, say:

This represents all the good and positive things in my life
I can now move forward with a happy heart

Snuff out both candles.

Keep the jar on your altar or somewhere you can see it. The jar is full of positive energy so keep it visible to remind you of all the good things. If you feel the jar's energy has waned, you can recharge it by giving it a shake and visualising white light entering it.

At some point you may feel that the jar has served its purpose. You can empty the feathers or seeds into the recycling or trash and rework the spell if you want to.

Release the Bindings Ritual

This ritual is set with the intent of letting go, releasing, purifying, and cleansing all that no longer serves you. Remember that when you clear out negative energy it leaves a void, so you must fill that void with positive intentions.

The Sumerian goddess Inanna lends her energy to this ritual. She is excellent at stripping things down to the core and removing that which is not needed.

This ritual can be done using the items listed below, or you can sit quietly in your space and just visualise the whole thing.

You will need:

+ A small dish of water with a pinch of salt added
+ One black candle
+ One white candle

+ Dark-coloured thread or twine (make sure to choose a natural fibre that will burn)
+ Fireproof dish
+ Scissors
+ Matches or a lighter
+ Something to eat and drink

Cast your circle. Walk around in a circle deosil (clockwise) or turn around on the spot if you are limited for space. Visualise a soft, glowing light forming a circle around you. As you walk the circle sprinkle the saltwater to create the boundary. When the circle is complete, visualise the light forming above you and below you to form a globe. As you cast the circle, say:

Circle of light
Circle of peace
Circle of protection
Circle this place

Call the quarters. Turn and face each compass direction, starting with the north and working deosil (clockwise). North is earth, east is air, south is fire, and west is water. As you face each compass direction in turn, say:

Element of earth, bringing stability and grounding
Please join me in this place
Blessings of earth
Element of air, bringing peace and clarity
Please join me in this place
Blessings of air
Element of fire, bringing energy and passion
Please join me in this place
Blessings of fire
Element of water, bringing emotion and calm
Please join me in this place
Blessings of water

As you light the black candle, say:

I call upon the ancient and wise goddess Inanna
And ask that you bring your strength, guidance, and support
To assist me with this rite
Blessings to you

Sit for a few moments and focus on the things that no longer serve you … those that hurt or damage you. What do you want to release or get rid of?

Then take the thread and wrap it around your ankles. (If it is easier, you can just tie it around one ankle rather than both.) Say:

These are the bindings that stop me from moving forward in my life

Then tie the thread around one of your wrists. (If you are working this ritual with another person present, they can tie both of your wrists and ankles for you and do the cutting. But if you are on your own, one wrist and one ankle are easier!) Say:

These are the bindings that stop me from taking hold of my own life
and decisions

Take the scissors. Cut the threads that bind your ankle, saying:

I cut the ties that bind me
May I walk free

Take the thread and light it in the candle flame, then drop it into the fireproof dish.

Cut the threads that bind your wrist, saying:

I cut the ties that bind me
I now take control

Take the thread and light it in the candle flame, then drop it into the fireproof dish.

Now light the white candle and take a few moments to visualise a white light emanating from the candle and washing over you, bringing positive, confident energy to you.

Take a sip of your drink, raising your glass to Inanna.

Take a few bites of your food.

Then close the ritual. Face the centre and hold your arms wide, saying:

My thanks to you, great goddess Inanna
For your strength, guidance, and wisdom
Please continue to guide and support me
With blessings and thanks

Face each direction in turn, starting with the west. Work widdershins (counterclockwise) and say:

Element of water
My thanks for lending your energy today
Blessings of water
Element of fire
My thanks for lending your energy today
Blessings of fire
Element of air
My thanks for lending your energy today
Blessings of air
Element of earth
My thanks for lending your energy today
Blessings of earth

Then walk the circle widdershins (counterclockwise) and say:

Circle of light
Circle of peace
Circle of protection
Circle this place
This circle is now open but never broken

Pour the rest of your drink and crumble some of your food onto the earth as an offering to Inanna.

Any remainder of the burnt threads should be disposed of in the trash or flushed down the toilet.

Bundle for Obstacles and Blockages

To begin, choose a piece of fabric that you associate with releasing and clearing. You will need a cord or ribbon to tie it with, or you could use a drawstring pouch.

Your obstacles and blockages bundle can be filled with anything that you feel drawn to add—with the exception of fresh food or herbs because those would go mouldy! You could add crystals, dried herbs, seeds, dried leaves, twigs, dried flower petals, small tokens, beads, buttons, coins, small ornaments, etc. Trust your intuition.

Sit quietly or meditate to decide which things to add. Reach out to a deity such as Inanna and ask what needs to go in. It might only be one or two items at first—you can add to it over time.

Each item is representative of your journey to release negative energy and replace it with positive energy. Charge each item individually before you pop it in the pouch. Hold each one in your hand and visualise positive energy entering it, releasing that which binds you.

This, for me, is a bit of a balance bundle. Part of it will include items to release you from the dark and the other part will have lighter items to remind you that you have let go and can move forward. Here are my suggestions:

+ Cords, which represent being bound to people, ideas, and issues
+ Anything connected to the water, such as shells and sea pebbles, to associate with the purification magic of the sea
+ Salt, which helps release, cleanse, and purify
+ A small, empty bottle to show that you have let go and are ready to receive new and positive energy
+ Herbs such as dried citrus peel, star anise, and rosemary

Keep the bundle on your altar or somewhere that you will see it. Use it when you meditate, either holding it on your lap or opening it up and handling each item in turn. You can also reach for it when you feel the need to let go. Draw upon the energy within to fill your mind and spirit with positive energy. Move forward unburdened.

ᘒ

On occasion, we all get stuck or bogged down with life's issues. But some-times it feels like everything grinds to a complete stop.

Find a method that works for you to remove any blockages or obstacles that are holding you back.

Release the negative energies you are holding on to, let go, and move forward.

If you find yourself struggling to overcome obstacles or break through blockages, refer back to this chapter for magical suggestions that might help.

CHAPTER SIXTEEN

Sleep Issues

O ften the negative issues we deal with can affect our sleep patterns and, in turn, being tired adds to our issues. It can become a very nasty cycle.

There are some obvious ways to improve the quality of your sleep, such as not drinking caffeine in the evening, but try to remember these simple ways to sleep better as well. Don't go to bed with unfinished business. Never go to sleep without resolving an argument. If you are busy at work or with a project and go to bed with your mind zipping about like a frog in a blender, then the chances are you won't be able to switch off enough to sleep. Jot down a few notes, taking the ideas out of your head and leaving them on the paper. Finally, establish a routine. This really helps. Get to know your own body clock and find the schedule that works for you.

I have included some tips for preventing nightmares in this chapter. Nightmares—where do they come from? What causes them? Dickens believed it might be undigested food (read *A Christmas Carol*, you'll see!), and I have no doubt that some foods will cause sleep disruption. More realistically, though, it is our subconscious that triggers nightmares. Our subconscious is a minefield of mixed-up emotions, thoughts, and brain waves firing off all over the place. Hopefully some of the suggestions I have made in this chapter will help if you do suffer from nightmares.

In this chapter you will find magical suggestions to help improve the quality of your sleep. Work with as many of them as you like. Follow your intuition and be guided by it as to what you choose to work with.

Affirmations. Regular positive statements can change the way we think about ourselves and our situations.

Colour Magic. Colour plays an important part in how we feel and can affect our emotions; work with it to boost positive energy.

Herbs. This section will contain my suggestions of herbs to work with in magical spell workings. Pick from my ideas or use your own—be guided by your intuition.

Foods. All foods have magical properties. I have given you some suggestions that can be eaten or used in spell work. I've also included a recipe in each chapter.

Herbal Teas. These can be created with herbs and spices that help alleviate negative issues. Work with my suggestions or use your own.

Incense and Oils. Scents can bring up strong emotions. Work with my suggestions to create incense blends or oil blends to use in ritual or spell work. You can also create these blends just because the scent will lift your mood!

Everyday Exercise. In this section you will find easy daily or regular routines to help get your positive energy flowing and get rid of the negative vibes.

Crystals. They hold such power in tiny, easy-to-handle form. Crystals can be worked with in all sorts of ways to help with all kinds of issues.

Meditation. Read through the script or even record it on your phone. Take some time out and work with the meditation for help and guidance.

Spell. You will find spells to help with any issue. Keep it simple and straightforward. If you don't have the items I have suggested, substitute them with whatever you feel is right. Personalise it; make the spell your own.

Ritual. The rituals included will not be too fancy or complicated. Often, the rituals connect with a deity and the elements to work some magic.

Magic Bundle. In this section you'll find my suggestions for creating a magic bundle to help you through your situation.

Affirmations for Sleep

Say these affirmations each night before you get into bed:

I am relaxed and comfortable.

I will get a full, restful night's sleep.

I am ready to relax and sleep.

Colour Magic for Sleep

If you saw sleep as a colour, what colour would you see? This will vary from person to person. For any negative emotion or issue that I want to release, I see black as a good colour to work with. White is also good because it is neutral. When I think of sleep, I think of a restful pastel colour. I like lilac.

Herbs for Better Sleep

These are for magical use, NOT consumption.

- Agrimony
- Bergamot
- Betony
- Chamomile
- Hops
- Hyacinth
- Passionflower
- Poppy
- Sweet pea
- Valerian
- Vervain

Foods for Better Sleep

These can be used magically and/or eaten.

- Lavender
- Milk
- Rosemary

+ Star anise
+ Thyme

Recipe: Hug in a Mug

Eating a big meal before bedtime is probably not advisable. However, if you struggle to slumber, a hot milk drink can help.

Magic of the Ingredients

+ Cardamom—love, passion, clarity, protection
+ Cinnamon—success, healing, psychic powers, protection, love, focus, spirituality
+ Cloves—love, clarity, protection, repels negativity, stress relief
+ Honey—happiness, healing, love, passion, spirituality
+ Milk—feminine power, goddess energy, moon magic, nurturing, love, spirituality
+ Nutmeg—luck, protection
+ Vanilla—love, spirituality, passion, creativity

You can charge or bless the ingredients as you add them to the mix or do so once the drink is made. Hold your hands over them and say:

Warm and comforting, bring sleep to me
So mote it be

Hug in a Mug

475 mL (16 fl oz) milk, dairy or plant based

1 teaspoon vanilla extract

1 cinnamon stick

4 cloves

2 cardamom pods

¼ teaspoon grated nutmeg

1 tablespoon honey

Pop everything into a saucepan and warm through over a low heat until just before it boils.

Remove from the heat, put a lid on the pan, and allow to infuse for 10 minutes.

Strain and serve. This makes enough for two mugs!

Herbal Teas for Better Sleep

These are some herbal teas that can be drunk on their own to help you drift off to sleep:

- Chamomile
- Lavender
- Rosemary
- Star anise
- Thyme

Try creating your own blends. Here are some of my favourite combinations:

- One teaspoon lavender flowers, one teaspoon chamomile, a slice of orange, and a few rose petals per mug of hot water
- One teaspoon rosemary, one teaspoon lemon balm, and one teaspoon chamomile per mug of hot water
- Hot milk is always a winner! Add in one teaspoon of honey or a piece of star anise for a flavour boost
- Hot milk with one teaspoon of lavender flowers
- Hot milk with one teaspoon of rosemary
- One teaspoon rosemary, one teaspoon thyme, and a spoonful of honey

Incense and Oil Blends for Sleep

Any of these can be used in spells, rituals, body care, anointing, cleansing, and more to help promote a peaceful night's sleep. Each one can be used on its own or mixed with others in a blend.

- Agrimony
- Bergamot

- Betony
- Chamomile
- Hops
- Hyacinth
- Lavender
- Passionflower
- Poppy
- Rosemary
- Star anise
- Sweet pea
- Thyme
- Valerian
- Vervain

Incense Blends

- One part rosemary, two parts thyme, and two parts chamomile
- Equal parts lavender, rosemary, and thyme
- One part thyme, two parts lavender, and a few drops bergamot essential oil

Essential Oil Blends

- Combine six drops chamomile, three drops poppy, and four drops lavender oil. Use in your bath or on an oil burner/diffuser or mix with a base oil to use on the body.
- Combine six drops lavender, six drops bergamot, and two drops rosemary. Use in your bath or on an oil burner/diffuser or mix with a base oil to use on the body.
- Combine four drops hyacinth, four drops lavender, and four drops sweet pea. Use in your bath or on an oil burner/diffuser or mix with a base oil to use on the body.

Everyday Exercise for Sleep

Your feet are an important part of your body and can be very telling, particularly if you partake in the holistic therapy of reflexology, which I wholeheartedly recommend. I receive reflexology treatments regularly and would not want to be without them. The sole of the foot is a map for the entire body. Give your tootsies a little TLC—you will feel the effects throughout your entire body.

Start with relaxation stretches for your feet: wriggle your toes and rotate your ankles.

Then, using your usual moisturiser, focus on the outside edge of your big toe. That is the spot that helps release melatonin into your bloodstream; it aids with sleep. Begin at the base of the toe and rub up and down the edge of the toe.

The ball of your foot represents the solar plexus, so massage there to help you relax.

The crease inside the big toe, just above the ball of your foot, is another good place to massage to release tension in your whole body.

Finish with a light massage all over both feet and you are done!

If you'd like an extra-relaxing experience, add a few drops of lavender oil to your moisturiser next time.

Crystals for Sleep

Carry crystals with you, use them in magical spells, or meditate with them. Remember to charge the crystal with your intent before use and cleanse it afterwards. Cleansing suggestions can be found in chapter 3 of this book.

+ **Amethyst** brings calm and balance to the mind and emotions.
+ **Ammonite** brings relaxation and protection from too much hectic energy.
+ **Angelite** relaxes and soothes.
+ **Celestite** is a very relaxing stone with a peaceful energy.
+ **Hematite** grounds you and brings stability.
+ **Howlite** is perfect to deal with insomnia. Place a piece under your pillow to bring about peace and deep sleep.
+ **Jade** soothes, reduces stress, and brings harmony.

+ **Labradorite** balances and replenishes you whilst you sleep. It also helps release negative patterns.

+ **Lapis lazuli** brings deep silence and a level of perspective that allows you to really find your intuition.

+ **Lepidolite** is calming and soothing, helping you to have a tranquil sleep.

+ **Moonstone** helps control the flow of energy and helps you connect with the energy of the moon.

+ **Rose quartz** brings its loving energy to help prevent nightmares and promote peaceful sleep with lovely dreams.

+ **Selenite** can recharge your energy as you sleep and also helps clear your chakras.

+ **Sodalite** brings a strong feeling of peace, making it perfect to bring about a good night's sleep.

Placing crystals around the bedroom can help promote a peaceful night's sleep, particularly if you place one crystal in each corner of the room. Black tourmaline and smoky quartz are very good for this.

Meditation for Sleep

This meditation will hopefully help you sleep better. This seems to have the best effect if you work with the meditation whilst in bed, right before you drift off to sleep. If you do meditate whilst in bed, please be mindful to extinguish lit candles and/or incense before sleeping—we don't want the house burning down whilst you slumber! If you want to try out this meditation during the day, you can also give it a try before a short nap.

Make yourself comfortable in a place where you won't be disturbed. If you feel drawn to, put on some light music, drumming, or chanting. Light your incense or oil blend if you would like.

As your world around you dissipates, you find yourself in a valley surrounded by mountains. The sun is beginning to set but is still above the horizon. The sky is a brilliant blue and streaked with hues of pink and orange. It is quite beautiful.

You look around and notice that the grass beneath your feet is really lush and thick. It feels like a comfortable mattress. You decide to sit down and find it so relaxing and welcoming that you lie down.

Beside you are small bushes with tall stems topped with pretty purple flowers. The scent is amazing. You reach up and touch one of the flowers. A connection is made and the name "lavender" pops into your head.

The plant asks what you need from it and encourages you to share your sleep issues with it. So, you talk…

The plant listens carefully and then gives you some advice…

You thank the plant and then make yourself comfortable, wriggling a little to find the best spot. The ground is so accommodating, and you soon find yourself relaxed and resting.

Watching the sky, you lie quietly as the streaks of clouds float in their kaleidoscope of colour. You watch as the sun slowly sets, disappearing below the horizon.

The sky begins to darken. Small, sparkly stars begin to appear one by one.

A light starts to creep across the sky, and you realise a crescent moon is now shining down upon you.

Lie there for as long as you want, watching the stars and soaking up the magic from the moon…

If you have just used this for a nap during the day, slowly and gently come back to this reality. Open your eyes. Wriggle your fingers and toes.

If you used the meditation to drift off to sleep, hopefully you will wake up feeling relaxed and refreshed.

Spell to Promote Restful Sleep

This spell is so simple and easy to do. Remember to work with a crystal that you feel drawn to. I recommend making this a part of your nightly routine.

You will need:

+ Sprig of lavender, thyme, or rosemary
+ Crystal of your choice (something grounding; smoky quartz is good)
+ Small pouch or envelope

Get ready for bed, close the curtains, and sit on the side of your bed.

Hold the crystal in your hand and draw upon the energy from it to ground yourself. Do a grounding exercise as well; it will help.

Next, chant:

With sweet dreams and for me a restful sleep
A promise to keep
With sweet dreams and for me a restful sleep
A promise to keep
With sweet dreams and for me a restful sleep
A promise to keep

Then take the herb and the crystal and pop them into the pouch or envelope. Place it under your pillow. If you find it uncomfortable to have this under your pillow, you can place it beside your bed. Say the chant each night before you go to sleep. Keep the pouch there until you feel it needs re-charging. This can be done by adding new herbs and cleansing and re-charging the crystal.

Ritual to Promote Restful Sleep

This ritual is set with the intent of helping you have a good night's sleep, but it also allows you to create your own sleep pillow. To create a sleep pillow, you will work with herbs and colours that you associate with rest, relaxation, and feeling calm.

The Tibetan goddess Blue Tara is called upon for this ritual. She is full of compassion and can aid with emotional and mental blockages to help you feel relaxed and refreshed.

This ritual can be done using the items listed below, or you can sit quietly in your space and just visualise the whole thing.

You will need:

+ Square piece of fabric or felt (or a pouch)
+ Needle and thread
+ Dried herbs and flowers to fill the pouch/sleep pillow
+ A few drops of a calming essential oil, such as lavender
+ One central candle to represent the goddess Blue Tara

+ Matches or a lighter
+ Something to eat and drink

Cast your circle. Walk around in a circle deosil (clockwise) or turn around on the spot if you are limited for space. Visualise a soft, glowing light forming a circle around you. When the circle is complete, visualise the light forming above you and below you to form a globe. As you cast the circle, say:

Circle of light
Circle of peace
Circle of protection
Circle this place

Call the quarters. Turn and face each compass direction, starting with the north and working deosil (clockwise). North is earth, east is air, south is fire, and west is water. As you face each compass direction in turn, say:

Element of earth, bringing stability and grounding
Please join me in this place
Blessings of earth
Element of air, bringing peace and clarity
Please join me in this place
Blessings of air
Element of fire, bringing energy and passion
Please join me in this place
Blessings of fire
Element of water, bringing emotion and calm
Please join me in this place
Blessings of water

As you light the central candle, say:

I call upon the ancient and caring goddess Blue Tara
And ask that you bring your compassion, guidance, and support
To assist me with this rite
Blessings to you

Next, make your sleep pillow. A sleep pillow is super simple to make. When I say "pillow" I don't mean something the size of the pillow on your bed—this design is much smaller. Something roughly the size of your hand should do the trick. This little pillow works really well to help you sleep and can be taken anywhere with you.

I make my sleep pillow with pieces of felt, but you can use scraps of fabric or even just a muslin or organza bag. Fill your sleep pillow with dried herbs and flowers. Dried lavender flowers or hops are excellent, but you could add in a mix of thyme and rosemary as well. Charge the herbs/flowers with the intent of a restful night's sleep before you put them inside the fabric.

Add in a few drops of essential oil. The oil can be used at regular intervals to boost the magic.

Finally, sew or tie the pillow securely.

It really is that simple: make a bag with felt or fabric and stuff it with dried herbs, flowers, and essential oil. Sew it up and there you go … a sleep pillow.

Take a sip of your drink, raising your glass to Blue Tara.

Take a few bites of your food.

Then close the ritual. Face the centre and hold your arms wide, saying:

> *My thanks to you, great goddess Blue Tara*
> *For your compassion, guidance, and wisdom*
> *Please continue to guide and support me*
> *With blessings and thanks*

Face each direction in turn, starting with the west. Work widdershins (counterclockwise) and say:

> *Element of water*
> *My thanks for lending your energy today*
> *Blessings of water*
> *Element of fire*
> *My thanks for lending your energy today*
> *Blessings of fire*
> *Element of air*
> *My thanks for lending your energy today*
> *Blessings of air*

Element of earth
My thanks for lending your energy today
Blessings of earth

Then walk the circle widdershins (counterclockwise) and say:

Circle of light
Circle of peace
Circle of protection
Circle this place
This circle is now open but never broken

Extinguish the lit candle.

Pour the rest of your drink and crumble some of your food onto the earth as an offering to Blue Tara.

Pop the sleep pillow in your bed, under your main pillow. You can give it a boost when you feel it needs it by sprinkling the fabric with a few drops of essential oil.

Bundle for Better Sleep

To begin, choose a piece of fabric that you associate with sleep and rest. You will need a cord or ribbon to tie it with, or you could use a drawstring pouch.

Your sleep bundle can be filled with anything that you feel drawn to add—with the exception of fresh food or herbs because those would go mouldy! You could add crystals, dried herbs, seeds, dried leaves, twigs, dried flower petals, small tokens, beads, buttons, coins, small ornaments, etc. Trust your intuition.

Sit quietly or meditate to decide which things to add. Reach out to a deity such as Blue Tara and ask what needs to go in. It might only be one or two items at first—you can add to it over time.

Each item is representative of your journey to promote a proper sleep pattern. Charge each item individually before you pop it in the pouch. Hold each one in your hand and visualise positive energy entering it, bringing peace and relaxation for a better night's sleep.

This bundle needs to contain relaxing, peaceful items. Here are my suggestions:

+ Herbs and flowers that make you think of sleep (hops and lavender are perfect for this)
+ Anything that makes you feel at ease and relaxed
+ Images of clouds and scenery that make you feel relaxed

Keep the bundle on your altar or somewhere that you will see it. Use it when you meditate, either holding it on your lap or opening it up and handling each item in turn. You can also reach for it when you feel the need to let go. Draw upon the energy within to fill your mind and spirit with positive energy.

Whether you struggle to sleep properly or suffer with nightmares, lack of sleep can have very adverse effects on your health and wellbeing.

Do what you can to find a method that helps you get a better night's sleep.

If you find yourself having a tough time sleeping, refer back to this chapter for magical suggestions that might help.

CHAPTER SEVENTEEN

Menses and Menopause

These ideas and suggestions may help you deal with the pain, discomfort, hormones, and life transitions that menses and menopause bring. I have decided to combine menses and menopause in this chapter because the symptoms are similar and both are hormonal issues.

In an ideal world, for a couple of days each month we would be allowed to stay on the sofa wrapped in a blanket with hot water bottles and a continual supply of chocolate. Unfortunately, reality dictates that most of us don't have the luxury to do that. We go to work, deal with people, and do other mundane tasks whilst gulping down painkillers and keeping a stack of sanitary towels on hand. For those of you going through menopause: if you can take time out on the bad days, do it—and don't feel guilty about it.

Do whatever helps you cope in whatever way fits your lifestyle. I have found that warning my family of my mood helps; then they can tiptoe around me if necessary!

If you are dealing with really uncomfortable menses or menopause symptoms, don't discount medication. Please do see your doctor; they can help. Some birth control medications may also help with heavy or prolonged periods.

In this chapter you will find magical suggestions to help with your menses or menopause symptoms. Work with as many of them as you like. Follow your intuition and be guided by it as to what you choose to work with.

Affirmations. Regular positive statements can change the way we think about ourselves and our situations.

Colour Magic. Colour plays an important part in how we feel and can affect our emotions; work with it to boost positive energy.

Herbs. This section will contain my suggestions of herbs to work with in magical spell workings. Pick from my ideas or use your own—be guided by your intuition.

Foods. All foods have magical properties. I have given you some suggestions that can be eaten or used in spell work. I've also included a recipe in each chapter.

Herbal Teas. These can be created with herbs and spices that help alleviate negative issues. Work with my suggestions or use your own.

Incense and Oils. Scents can bring up strong emotions. Work with my suggestions to create incense blends or oil blends to use in ritual or spell work. You can also create these blends just because the scent will lift your mood!

Everyday Exercise. In this section you will find easy daily or regular routines to help get your positive energy flowing and get rid of the negative vibes.

Crystals. They hold such power in tiny, easy-to-handle form. Crystals can be worked with in all sorts of ways to help with all kinds of issues.

Meditation. Read through the script or even record it on your phone. Take some time out and work with the meditation for help and guidance.

Spell. You will find spells to help with any issue. Keep it simple and straightforward. If you don't have the items I have suggested, substitute them with whatever you feel is right. Personalise it; make the spell your own.

Ritual. The rituals included will not be too fancy or complicated. Often, the rituals connect with a deity and the elements to work some magic.

Magic Bundle. In this section you'll find my suggestions for creating a magic bundle to help you through your situation.

Affirmations for Menses

Menstruation is a reminder that I am a woman.
Menstruation is a gift of life.
I will get through this.

Affirmations for Menopause

Menopause is part of my journey.
Life brings changes and transitions.
I will get through this.

Colour Magic for Menses and Menopause

If you saw menses or menopause as a colour, what colour would you see? This will vary from person to person. For any negative emotion or issue that I want to release, I see black as a good colour to work with. White is also good because it is neutral.

I gotta go with the obvious here—for me, it is red. Red is a colour that has mixed meanings: power and passion, anger and frustration…which pretty much sums it up, really!

Herbs for Menses and Menopause

These are for magical use, NOT consumption.

+ Alexanders
+ Alyssum
+ Carnation
+ Chamomile
+ Cramp bark (guelder rose)
+ Elm
+ Frankincense
+ Holly
+ Hyacinth
+ Nettle
+ Passionflower

+ Patchouli
+ Rue
+ Skullcap
+ Witch hazel
+ Yarrow

Foods for Menses and Menopause

These can be used magically and/or eaten.

+ Chocolate
+ Cinnamon
+ Coriander
+ Cumin
+ Dill
+ Fennel
+ Garlic
+ Ginger
+ Lavender
+ Lemon balm
+ Marjoram
+ Mint
+ Star anise
+ Turmeric

I also recommend milk or wine.

Recipe: Chocolate Cookies

Well, it had to be chocolate to deal with periods, didn't it? Cookies are very much a feel-good food, and they're portable as well! They fit nicely in your bag for when you are out and about.

Magic of the Ingredients

- ✦ Butter—feminine power, antidepression, goddess energy, nurturing, love
- ✦ Chocolate—positive energy, happiness, love
- ✦ Sugar—to make life sweet!

You can charge or bless the ingredients as you add them to the mix or do so once the cookies are made. Hold your hands over them and say:

Blood of my body within me
Chocolate will help me be pain free

Chocolate Cookies

340 g (12 oz) chocolate

115 g (4 oz) butter

3 large eggs

275 g (10 oz) sugar

2 teaspoons vanilla extract

65 g (2 oz) plain (all-purpose) flour

½ teaspoon baking powder

¼ teaspoon salt

125 g (4 oz) chocolate chips

Preheat oven to 180°C (350°F).

Line a baking tray with baking parchment.

Melt the chocolate and butter in a bowl over a pan of simmering water (or use the microwave). Leave to cool completely.

Put the eggs into a bowl and beat for 30 seconds, then add the sugar and vanilla and beat for 15 minutes, or until the mixture is light and fluffy.

Add the cooled chocolate, flour, baking powder, and salt. Beat until everything is well blended.

Add the chocolate chips and fold them in.

Dollop approximately 20 spoonfuls of the mixture onto the baking tray, making sure to leave space around them. (They will flatten and spread while cooking.)

Bake for about 20 minutes. You will know they are done when the tops of the cookies are cracked slightly.

Cool on a wire rack.

Herbal Teas for Menses and Menopause

These are some herbal teas that can be drunk on their own to help alleviate period pains or menopause symptoms:

+ Chamomile
+ Chocolate
+ Cinnamon
+ Coriander
+ Cumin
+ Fennel
+ Ginger
+ Lavender
+ Lemon balm
+ Marjoram
+ Milk
+ Mint
+ Nettle
+ Star anise
+ Turmeric

I also recommend drinking wine (in moderation, of course).

Try creating your own blends. Here are some of my favourite combinations:

+ One teaspoon lavender and one teaspoon lemon balm per mug of hot water
+ One teaspoon nettle and one teaspoon lemon balm per mug of hot water
+ Hot chocolate with whipped cream and chocolate flakes—perfect for if you've had a really bad day
+ Hot chocolate with a pinch of cinnamon

+ Hot chocolate with a pinch of cinnamon, a pinch of ginger, and a pinch of star anise
+ Hot milk with one teaspoon of cinnamon and a slice of root ginger
+ One teaspoon fennel, half a teaspoon coriander seeds, and a slice of root ginger per mug of hot water
+ Hot milk with one teaspoon of turmeric

Incense and Oil Blends for Menses and Menopause

Any of these can be used in spells, rituals, body care, anointing, cleansing, and more to help ease period pains or menopause symptoms. Each one can be used on its own or mixed with others in a blend.

+ Carnation
+ Chamomile
+ Chocolate (cocoa nibs)
+ Cinnamon
+ Coriander
+ Cumin
+ Fennel
+ Frankincense
+ Ginger
+ Hyacinth
+ Lavender
+ Lemon balm
+ Marjoram
+ Mint
+ Nettle
+ Passionflower
+ Patchouli
+ Star anise
+ Turmeric

Incense Blends

+ One part frankincense, one part cinnamon, and one part star anise. If you'd like, add a dash of red wine
+ Equal parts mint, ginger, fennel, and cinnamon
+ One part lavender, one part hyacinth, and two parts passionflower
+ One part nettle, two parts mint, and one part marjoram
+ Equal parts cocoa nibs, cinnamon, and star anise
+ One part lemon balm, one part coriander, one part ginger, and two parts cocoa nibs

Essential Oil Blends

+ Combine six drops chamomile, three drops carnation, and six drops coriander. Use in your bath or on an oil burner/diffuser or mix with a base oil to use on the body.
+ Combine six drops frankincense, four drops patchouli, and four drops ginger. Use in your bath or on an oil burner/diffuser or mix with a base oil to use on the body.
+ Combine six drops mint, four drops fennel, and six drops lemon balm. Use in your bath or on an oil burner/diffuser or mix with a base oil to use on the body.
+ Combine four drops ginger, four drops coriander, four drops cinnamon, and four drops frankincense. Use in your bath or on an oil burner/diffuser or mix with a base oil to use on the body.

Everyday Exercise for Menses and Menopause

Stuff happens. Change is a part of life, and this includes the changes that Mother Nature likes to throw at us. We cannot stop menses or menopause from happening. Although, in the case of really bad periods, I would always recommend going to see your doctor. There are things that can be done to help ease the situation.

However, for most people, periods happen. For most people, periods show up every month for years. We have to learn to deal with them. Menopause happens, whether we like it or not. Ain't nothing gonna change that either. Again, we have to learn to deal with it. (Yep, I am saying this through gritted teeth because even though I know it is true, that doesn't mean I like it.)

Enjoying life regardless of where you're at in your cycle is all about self-care and working out the best way for you to deal with symptoms. A big part of this is taking time out for yourself. We all have busy lives, but it might be a case of learning to say, "No, I can't go out tonight!" and spending the evening wrapped up in a blanket with a hot water bottle and a good book.

Make sure there is time in your life for you to practice self-care. Learn what soothes your body, your spirit, and your soul. You know better than any-one else how your body works and responds to things.

Find a little daily ritual you can do to cope with your symptoms, and make sure you allow yourself the time to do it! Do not, under any circumstances, feel guilty for looking after yourself!

Crystals for Menses and Menopause

Carry crystals with you, use them in magical spells, or meditate with them. Remember to charge the crystal with your intent before use and cleanse it afterwards. Cleansing suggestions can be found in chapter 3 of this book.

- **Bloodstone** does what it says on the tin: it helps with all types of blood issues, including regulating heavy periods.
- **Carnelian** helps with menstrual issues and is associated with the ovaries and testes.
- **Chrysocolla** is soothing for menstrual cramps and PMS.
- **Citrine** balances hormones and gives a boost of energy.
- **Clear quartz**, especially a double-point piece, absorbs and discharges energy at each end, so it can help with flow and changes.
- **Fluorite** brings emotional stability.
- **Garnet** is calming and balancing for the emotions during PMS and menstruation.
- **Green tourmaline** heals and brings a balance for both male and female energy.
- **Jasper** supports healing and brings stability to blood flow and balance to the body.

+ **Labradorite** helps reduce PMS pain.

+ **Lapis lazuli** is full of healing and calming energy, particularly for your menstrual cycle.

+ **Malachite** helps with menstrual problems and irregularities.

+ **Moonstone** is a full-on feminine energy stone that brings balance to your hormones and menstrual cycle.

+ **Opal** relieves menstrual pain, PMS, and all kinds of reproductive issues.

+ **Rose quartz** is loving, calming, and brings a healing, feminine energy that supports the reproductive system.

+ **Smoky quartz** can ground your hot flashes.

+ **Snowflake obsidian** is a balancing stone.

+ **Turquoise** boosts your mood and helps balance emotions.

Meditation for Menses and Menopause

This meditation will help support you through your monthly menstrual cycle or, when the time comes, your menopause. Practice this meditation when any symptoms or issues arise with either.

Make yourself comfortable in a place where you won't be disturbed. If you feel drawn to, put on some light music, drumming, or chanting. Light your incense or oil blend if you would like.

As your world around you dissipates, you find yourself standing barefoot on dusty ground. In front of you is a large, rustic-style yurt. You can hear voices quietly talking inside, and it sounds like someone is singing.

The tent flap opens and a young woman looks out. She beckons you to come inside, so you do.

It is warm inside the yurt, and there is a small fire in the centre. Smoke curls toward a vent in the roof.

Candles are lit all around, and the light shows you that the yurt is filled with all ages, from teenagers to elders. People are seated cross-legged on the floor or comfortably on pillows and low stools. The young woman that ushered you in invites you to take a seat. You find a spot that is comfortable.

The singing you heard gets slightly louder as more voices join in the song. Someone starts to drum a beat.

You allow the sound to wash over you.

The young woman comes over and offers you a cup with warm liquid inside. You accept it with thanks and sip it slowly. The liquid is delicious and soothing.

A large platter is passed around. It is filled with a variety of dried fruits and nuts. You take a handful and munch happily.

One of the elders comes and sits beside you, explaining that they are the village healer. They ask if you have any health issues you want to talk about. You find yourself opening up and talking about issues and matters that concern you…

When you have finished, advice is given to you. Take note of what is said…

When the village healer has finished speaking, thank them.

You get up to leave and the young woman appears to escort you back out. As you are about to leave the yurt, she hands you some white flowers tied together with a red ribbon. You thank her, and then she is gone.

As you look at the flowers, a connection is made and the name "guelder rose" pops into your head. Listen, the flowers have a message for you…

When you are ready, you take a few steps away from the yurt and turn around to take a last look. Know that you can come back here any time you need.

Slowly and gently come back to this reality. Open your eyes and wriggle your fingers and toes.

Eat and drink something.

Jot down any thoughts or images that came to mind during your meditation. It can be useful to refer back to them later.

Spell to Release Pain

If you have bad period pains, this spell can help ease them. It is really simple. By using visualisation, you can move the pain from your body and send it into the pebble. You might see the pain as a particular colour—go with it. I like to visualise a white or blue light when working with healing energy, but you may find yours is different. Trust your intuition.

You will need:

+ Pebble

+ Your visualisation skills

Sit quietly and place the pebble on your womb. (Note: this spell works with all kinds of body pain. Just place the pebble at the source of your discomfort.)

See the pain streaming out of your body and into the pebble. Visualise it as a beam of light. Allow the pain to leave your body and fill the pebble.

Visualise a white or blue light coming from your heart or through the top of your head down to the womb, filling it with healing energy.

When you are finished, take the pebble and throw it as hard and as far as you can. The pebble can be thrown into the sea or a river. You may prefer to throw the pebble across a field or garden. Alternatively, throw it in the trash.

Ritual to Celebrate the Flow of Life

I sat and pondered for quite a while about a ritual to deal with menses and menopause. Nothing seemed to fit. Then I realised the ritual ought to be about celebrating the changes and transitions we go through in life. A rite of passage, perhaps? Some cultures celebrate the menarche (when a girl gets her first period), and for boys the age of thirteen is often celebrated as a step into adulthood. The transition to crone (when a woman has finished menopause and/or feels ready to embrace older age) or sage (the equivalent male version of a crone) has been marked by some as well.

Therefore, this ritual is all about celebrating life and the changes that it brings, whether those changes are menstruation, menopause, or just a shift in how you deal with life.

I work with Mary Magdalene for this ritual because she has such a powerful feminine energy and also brings healing with her.

This ritual can be done using the items listed below, or you can sit quietly in your space and just visualise the whole thing.

You will need:

+ One central candle to represent Mary Magdalene
+ Three crystals or tumble stones (to represent your past, your present, and your future)
+ Photos of yourself or items that bring you memories from your past
+ A current photo of yourself, if you have one
+ Matches or a lighter
+ Something to eat and drink

Cast your circle. Walk around in a circle deosil (clockwise) or turn around on the spot if you are limited for space. Visualise a soft, glowing light forming a circle around you. When the circle is complete, visualise the light forming above you and below you to form a globe. As you cast the circle, say:

Circle of light
Circle of peace
Circle of protection
Circle this place

Call the quarters. Turn and face each compass direction, starting with the north and working deosil (clockwise). North is earth, east is air, south is fire, and west is water. As you face each compass direction in turn, say:

Element of earth, bringing stability and grounding
Please join me in this place
Blessings of earth
Element of air, bringing peace and clarity
Please join me in this place
Blessings of air
Element of fire, bringing energy and passion
Please join me in this place
Blessings of fire
Element of water, bringing emotion and calm
Please join me in this place
Blessings of water

As you light the central candle, say:

I call upon the ancient and supportive goddess Mary Magdalene
And ask that you bring your compassion, guidance, and support
To assist me with this rite
Blessings to you

Now take some time to sit and sift through photographs of yourself from the past. Focus on the good memories of each stage in your life so far. Note the transitions and the points in your life where it has moved: schools, college, births, relationships, friendships, deaths, career moves, spiritual shifts … anything where your life turned.

Hold the first crystal in your hand, the one that represents the past, and say:

I acknowledge, recognise, accept, and give thanks
For all the changes and transitions that have happened in my life so far
Each one has helped to make me the person that I am now

Place the crystal in front of the central candle.

Sit for a while and focus on the present. Look at a current image of yourself if you have one. Think about your life now. Who surrounds and supports you? What do you do? Where are you at in life?

Take the second crystal in your hand, the one that represents the present, and say:

I acknowledge, recognise, accept, and give thanks
For all that has led me to my life as it is now

Place the crystal in front of the central candle.

Sit quietly and meditate. Allow your mind to be led where it needs to go. Mary Magdalene will help guide you if necessary. Be guided on a journey that gives you advice and guidance about your future …

Take the third crystal in your hand, the one that represents your future, and say:

I acknowledge, recognise, accept, and give thanks
That life presents me with changes and transitions
That it flows ever onwards
Leading me on the pathway that I need to follow

Place the last crystal in front of the central candle.

Take a sip of your drink, raising your glass to Mary Magdalene.

Take a few bites of your food.

Then close the ritual. Face the centre and hold your arms wide, saying:

> *My thanks to you, great goddess Mary Magdalene*
> *For your compassion, guidance, and wisdom*
> *Please continue to guide and support me*
> *With blessings and thanks*

Face each direction in turn, starting with the west. Work widdershins (counterclockwise) and say:

> *Element of water*
> *My thanks for lending your energy today*
> *Blessings of water*
> *Element of fire*
> *My thanks for lending your energy today*
> *Blessings of fire*
> *Element of air*
> *My thanks for lending your energy today*
> *Blessings of air*
> *Element of earth*
> *My thanks for lending your energy today*
> *Blessings of earth*

Then walk the circle widdershins (counterclockwise) and say:

> *Circle of light*
> *Circle of peace*
> *Circle of protection*
> *Circle this place*
> *This circle is now open but never broken*

Snuff out the central candle.

Pour the rest of your drink and crumble some of your food onto the earth as an offering to Mary Magdalene.

Your crystals can be put on your altar, beside your bed, or in your magic bundle. If you'd like, you can keep the photos out on display as a visual reminder of the work you've done.

Bundle for Menses and Menopause

To begin, choose a piece of fabric that you associate with transformation. You will need a cord or ribbon to tie it with, or you could use a drawstring pouch.

Your bundle can be filled with anything that you feel drawn to add—with the exception of fresh food or herbs because those would go mouldy! You could add crystals, dried herbs, seeds, dried leaves, twigs, dried flower petals, small tokens, beads, buttons, coins, small ornaments, etc. Trust your intuition.

Sit quietly or meditate to decide which things to add. Reach out to a deity such as Mary Magdalene and ask what needs to go in. It might only be one or two items at first—you can add to it over time.

Each item is representative of your journey so far. Charge each item individually before you pop it in the pouch. Hold each one in your hand and visualise positive energy entering it, bringing peace so you can easily adapt to life's changes.

This is your life in a bag, basically. Here are my suggestions:

+ Your three crystals from the Flow of Life ritual
+ Photos that remind you of important times in your life
+ Mementos of life events: invites, hospital bands, tickets, badges... whatever you relate to
+ Herbs and flowers that represent your cycle or stage in life, such as cinnamon, star anise, or coriander

Keep the bundle on your altar or somewhere that you will see it. Use it when you meditate, either holding it on your lap or opening it up and handling each item in turn. You can also reach for it when you feel the need to let go. Draw upon the energy within to fill your mind and spirit with positive energy.

Life is a journey. Dealing with menses, menopause, and all the symptoms and experiences that they bring can be a challenge. But remember: without periods, there would be no new life.

Find what works best for you and your cycle and deal with it to the best of your abilities. Don't let it rule your life!

If you find yourself dealing with painful periods or struggling through menopause symptoms, refer back to this chapter for magical suggestions that might help.

CHAPTER EIGHTEEN

༄

Transitions
and Changes

We all go through changes in our lives. Some we make ourselves; others are forced upon us. It might be changes in your body, such as puberty or menopause, but it could also be just a certain point in your life where you feel the need to change. We all experience huge shifts in our emotions and feelings on occasion. Life is fluid and ever-changing. Over the years, I have learnt that changes are usually necessary.

To help deal with all the emotional issues within this book, you will need to make some changes, break some patterns, and go through some transitions. Know that whilst it will take work on your part and some of it will be difficult, the end result will be totally worth it.

There are some herbs, plants, flowers, and crystals that you can add to your workings to help cause change. Add them into the other exercises, spells, and rituals included within this book to help you deal with the transitions that take place. For example, if you were working with chapter 14 and wanted to bring about some positive change, you could incorporate some of the herbs from this chapter. And for any of life's transitions, you can carry a crystal with you that helps make the journey a smooth one. But for now, work with individual suggestions to start your journey of transformation.

In this chapter you will find magical suggestions to help you make and deal with changes. Work with as many of them as you like. Follow your intuition and be guided by it as to what you choose to work with.

Affirmations. Regular positive statements can change the way we think about ourselves and our situations.

Colour Magic. Colour plays an important part in how we feel and can affect our emotions; work with it to boost positive energy.

Herbs. This section will contain my suggestions of herbs to work with in magical spell workings. Pick from my ideas or use your own—be guided by your intuition.

Foods. All foods have magical properties. I have given you some suggestions that can be eaten or used in spell work. I've also included a recipe in each chapter.

Herbal Teas. These can be created with herbs and spices that help alleviate negative issues. Work with my suggestions or use your own.

Incense and Oils. Scents can bring up strong emotions. Work with my suggestions to create incense blends or oil blends to use in ritual or spell work. You can also create these blends just because the scent will lift your mood!

Everyday Exercise. In this section you will find easy daily or regular routines to help get your positive energy flowing and get rid of the negative vibes.

Crystals. They hold such power in tiny, easy-to-handle form. Crystals can be worked with in all sorts of ways to help with all kinds of issues.

Meditation. Read through the script or even record it on your phone. Take some time out and work with the meditation for help and guidance.

Spell. You will find spells to help with any issue. Keep it simple and straightforward. If you don't have the items I have suggested, substitute them with whatever you feel is right. Personalise it; make the spell your own.

Ritual. The rituals included will not be too fancy or complicated. Often, the rituals connect with a deity and the elements to work some magic.

Magic Bundle. In this section you'll find my suggestions for creating a magic bundle to help you through your situation.

Affirmations for Transitions and Changes

I embrace the changes in my life.
I accept that change happens for a good reason.
It is time to move on to the next part of my journey.
Bring it on!

Colour Magic for Transitions and Changes

If you saw change as a colour, what colour would you see? This will vary from person to person. For any negative emotion or issue that I want to release, I see black as a good colour to work with. White is also good because it is neutral.

For me, it would have to be a gradient, which is something that starts as one colour and transitions to another, or a darker colour that gradually fades. Change could also be something two-toned or shimmery. Remember that changes and transitions are positive, so lean toward strong, happy colours.

Herbs for Transitions and Changes

These are for magical use, NOT consumption.

+ Birch
+ Carnation
+ Cramp bark (guelder rose)
+ Holly
+ Lavender
+ Poppy
+ Rose
+ Skullcap
+ St. John's wort
+ Sweet pea
+ Vervain

Foods for Transitions and Changes

These can be used magically and/or eaten.

+ Black pepper
+ Cinnamon
+ Cumin
+ Garlic
+ Ginger
+ Lemon balm
+ Plums

Recipe: Chai Tea Cupcakes

Chai is a beautiful flavouring of spices that really lifts these cupcakes and adds a punch of power. This is one of my favourite cupcake recipes. The spices will help you with any transitions, and eating cake always makes people happy!

Magic of the Ingredients

+ Butter—peace, spirituality
+ Cardamom—love, passion, clarity, uplifting, protection
+ Cinnamon—success, healing, power, protection, focus, spirituality
+ Cloves—love, money, exorcism, clarity, protection, abundance, repels negative energy, stress relief, truth
+ Eggs—fertility, creation, life, new beginnings, divination
+ Milk—feminine power, goddess energy, moon magic, nurturing, love, spirituality
+ Nutmeg—money, luck, protection
+ Sugar—to make life sweet!

You can charge or bless the ingredients as you add them to the mix or do so once the cupcakes are made. Hold your hands over them and say:

Cupcakes sweet and filled with spice
Help with changes and keep things nice

Chai Tea Cupcakes

For the cupcakes:

    250 g (9 oz) self-rising flour

    ½ teaspoon sodium bicarbonate (baking soda)

    250 g (9 oz) sugar

    ½ teaspoon ground cloves

    ½ teaspoon ground cinnamon

    ½ teaspoon ground cardamom

    250 g (9 oz) butter

    4 large eggs

    3 tablespoons milk

For the icing:

    300 g (10½ oz) butter

    675 g (23½ oz) icing sugar

    4 tablespoons milk

    2 tablespoons demerara sugar

    1 teaspoon ground cinnamon

    ¼ teaspoon ground nutmeg

    Pinch ground cloves

Preheat the oven to 170°C (375°F).

Pop the flour, sodium bicarbonate, sugar, and spices into a large bowl. Add the butter and the eggs and beat for about a minute.

Add the milk and whisk until the ingredients are all incorporated.

Fill twelve muffin cases with the mixture and bake in the oven for 20 minutes. Leave to cool.

To make the icing, beat the butter until pale and smooth.

Pop the icing sugar in a large bowl and gradually add the butter, beating well as you go.

Add in the milk and beat until combined.

When the cakes are cool, ice the top.

Then mix the demerara sugar with the spices and sprinkle this mixture over the iced cupcakes.

Herbal Teas for Transitions and Changes

These are some herbal teas that can be drunk on their own to help make changes smooth:

+ Black pepper
+ Cinnamon
+ Cumin
+ Ginger
+ Lavender
+ Lemon balm
+ Rose

Try creating your own blends. Here are some of my favourite combinations:

+ One teaspoon dried lavender flowers, a few rose petals, and a splash of lemon juice per mug of hot water
+ Half a teaspoon ground cinnamon, a slice of root ginger, and a few rose petals per mug of hot water
+ Two teaspoons dried lemon balm and half a teaspoon ground cinnamon per mug of hot water
+ One teaspoon dried lemon balm and a few rose petals per mug of hot water

Incense and Oil Blends for Transitions and Changes

Any of these can be used in spells, rituals, body care, anointing, cleansing, and more to help you be comfortable with change. Each one can be used on its own or mixed with others in a blend.

+ Birch
+ Black pepper
+ Carnation
+ Cinnamon
+ Cumin
+ Ginger

- Holly
- Lavender
- Lemon balm
- Poppy
- Rose
- Sweet pea
- Vervain

Incense Blends

- Equal parts cinnamon, ginger, and lemon balm
- One part frankincense resin, two parts ginger, and one part black pepper
- Equal parts copal resin, lavender, and rose
- Equal parts rose, cinnamon, and cumin

Essential Oil Blends

- Combine six drops ginger, three drops black pepper, and three drops cinnamon. Use in your bath or on an oil burner/diffuser or mix with a base oil to use on the body.
- Combine six drops lemon balm and six drops ginger. Use in your bath or on an oil burner/diffuser or mix with a base oil to use on the body.
- Combine six drops rose and six drops lavender. Use in your bath or on an oil burner/diffuser or mix with a base oil to use on the body.
- Combine four drops rose, two drops sweet pea, and six drops lemon balm. Use in your bath or on an oil burner/diffuser or mix with a base oil to use on the body.

Everyday Exercise for Transitions and Changes

Transitions and changes are often just different ways of doing things or looking at something from a different perspective. We can get stuck in a rut or set in our ways with the usual routines. Try taking a step back and looking at things from a different perspective. If you feel overwhelmed by changes or are worried about transitions that are happening, this may help.

Settle yourself down in a place you are familiar with or a place where you have a familiar view; it could be your garden or any room in your house. Now look at it from a different perspective. You could lie down on the ground and look at the flower bed from a worm's viewpoint, or you could sit in your living room but pick a different chair than the one you normally sit in.

Once you've found a different perspective that is comfortable, spend some time in your new position and take in all the details. How do things look from another angle? Now apply that mindset to the changes that are happening in your life. It will hopefully give you some clarity.

Crystals for Transitions and Changes

Carry crystals with you, use them in magical spells, or meditate with them. Remember to charge the crystal with your intent before use and cleanse it afterwards. Cleansing suggestions can be found in chapter 3 of this book.

+ **Amethyst** guides you from the old to the new.

+ **Apache tears** bring support to help you through transitions and difficult times.

+ **Chrysocolla** helps you to deal with whatever life throws at you.

+ **Garnet** brings confidence and the ability to switch your survival instincts into action, helping you to deal with new situations.

+ **Jet** is very grounding and protecting. It works to stabilise your energies.

+ **Labradorite** gives you clarity of thought and direction.

+ **Malachite** is all about balance and endurance.

+ **Moonstone** brings a calming and peaceful energy to help guide you to make the right decisions.

+ **Rutilated quartz** helps to recognise the truth and to understand changes and transitions.

+ **Tourmaline** brings clarity and understanding to accept and work with changes.

+ **Tree agate** brings the power of nature, stability, and the flexibility to weather any storm.

Meditation for Transitions and Changes

Make yourself comfortable in a place where you won't be disturbed. If you feel drawn to, put on some light music, drumming, or chanting. Light your incense or oil blend if you would like.

As your world around you dissipates, you find yourself in a garden. You are lying on the grass near a flower bed. The sun is warm on your skin and the air is fresh and sweet.

Take a few deep breaths in and enjoy the scented air. The flower bed beside you is full of beautiful flowers of all sizes, shapes, and colours.

Take some time to have a look at them but stay lying on the grass. This way you can see the flowers from ground level.

The flowers are full of buzzing bees, and you watch them hop from flower to flower covered in dusty, yellow pollen.

Then you notice something on a large leaf close to you. It looks like a tiny pod made from mouldy, dark grey leaves. It looks unpleasant and is probably something that should be picked off the plant and put in the compost.

As you look, it starts to move ...

Piece by piece, the bits of grey covering start to peel back, small pieces falling away.

Something appears to be emerging from inside. Slowly but surely, a creature is releasing itself from the folds of the dusty grey tomb it was encased in.

When it is finally out completely, it reveals stunning, vibrant wings. You have just watched a butterfly emerge from its chrysalis.

From the ugliness of dead and decaying leaves, a fabulous butterfly appeared. The wings flap and the colours dance. Then it takes flight ...

You watch as it flutters majestically up into the air and across the tops of the flowers.

Take some time to think about this amazing transformation and how it echoes your own life and any situation.

The butterfly began life as something completely different. It then transitioned into a wonderful creature.

When you are ready, slowly and gently come back to this reality.

Open your eyes and wriggle your fingers and toes.

Have a drink and something to eat.

Jot down any thoughts or images that came to mind during your meditation. It can be useful to refer back to them later.

Spell for Transitions and Changes

This candle spell will help put change into motion. This spell encourages you to let go of the past habits, lifestyle, or patterns and move forward with the new. Your mirror is used to reflect this restorative energy back to you.

You will need:

+ One black candle for the past

+ One white candle for transitions

+ One green candle for moving forward

+ Matches or a lighter

+ A mirror large enough to sit all three candles in front of

Start by placing your mirror in front of you. Put the black candle to your left, the white candle in the centre, and the green candle to the right.

Sit quietly and then light the black candle. This is the old, the past, the part of yourself or your life you want to let go of. Focus on that for a moment, watching the candle flame as you do. Then say:

I let go of the past
I release it at last

Snuff out the black candle.

Now light the white candle and focus on what changes need to be made to create the new you, your new life, or your new pathway. Sit watching the flame as you visualise. Then say:

These changes I make
This positive move I take

Now take the white candle and light the green candle from it.

Sit quietly and watch the green candle flame as you visualise the new you, your new situation, or your new way of thinking. See it all clearly in your mind's eye. Then say:

I embrace this new task
I move forward at last

When you are ready, snuff out the white and green candles.

I suggest you repeat this spell for three days in a row. Then leave it set up. You can relight the candles and repeat the chants until the spell has worked.

If you have candle stubs left, they can be buried or thrown in the trash.

"Bring on the Changes!" Ritual

This ritual is set with the intent to help guide you through any changes or transitions. Although change can be difficult at times, it is often necessary. Use this ritual to help you work through the process.

I have called upon the Egyptian goddess Isis for this ritual as she is excellent to work with for support and guidance during changes and transitions.

This ritual can be done using the items listed below, or you can sit quietly in your space and just visualise the whole thing.

You will need:

+ Large piece of paper
+ Pen
+ One central candle to represent the goddess Isis
+ Matches or a lighter
+ Something to eat and drink

Cast your circle. Walk around in a circle deosil (clockwise) or turn around on the spot if you are limited for space. Visualise a soft, glowing light forming a circle around you. When the circle is complete, visualise the light forming above you and below you to form a globe. As you cast the circle, say:

Circle of light
Circle of peace
Circle of protection
Circle this place

Call the quarters. Turn and face each compass direction, starting with the north and working deosil (clockwise). North is earth, east is air, south is fire, and west is water. As you face each one, say:

Element of earth, bringing stability and grounding
Please join me in this place
Blessings of earth
Element of air, bringing peace and clarity
Please join me in this place
Blessings of air
Element of fire, bringing energy and passion
Please join me in this place
Blessings of fire
Element of water, bringing emotion and calm
Please join me in this place
Blessings of water

As you light the central candle, say:

I call upon the strong and wise goddess Isis
Hear my prayer and bring your guidance and strength
To assist me with this rite
Blessings to you

Take your sheet of paper and your pen. Now we are going to begin a journey. Start at the outer edge of the paper and begin to draw a curved line. This line is the beginning of a spiral. The spiral line will slowly go toward the centre of the paper. Keep drawing, bringing the line of the spiral gently inwards, until you reach the centre point.

Now put the spiral drawing down in front of you. Sit comfortably and fix your eyes upon the outer edge and the starting point of the spiral.

Slowly follow the spiral inwards with your eyes (or your finger) on the paper. Begin by visualising the old habits or patterns that you want to leave behind. Say:

Now in my past
Left behind

As you move your eyes or your finger inwards, start to visualise a smooth transition, the things you need to do in order to make your transformation. Say:

These changes I make
My future path to take

When you finally reach the centre of the spiral, take some time and visualise your goal. Say:

The changes I willingly make
Success of the chances I take

Ask the goddess Isis to help you on your transitional journey and thank her in advance for her help and assistance.

Fold the paper up several times.

Take a sip of your drink, raising your glass to Isis.

Take a few bites of your food.

Then close the ritual. As you snuff out the central candle, say:

My thanks to you, great goddess Isis
For your guidance and strength
Please continue to guide and support me
With blessings and thanks

Face each direction in turn, starting with the west. Work widdershins (counterclockwise) and say:

Element of water
My thanks for lending your energy today
Blessings of water
Element of fire
My thanks for lending your energy today
Blessings of fire
Element of air
My thanks for lending your energy today
Blessings of air
Element of earth
My thanks for lending your energy today
Blessings of earth

Then walk the circle widdershins (counterclockwise) and say:

Circle of light
Circle of peace
Circle of protection
Circle this place
This circle is now open but never broken

Pour the rest of your drink and crumble some of your food onto the earth as an offering to Isis.

The spiral paper can be placed on your altar until your transitions are complete.

Bundle for Transitions and Changes

To begin, choose a piece of fabric that makes you feel calm and grounded. You will need a cord or ribbon to tie it with, or you could use a drawstring pouch.

Your bundle can be filled with anything that you feel drawn to add—with the exception of fresh food or herbs because those would go mouldy! You could add crystals, dried herbs, seeds, dried leaves, twigs, dried flower petals, small tokens, beads, buttons, coins, small ornaments, etc. Trust your intuition.

Sit quietly or meditate to decide which things to add. Reach out to a deity such as Isis and ask what needs to go in. It might only be one or two items at first—you can add to it over time.

Each item is representative of your journey to go with the flow. Charge each item individually before you pop it in the pouch. Hold each one in your hand and visualise positive energy entering it, bringing calm and peace and allowing you to go with the flow.

Here are my suggestions:

+ Your spiral drawing
+ Image of a butterfly
+ Small mirror
+ Piece of labradorite
+ A few rose petals
+ Stick of cinnamon

Keep the bundle on your altar or somewhere that you will see it. Use it when you meditate, either holding it on your lap or opening it up and handling each item in turn. You can also reach for it when you feel anxious about change. Draw upon the energy within to fill your mind and spirit with calming and peaceful energy.

In order to make changes, we have to break patterns in our behaviour.

These suggestions should help make those transitions smooth and give them a nudge along, but remember to be open to whatever comes your way.

Changes and transitions can be made by choice or they can be forced upon us. Either way, it is easier to embrace and accept them rather than fight against them.

Make the best of what life gives you.

If you find yourself struggling to adjust to transitions and changes, refer back to this chapter for magical suggestions that might help.

PART THREE
GUIDANCE AND MOVING FORWARD

CHAPTER NINETEEN

❦

The Magical Pantry

L isted here are the herbs, plants, and foods I like to keep in my cupboard for magical use. These plant material suggestions are just a guide. If you are drawn to use something else or can't easily get hold of them, follow your intuition. Whilst one or two of them are specific, most of them can be utilised to cover all the issues we are dealing with in this book.

I grow as many of these plants and flowers in my garden as I can squeeze in. That way I know they are organic, and they have my energy added to them already. I collect and dry all the flower petals, leaves, thorns, and seed heads. However, I also source ingredients from local farmers markets and Asian supermarkets. It doesn't matter if you cannot grow them yourself; source them locally and within your budget. If you are buying them, it is advisable to cleanse them before use. Just visualise a bright white light surrounding them. Charge each ingredient with your intent before use.

Don't spend lots of money purchasing special "magical" packets of herbs—they are the same herbs that you buy in the supermarket. I also keep any "out of date" dried herbs and ingredients such as flour and oats. Most dried herbs and spices don't really go out of date, they just lose the strength of their flavour, but they are perfectly good to use in magical workings. Don't waste anything!

I have listed the ingredients and plants for magical use, but some are good to use in herbal teas as well. Please be very careful when taking any herbal supplements or remedies. Particular care should be taken if you are pregnant, have a medical condition, or are taking any kind of over-the-counter medication. Seek professional advice first.

If you are using any essential oils, please DO NOT put them directly on the skin; always dilute with a carrier oil first. You may have an allergic reaction. Some essential oils can also sting when in direct contact with the skin. I would also advise against ingesting essential oils.

Agrimony
(Agrimonia eupatoria)

Magical Properties: Dispels negativity, reverses
spells, aids spiritual healing, cleanses the aura,
sleep, happiness, luck, love, protection

Agrimony has tall spikes of yellow flowers that are seen growing between fields, on roadsides, and in hedgerows. Dry the flowers and the leaves to use for magical purposes. Use agrimony in spells to bring about calm, soothe anxiety, and help release negative emotion.

Agrimony can also bring in protection against negative energy. Pop some dried agrimony beneath your pillow and it will help bring a peaceful sleep. As it is an air herb, it will also help bring clarity to your thoughts. Burn agrimony as an incense to clear the air, cleanse your aura, and lift the general mood.

Alexanders
(Smyrnium olusatrum)

Magical Properties: Sea magic, intuition, emotions, cleansing, releasing

The Alexanders plant blossoms in the springtime. The buds are safe to eat and will bloom into lime-green flowers. Often found close to the ocean, it can also survive inland on any chalky soil type.

The Romans brought the plant to Britain; it was known then as "parsley of Alexandria." Its connection to the ocean brings in sea magic and spells for working with your intuition and emotions. Used medicinally for cleansing your system, Alexanders can be used in magical workings for purifying and releasing.

Aloe
(Aloe vera)
Magical Properties: Luck, protection,
calming, moon magic, psychic abilities

Aloe vera is a common house plant with long, sap-filled leaves that carry spikes along the edges. The sap inside the leaves is excellent for soothing burns. The dried leaves can be used in incense blends for moon magic and working with moon goddesses. Aloe juice is very soothing and can help bring calming energy. Keep one in your home in a warm place like a windowsill.

Alyssum
(Alyssum spp. & Lobularia spp.)
Magical Properties: Protection, maiden magic,
peace, calming, balance, spirituality

Grown as an annual, *Alyssum* comes in various varieties that are all covered in sprays of white, red, yellow, or purple flowers. It has a long flowering period covering the summer right into early autumn. Dried, the flowers can be used in spell work for your home and family. They keep the peace and help calm any situation or argument. Keep a pinch of dried *Alyssum* flower on you to help balance out your emotions.

Basil
(Ocimum basilicum)
Magical Properties: Wealth, money, prosperity, love,
exorcism, protection, happiness, peace

Basil is quite a tender plant. It loves warmth and doesn't tolerate being outside during the winter in most climates. Keep a pot indoors on your windowsill and it will last a good while.

Basil comes in a variety of types including Greek, lemon, Thai, purple, mint, and cinnamon. Each one has a unique scent.

Basil is one of the herbs traditionally known as a "witch's herb." The leaves are useful in spell work; write something you want to banish on a leaf and burn it or leave it out in the sun to dry. Another option is to write a wish or desire on a basil leaf and then eat it to activate the magic.

Dried basil works very well in incense blends to purify and exorcise. Add basil to protection powders and incense blends to bring calm and peace into your home, or eat it to absorb the magic.

Benzoin
(Styrax benzoin)
Magical Properties: Prosperity, purification,
calming, confidence, love, lust

Benzoin comes from an Indonesian tree. The part we use in magic and incense is the solid resin. Benzoin swoops in with a soothing and calming energy, but it also carries a good punch of confidence. Being a resin, it creates lots of smoke when burnt on charcoal, so it can be used effectively for cleansing and purification.

Bergamot
(Monarda didyma, Mondarda fistulosa)
Magical Properties: Abundance, meditation,
sleep, dreams, clarity, friendship

Bergamot is a beautiful addition to any summer garden, bringing bright red, white, or pink flowers. It has large oval leaves with toothed points. It is a member of the mint family.

I love the folk name for bergamot. It's called "bee balm" because our favourite stripy insects absolutely love this plant.

Use the dried flowers and leaves for magical purposes. Create a bergamot sleep pillow for interesting dreams and a peaceful sleep. Take a bergamot leaf and rub it between your hands to encourage strong, happy friendships. For a boost to your psychic skills, add a pinch of dried bergamot to your incense blends.

Betony (Wood)
(Stachys officinalis)

Magical Properties: Love, purification, clarity, protection, anti-intoxication, fends off nightmares, antidepression, memory, stress relief

Wood betony is such a pretty little plant. It's often found in the wild, although you can purchase it for your garden too. It prefers to grow wild in woodland clearings, in hedgerows, and out on the heath. The flowers are purple in colour and look like little orchids. Use the leaves and flowers in magic, but make sure to pick the flowers when they are still buds.

Betony is a powerful herb for protection. It wields against evil and negative energy exceptionally well—and against snakes, just in case you need it. During the Middle Ages it was used as an herb for protection against Witchcraft.

This is the perfect herb to use in magical workings to dispel personal fears, to help you face your own inner demons, and to bring some stress relief. Keep betony with you for concentration, focus, and to boost your memory. It can help you when taking tests or exams, or it can just be used because you have a brain like a sieve (that would be me).

Betony is all about balance as it is associated with the solar plexus. Placed under your pillow, betony can help to keep away nightmares. A bath with betony flowers added can help drown your fears and ease depression. Place betony leaves in bottles or pouches and disperse them around the house to calm or prevent arguments. If you feel a bit uncomfortable and can't quite pinpoint where or why, betony can help to calm the energy.

Birch
(Betula pendula, Betula pubescens,
Betula lenta, Betula alba)

Magical Properties: Purification, protection, exorcism, new beginnings, courage, fertility, love, release

Possibly one of the most recognisable trees, birch has bright white bark and light green leaves. Birch is a tree of beginnings and changes. It was the first type of tree planted by settlers when they found their new home.

Birch can give you the courage to release your fears and seek new beginnings. The twigs of a birch tree can be used for cleansing and purification. Create a small hand broom out of birch twigs by tying them together with twine or ribbon, then use the broom to sweep negative energy from your home. Looking to attract love? Burn a few birch leaves to clear the pathway and allow new love to find you.

Black Pepper
(Piper nigrum)

Magical Properties: Protection, exorcism, reduces jealousy, repels negativity, strength, confidence, prevents gossip

The pepper tree can grow up to twenty feet tall. The little berries, which are red when picked, turn black when laid out in the sun to dry. Basically, we eat suntanned peppercorns!

Peppercorns are really useful in all kinds of spell workings. Add them to sachets, amulets, bottles, powders, and pouches. They bring a powerful punch of protection magic but also work well to create personal and physical boundaries. They bring out your inner strength and help boost your confidence with their fiery pepper.

If you gargle with black pepper it can numb your tongue (don't try this), so it makes sense to use it in magical workings to stop any gossip. Ever had a visitor to your home that you hope never returns? Once they finally leave the house, throw a mixture of black pepper and salt out the door after them. This should prevent them from returning any time soon.

Black Tea
(Camellia sinensis)

Magical Properties: Meditation, courage, strength, prosperity

Any time something terrible happens in Britain, the first thing we do is make a cup of tea. It has that soothing kind of feeling that can help right any wrong. To sit down at the end of the day and sip a cup of tea is both relaxing and calming. A cup of tea will always make you feel better. By creating your own blend of tea, you can also use it for any kind of magical intent.

Black tea is a sun and fire herb, so it has lots of fiery energy. Add tea leaves to magical workings for courage, strength, and prosperity. You can also use it just to relax and unwind. Black tea provides a really good base for creating magical blends by adding other ingredients. You don't have to use loose leaves; you can experiment with tea bags too. In fact, the process of making tea is a bit of a ritual in itself. Some cultures have whole ceremonies dedicated to making tea. And once you have drunk your cuppa, you can read the tea leaves!

Tea Leaf Reading

Tea leaf reading, or tasseography, is fairly simple to do. First of all, you need to make a cup of tea…that was pretty obvious, wasn't it? You will need to use loose leaf tea. (If you don't have loose leaf tea, you can open a tea bag.) Make the tea in a pot, letting it steep for a few minutes.

Whilst the tea is brewing, use this time to ground and centre yourself. Allow your mind to become calm. Then pour yourself a cup of tea, using a plain, light-colour cup if you have one.

Slowly sip the tea (avoiding the tea leaves). If you have a question in mind, think about it as you drink your tea.

Leave a small amount of tea in your cup, then hold your nearly empty cup in your hand and swirl it around three times. The tea leaves should disperse around the inside of the cup. Carefully dump out the remaining liquid by turning your cup over into a saucer. Wait for a count of three, then turn your cup back over.

If your cup has a handle, begin reading the tea leaves from that point, working clockwise. If the cup doesn't have a handle, start at the twelve o'clock position.

Read what you see. Trust your intuition on this. What do the images mean to *you* personally? Look at the shapes and images. Pay attention to any words that pop into your head.

Blueberries
(Cyanococcus)
Magical Properties: Calm, peace, protection, passion, fertility

Blueberries are the delicious, indigo-blue fruits that are produced on a perennial flowering plant. The blueberry brings calming and accepting energy along with a bit of protection too. The fruit can be used to help prevent psychic attacks.

You can add the dried berries and leaves to pouches, bottles, or incense blends—pop them in your mouth too! Whether you eat them fresh or inside a blueberry muffin, they are equally magical and delicious.

Carnation
(Dianthus caryophyllus)
Magical Properties: Healing, strength, protection, release, courage

Carnations are the flowers often found in bunches at supermarkets or petrol stations. They are extremely long lasting as a cut flower and come in a dizzying array of colours.

Carnations are my go-to flower for any kind of healing spell work. The humble carnation also carries the magical energy of courage. There is a reason the flower is often worn in a buttonhole. To release negative energy, thoughts, or emotions, hold a carnation flower in your hand and let the negative energy flow from your body and mind into the flower. Once fully released, the flower can be disposed of, taking your negative energy with it. Burn it, throw it in the trash, wash it away, throw the petals to the wind, or bury it (just don't bury it on your property!).

Carnations lend themselves perfectly to colour magic. Trust your intuition and be guided by the colour of the flower and what it means to you for your magical workings.

Celandine
(Chelidonium majus)
Magical Properties: Happiness, protection,
release, escape, assists with legal matters

Celandine is often thought of as a weed because of its spreading habit. It carries yellow flowers and dark green leaves through the summer months.

Add celandine to amulets, pouches, and bottles created for happiness. Abusive relationships or bad situations can benefit from a pinch or two of dried celandine, which will help remove you from the situation. When used in magic, celandine can also help free you from any self-imposed limitations.

Celandine is toxic if ingested.

Celery
(Apium graveolens)
Magical Properties: Clarity, passion, peace

Celery has a very strong flavour; it is one that you will either love or hate (I am the former). You can eat the stalks, the leaves, and the seeds of this plant—they all have that familiar flavour.

Use the stalks in recipes but also in magical workings to bring a boost of passion and lust. The seeds are excellent in spell work for matters of the mind, bringing clarity and concentration. Passion, lust, clarity, and concentration is an interesting combination! Add the seeds to any magical workings to bring about peace and a calming influence.

Chamomile
(Chameamelum nobile, Anthemis nobilis)
Magical Properties: Sleep, dreams, love, calm,
money, relaxation, purification, balancing

Mostly grown as a cultivated plant, chamomile does grow wild in some places. It is a really pretty daisy-like flower with feathery leaves. It makes a lovely alternative to a grass lawn.

To spread the magic, you can use the dried flowers and leaves or a chamomile tea bag. Chamomile creates a good energy for a pre-ritual bath. Add chamomile to your bath to cleanse and purify your body and to bring a sense of peace and calm. Chamomile flowers or a tea bag can be dropped into a bucket of hot water to use as a floor wash, clearing negative energy around your home. Add the dried flowers to a sleep pillow to aid prophetic dreams and bring about a good night's sleep. Chamomile makes an excellent herb for cleansing and balancing your chakras, particularly the throat chakra.

Chives
(Allium schoenoprasum)
Magical Properties: Exorcism, repels negativity,
breaks bad habits, protection

Because they are part of the onion family, chives have the same oniony flavour. Eat the green tube stalk of the plant. You can eat the pretty purple flowers too.

During the Middle Ages, if you felt a bit low or depressed you were fed chives to dispel negative energy and uplift your spirits. This is possibly why chives are also used in exorcism rituals.

Use chives to help break any destructive or negative patterns and cycles that you have found yourself in. Chives bring protection. They are also useful to keep you away from evil temptation…if you want to be kept away…

Chocolate
(Theobroma cacao)
Magical Properties: Prosperity, positive energy, happiness, love

When I take on a subject, I take it very seriously and do as much research as I possibly can. The subject of chocolate was no exception! Rest assured it was thoroughly investigated, mostly on a practical level.

Our favourite ingredient comes from a bean—the cacao bean to be exact. Add in cocoa solids, cocoa butter, fat, and sugar (often with some milk powder for good measure) and you have chocolate. The darker the chocolate is, the more cocoa content it has. So, for example, if you take cocoa butter, sugar, and milk, you have created white chocolate. (In my humble opinion, this is a chocolate imposter.)

You can add squares or gratings of chocolate to spell work, but it does get a bit messy. If you want to use chocolate in spell work, you can use hot chocolate or even chocolate cake as an excellent base for adding other ingredients. However, I find cocoa powder is much easier to use for magical purposes.

Use chocolate in any magical working for feel-good or uplifting energy. It is a proven fact that chocolate makes you feel good and uplifts your mood and emotions. Chocolate has a direct link to the heart chakra, so it brings lots of love energy. Being given chocolates always makes me feel loved!

Cinnamon
(Cinnamomum verum)
Magical Properties: Success, healing, power, psychic powers, protection, love, focus, lust, spirituality, changes

This is not only one of my favourite flavours, but as a magical ingredient it covers so many different intents. Cinnamon is made from the bark of a tree. You can purchase the familiar rolled cinnamon sticks or ground cinnamon for culinary or magical use. A cheaper option that is just as powerful for magical use is cassia bark, often used in Asian cooking.

Cinnamon works really well in incense but can be used in all magical spell work. Add a pinch of ground cinnamon to boost magic. It brings focus, concentration, a spiritual connection, psychic boost, strength, success, and courage. It is a very useful ingredient.

Cloves
(Syzygium aromaticum)
Magical Properties: Love, money, exorcism, clarity, protection, abundance, repels negativity, prevents gossip, stress relief, truth

The dark cloves we are familiar with are the seeds of a small evergreen tree. They have a powerful taste and scent that works very well for cleansing and clearing energy.

If you want to keep the harmony within a group of friends or family, give them a clove each or bake a big apple pie spiced with ground cloves. The magic of cloves brings in friendship and peace. To keep gossip out of your home and bring in protection, hang a bag of cloves over your doorway.

Columbine
(Aquilegia canadensis, Aquilegia vulgaris)
Magical Properties: Love, courage, faeries, clarity, reduces jealousy

Columbine grows wild in fields and meadows but can also be cultivated for your garden. They self-seed all over the place. Columbine comes from the Latin word for dove, *columba*. When you look at the flower it resembles five birds sitting together, which explains the nickname. You need to take a closer look at the plant to see what I mean.

The leaves and flowers can be used in magical workings to dispel jealousy, bring courage, and help you see things clearly. Take a bath with columbine seeds or flowers added to get a fresh and clear view on any situation.

Columbine is toxic if ingested.

Coriander/Cilantro
(Coriandrum sativum)
Magical Properties: Health, healing, peace, love,
release, wealth, protection, repels negativity

This plant is called coriander in the UK and cilantro in the US—different names, but exactly the same plant. This seems to be a love-it-or-hate-it kind of herb. Some say it tastes like soap. Personally, I love the flavour of coriander in small doses, as the flavour can be overpowering.

It is an annual herb that has pretty, bright-green leaves. The flowers are lilac and produce small, sphere-shaped seeds. The seeds carry a nice orange flavour. Coriander can be used to bring protection, particularly with any astral or psychic work. It has a strong protective energy too.

To bring a peaceful and calm atmosphere into your house, hang a bunch of fresh coriander above your doorway. Keep coriander on you to attract love. It can also be useful to help you let go of past issues and move forward. Coriander is a seriously good plant for all health and healing magic.

Cowslip
(Primula veris)
Magical Properties: Healing, peace, calm, treasure, youth, anti-visitor

This pretty yellow flower grows in the wild but can also be cultivated for the garden. It is a good sign of spring.

Keep a pot of cowslip indoors to keep the air peaceful and calm. Dried cowslip flowers popped under your front doormat will keep out those visitors that you don't want to see.

Cramp Bark (Guelder Rose)
(Viburnum opulus)
Magical Properties: Relaxing, meditation, stress relief,
releases tension, antianxiety, healing, rebirth, protection

With green leaves that gain a touch of red in the winter, white flower heads in the summer, and scarlet berries in autumn, the cramp bark tree is pretty year-round. You can eat the berries and use the bark medicinally.

Cramp bark is the plant to use for any kind of goddess magic or reproductive issues. It holds a large amount of feminine energy as well as the energy of the dark goddess and of Samhain. The bloodred berries can be used to represent death and rebirth or used instead of blood in magic. Squish the berries and you can use the juice as a red ink. Both the bark and the berries work well in protection workings.

Cyclamen
(Cyclamen spp.)
Magical Properties: Happiness, self-esteem,
protection, fertility, love, lust, fends off nightmares

Flowering in very early spring and sometimes during a mild winter, *Cyclamen* has red, pink, or white flowers. The flower stalks emerge from fans of ivy-shaped leaves.

Bring a pot of *Cyclamen* into the house to give you a happy, loving, and protected energy and to increase your self-esteem. If you want to keep nightmares at bay and dispel negative energy, put a pot of *Cyclamen* in your bedroom.

Cyclamen is toxic if ingested.

Cypress
(Cupressus sempervirens)
Magical Properties: Release, binding, helps with grief, protection, healing

"Tree of Death" is the very dramatic folk name for the cypress tree. It does make it a useful tree to work with for easing grief and any reincarnation, death, and rebirth magical workings.

Cypress can be used as an ingredient for binding spells and releasing magic. To bring protection and blessings to your home and family, hang a piece of cypress over your doorway.

Dill
(Anethum graveolens)
Magical Properties: Protection, love, lust, money,
reduces jealousy, balance, clarity, knowledge, magic

A hardy, annual herb, dill has pretty lacy leaves along with tall stems topped with yellow flowers.

The seeds of dill are easiest to work with for magic. Place the seeds around your house for protection. Use dill seeds in spell work to counteract any jealousy. Dill can be used to bring balance between your conscious and unconscious mind along with clarity and insight.

Elm
(Ulmus)
Magical Properties: Love, balance, luck, energy, psychic powers

Found throughout most of the Northern Hemisphere, the elm tree can grow to be more than 150 feet tall. It is a beautiful tree with inverted triangle leaves. The elm tree is often found in the underworld in Greek mythology. Celtic myths place the elm at crossroads and entrances to the fairy world. Elves are apparently quite taken by the elm tree as well.

Use elm to balance both the heart and the mind, to enhance your psychic powers, and to bring love to you.

Elm sap can be an irritant to the skin.

Fennel
(Foeniculum vulgare)
Magical Properties: Healing, purification, protection,
courage, confidence, fertility, initiation

A tall plant with bright green stems and feathery leaves, fennel has bright yellow flowers during the summer months that develop into the aniseed-flavour seeds we are familiar with. Fennel root also makes a very pleasant vegetable. If you don't like aniseed, then you won't like the fennel seeds or the root—it is quite a strong flavour.

The strong scent and taste make fennel excellent to use for cleansing and purifying. Add it to incense blends and bathwater for that purpose. It clears the mind, the body, the soul, and any space around you. This is not just a fresh waft; it's a really good kick-everything-out kind of cleanse. This also makes fennel excellent for protection and healing spell work.

To bring confidence and courage, eat or carry fennel seeds with you. Fennel can also help release that which no longer serves you and clear the way ahead, so it works particularly well in initiation rituals and spells.

Frankincense
(Boswellia spp.)
Magical Properties: Purification, spirituality,
relaxation, focus, love, abundance

If you ever see an image of a Boswellia tree, it looks old and craggy, often growing out of rocks in desolate areas. It is this tree that provides the resin we use as frankincense. This is probably my personal favourite scent for incense. Bear in mind, as with all resin, it does make a lot of smoke when burnt on charcoal.

It is a very spiritual and uplifting scent which cleanses and purifies the body, spirit, and soul. It also brings focus, clarity, and a general feeling of well-being.

Garlic
(Allium sativum)
Magical Properties: Healing, protection, hex breaking, repels
negativity, lust, strength, courage, antidepression

Garlic is excellent for your health and for magic. The sulphur compound found within garlic cloves is the good stuff; it brings health benefits. If you are worried about psychic attacks, then garlic is your go-to magical ingredient.

Work with garlic to break any hexes and disperse negative energy. I like to use garlic salt as it combines the magical properties of garlic with salt magic. It is also easier to use in bottles, pouches, and powders.

Don't throw away the white papery skin of a garlic clove—this can be used in magical workings. It has the same power as garlic bulbs but with less scent and lasts longer. The skin can also be burnt to bring prosperity, clear out negative energy, and help ease depression.

Hanging garlic cloves up in your home wards against evil and brings in protection against thieves.

Ginger
(Zingiber officinale)
Magical Properties: Healing, power, love,
passion, success, prosperity, protection

The root of this plant gives us the fresh or dried ginger we are familiar with. Medicinally and magically, ginger brings healing to the table in any workings. A pinch of ginger will speed up any workings and help bring a successful ending. It also has a fiery punch of energy so it can be added to any magic to give it a big boost of energy. You can also eat a piece of ginger before working any magic to help boost your own personal power.

Grapefruit
(Citrus × paradisi)
Magical Properties: Happiness, spirit work,
purification, antidepression, energy

Take a pomelo and a sweet orange, combine them, and you get a grapefruit. It is a totally happy fruit that will uplift your spirits and enhance your mood and emotions. The grapefruit refreshes and sparks your psychic abilities, waking up your whole body and mind. Grapefruit also had a wonderful cleansing and purifying energy.

Grapes
(Vitis vinifera)
Magical Properties: Spirituality, fertility,
moon magic, offerings, love, happiness

Grown on gnarly, twisting, woody vines, grapes can be eaten fresh or made into all kinds of things. Raisins are the result of dried grapes and, of course, if you squash and ferment them it makes wine.

You can use fresh grapes in spell work, but it is probably easier and less messy to use raisins, sultanas, or vine leaves. Grapes can help you connect with spirit, enhance your visions and dreams (too much wine also has that effect), and give you a big spiritual boost.

Grapes have a strong lunar connection, so moon magic is perfect for grapes. Grapes also make an excellent and well-received offering to most deities.

Whilst wine does bring happiness and love, be careful of too much intake.

Green Tea
(Camellia sinensis)
Magical Properties: Energy, health, prosperity, cleansing,
repels negativity, love, passion, longevity, immortality

If you take fresh leaves from the tea plant and don't oxidise and ferment them as you do with black tea, you get green tea. Now globally recognised as a healthy tea to drink, Chinese and Indian medicine has been promoting the health benefits of green tea for a very long time. We have Chinese monks up in the Himalayas to thank for the discovery of green tea.

Holly
(Ilex aquifolium, Ilex opaca)
Magical Properties: Protection, luck, dreams, balance, success

Perhaps one of the most iconic plants of the festive season, holly is an evergreen shrub but can also grow into a tree if not kept in check. With dark green leaves and scarlet berries, it is a big part of Yule celebrations. It is also burnt during Imbolc rituals.

For prophetic dreams and visions, hang holly above your bed. To keep out evil spirits (and next door's cat) and to protect against lightning, plant holly around your house. Bring holly into the home at the winter solstice and it will ensure a happy, successful, and balanced coming year.

Holly berries are highly toxic if ingested.

Hops
(Humulus lupulus)
Magical Properties: Dreams, sleep, aphrodisiac

Hop flowers are used primarily to create beer, but they are really magical too.

For centuries they have been used to prevent nightmares, bring good dreams, and ensure a sound night of sleep. They make a good addition to any sleep pillow. Dried hop flowers can be added to your bathwater just before bedtime to help make you feel sleepy. Wash your floors, window frames, and the surfaces of your home with a warm water and hop mix to keep the air calm and peaceful.

If you are in a low place, avoid hops. They can bring you down even further.

Hyacinth
(Hyacinthus orientalis)
Magical Properties: Love, happiness, peace,
sleep, fends off nightmares, abundance

Hyacinth is highly scented and very pretty with spring flowers that are produced from bulbs. You can find hyacinth flowers in shades of white, yellow, purple, and pink. With such a strong scent, the hyacinth is very powerful. It brings peace, calm, and happiness. But do watch out for hay fever!

If you want to keep nightmares away, pop a hyacinth on your bedside table. Hyacinth bulbs are poisonous if ingested.

Hypericum
(Hypericum spp.)
Magical Properties: Protection, health, strength,
love, divination, happiness, abundance, truth

You may be familiar with the medicinal plant St. John's wort, which is sometimes used to treat depression. It is a specific variety—*Hypericum perforatum*. If you are using the plant for magical purposes, however, any of the plants in the *Hypericum* genus work just as well. The *Hypericum* is a shrub that produces year-round displays: green leaves often turn red at the edges in autumn, bright yellow flowers last all summer long, and then the plant becomes covered in red or black seeds.

Ruled by the sun, St. John's wort can be used to bring light into the dark. With such a strong antidepression link, it works well in magical spells for bringing an uplifting and happy energy.

Apparently, St. John's wort was one of the plants placed in the mouth of a person accused of Witchcraft. It was supposed to force them to confess to their wicked ways. How the poor person was supposed to talk—let alone confess—with a mouthful of leaves, I don't really know. However, I have found that St. John's wort works well in any spells that seek the truth.

Knotweed
(Polygonum aviculare)
Magical Properties: Binding, health, clarity, relieves worries

Knotweed is not a plant you really want to find in your garden because it does have a habit of winding around everything and being really difficult to get rid of. I know some people like that, though…

If you need to offload your worries and cares, then talk to this plant. Once you've finished, burn the knotweed so it can release your worries and cares for you. Knotweed also brings the ability to improve your health. Use knotweed in any workings to gain clarity and clear vision. Because it is a plant that winds around all other plants, knotweed works exceptionally well in binding spells.

Lavender
(Lavandula angustifolia)
Magical Properties: Happiness, peace, love, protection, sleep, clarity, faeries, strength

Probably one of the most recognised flowers, lavender grows on green shrubs with pretty grey leaves. The purple flowers have a beautiful scent during the summer months and retain the scent when they are dried.

Lavender helps bring clarity to your thoughts and mind. It is a calming and peaceful flower that brings tranquillity and happiness with it. Use in sleep pillows to help bring rest and relaxation. Add lavender to your floor wash or bathwater to share the energy. To keep peace in your home and protect against negative energy, hang a bunch of lavender over your doorway or grow some around your property. Lavender provides you with inner strength and protection against any kind of emotional abuse.

Lemon
(Citrus × limon)

Magical Properties: Purification, moon magic, happiness,
decisions, uplifting, love, protection, friendship, fidelity

Lemons are not just for your gin and tonic! The lemon is sacred to the moon and also brings a burst of colourful, happy energy. The lemon scent is refreshing and uplifting, which helps provide clarity of mind and assists with decision-making.

The juice of a lemon is very acidic, so it can be used in magic for purification and cleansing. Lemon juice can be added to blessed water or a ritual bath. I like to use dried lemon peel or lemon leaves in incense blends. I also add them to spiritual washes and pouches.

Lemon Balm
(Melissa officinalis)

Magical Properties: Success, healing, antidepression,
boosts memory, love, antianxiety

This lovely lemon-scented plant grows all over my garden and has to be restrained—otherwise it would take over! Bees absolutely love the tiny flowers. It is part of the mint family, which explains the similarity of the leaves. The Elizabethans used lemon balm in their food and drink as they believed it provided relief for depression and aided their memory.

Lemon balm also eases anxiety and promotes balance and calm. To work a quick spell for happiness, write your wish on a lemon balm leaf and leave it out to dry (either on your altar or in the sunshine). Once the magic has worked, you can burn the leaf.

Lettuce
(Lactuca sativa)

Magical Properties: Fertility, meditation, astral travel, calm

Usually we find lettuce in our sandwich or salad bowl, but it has some wonderful magical uses!

Lettuce can help you meditate and bring a calm and centred focus for any kind of astral- or dreamwork. It doesn't dry well so I don't recommend using it in pouches, incense, or witch bottles. Give lettuce as an offering or eat it to absorb the magic. It works well in fertility spells, not just for babies but for any new ideas, projects, directions, or journeys. Eating lettuce can bring calm and peace to your well-being.

Lungwort
(Pulmonaria officinalis)
Magical Properties: Healing, cleansing, releasing, calming

This pretty perennial has large oval leaves covered in white spots. It's naturally covered in white spots, and no, they're not contagious…Lungwort sports pretty purple-pink flowers. The leaves are covered in bristly hairs. Lungwort leaves are similar to the leaves of a borage (starflower), probably because they are both members of the *Boraginaceae* family. It is often found in the wild but can also be cultivated. It was originally believed to be good for pulmonary problems as the leaves were thought to resemble lung tissue. It does make a good herb for magical healing work!

Lungwort works well for cleansing and releasing emotional blockages. Use it in situations where there doesn't seem to be a resolution. It can bring a good calming and soothing energy to your home.

Marjoram
(Origanum majorana)
Magical Properties: Love, happiness, health,
protection, marriage, helps with grief

Marjoram grows wild on grassland and waste ground, and obviously in our gardens too! During the summer months, it is covered in lilac flowers.

Marjoram is a bundle of happiness and works extremely well to help ease depression. It also promotes healing for grief. Add marjoram to your antidepression spells or recipes. If you don't have marjoram, you can use oregano. It is much more common to find oregano in a kitchen, and it shares the same magical properties.

Milk

Magical Properties: Feminine power, creativity, antidepression, goddess energy, moon magic, nurturing, offerings, love, spirituality, faeries

Milk has many sources. It comes from animals of various sorts: cows, sheep, goats, yaks…No matter where it comes from, it all has magical properties! The mother produces milk to feed her infant, so it has a wonderful nurturing, caring energy. It also carries feminine power. The moon rules milk of all kinds, so you also get moon magic and goddess energy in this one drink. What a bargain!

Each type of milk will also have specific magical qualities associated with the type of animal it came from. If you don't like milk, no worries—this magic also transfers into any product made from milk, so pick up some butter or yogurt.

Milk makes a brilliant offering to any deity. It's also a great option for offerings to the world of the Fae. Pour milk onto the ground after a ritual as an offering.

Mint
(Mentha spp., Mentha piperita)

Magical Properties: Money, healing, exorcism, protection, cleansing, calming

Often found in gardens or in herb beds, mint is a highly scented perennial that has masses of pungent green leaves and lilac flowers. It can also be found in the wild, usually in damp woodlands or beside streams. There are many varieties of mint. If you decide to grow mint in your garden, I would advise keeping it restricted to a pot. If you let it grow freely in the ground, it will take over!

There are so many ways to use mint in your everyday life. With its cooling properties, mint can calm down any situation. It also works well for healing spells. Drink mint tea or iced mint water to cleanse and purify your body. Drinking mint tea also helps keep communications amicable. Use the scent to uplift and bring in positive energy. Add mint leaves or mint tea bags to hot water to create a floor and surface wash that will cleanse and purify your home. For a restful and peaceful sleep, pop a few mint leaves under your pillow.

To keep negative energy away and provide protection for your home, sprinkle dried mint or grow mint plants around your property. It also works well for travel spells.

Mustard
(Brassica juncea, Brassica nigra, Sinapis hirta)
Magical Properties: Clarity, psychic abilities,
protection, astral travel, faith, success

You are probably more familiar with mustard in its condiment form. The seeds are ground and mixed with water, salt, and (usually) lemon juice to create the yellow paste. For spell work, I recommend using the small mustard seeds because it is easier and less messy.

Mustard brings a sharp and fiery energy. It can increase your psychic abilities and bring clarity of thought and situational insight. In the Atharva Veda scripts and Tamil literature, white mustard seeds are mentioned as a use for preventing ghosts and keeping evil spirits away. I like to use black mustard seeds in binding spells or to protect against those that are causing grief or harm. Mustard also has protective qualities, especially for mothers and newborn babies.

Nettle
(Urtica dioica)
Magical Properties: Healing, protection, lust, money, exorcism

The humble stinging nettle grows around the world and on almost any type of soil. It can grow quite tall, around four or five feet in some cases. The leaves are heart shaped with toothed edges. The coarse hairs that grow on the stems and leaves cause that itchy, "stinging" feeling. During the summer the plant carries bunches of green catkins, with female and male flowers growing on separate plants.

History tells us that nettles were used quite frequently to protect against witches and demons. Nettles make a good ingredient in spell work to remove curses and send hexes back to their source. The nettle also provides protection against negative energy and danger of all kinds.

Use nettle to exorcise and ward against ghosts and evil spirits. Crush dried nettled into a powder and sprinkle around your property; this will protect against negative energy. Nettles work well in any kind of healing spell.

Orange
(Citrus × sinensis)
*Magical Properties: Love, happiness, uplifting,
generosity, purification, clarity, energy, fidelity*

A happy, bright, and sunshiny fruit, the orange brings love and happiness. The orange can be used to purify and cleanse body, mind, and soul.

Orange juice can be served in ritual to help the energy flow. Use orange juice or dried orange peel to make a drink that will help provide clarity and uplifting energy.

Passionflower
(Passiflora)
Magical Properties: Love, calm, peace, sleep, friendship

Passionflower is a climbing plant with the most amazing and unusually shaped flowers, followed by oval fruits.

This plant is all about love and passion, but it also brings a good energy for calm and peace. Use passionflower in any type of working for friendship issues. Add it to dream pillows to help bring a good night's sleep.

Patchouli
(Pogostemon cablin)
*Magical Properties: Grounding, earth magic, prosperity,
money, protection, sex magic, balance, calm*

A member of the mint family, the patchouli plant has tall stems topped with pale pink or white flowers. It is a tropical plant so won't grow in colder climates. Used for centuries in medicine and perfume, patchouli carries a very particular, strong, earthy scent. Use it for grounding and any kind of earth magic.

Patchouli will give you a direct connection to Mother Earth and the earth elementals. Patchouli also carries a balancing energy that swoops in with peace and tranquillity. Use dried patchouli if you can get it, but the essential oil works well. In a pinch I have also used patchouli incense sticks, crushed into a powder.

Patchouli essential oil is toxic if ingested.

Pine
(Pinus spp.)
Magical Properties: Centring, focus, dragon magic, protection,
truth, abundance, purification, fertility, healing

Often associated with Yule, pines are evergreen conifers with thick bark and green needles. These aren't just for the colder months—pine has wonderful properties that can be utilised year-round.

Pine brings a very strong energy of protection for your home, yourself, or your sacred space. It also provides a welcoming feeling of hospitality. Breathe in the scent of pine to centre and focus your thoughts and mind.

Pine works perfectly in truth spells or when you wish to uncover secrets or hidden knowledge. Add pine essential oil or a handful of pine needles to your floor and surface wash.

Plum
(Prunus spp.)
Magical Properties: Love, spirituality, relaxation,
passion, longevity, wisdom, rebirth

Plums are a delicious fruit that come in lots of different varieties. I particularly like the yellow plums. I recommend working with the plum stones, but you can also eat the flesh of the fruit to absorb its magic.

Plum can increase your spiritual connection. In ancient Egypt and Greece, the plum was used to help bring relaxation to the body and the mind. Mention of the humble plum dates back as early as 479 BCE. Confucius wrote about the plum tree in Chinese myths, and the Chinese believe it to be a symbol of great wisdom, long life, and resurrection.

Poppy Seeds
(Papaver somniferum)
Magical Properties: Calm, peace, luck, protection, invisibility, prosperity

Poppy seeds are delicious. They are often used in baking recipes like cakes, breads, or muffins, but they do have a wonderful magical energy as well.

Sprinkle them onto your meal or add them to spells for prosperity and protection. Poppy seeds bring a peaceful and calming energy.

Pulsatilla/Pasqueflower
(Anemone pulsatilla, Pulsatilla vulgaris)
Magical Properties: Protection, healing, health

Pulsatilla is a perennial plant that flowers in the spring. It is often referred to as pasqueflower or anemone. It has long stems topped with a single flower, usually in a bright colour.

Use the petals or leaves in any kind of health or healing spell work. Pulsatilla brings protection and helps to dispel negative energy.

Pulsatilla is poisonous.

Rhubarb
(Rheum rhabarbarum)
Magical Properties: Willpower, releases worry, love, protection

Usually found in sweet pies and cakes, rhubarb is actually classified as a vegetable. It can help increase your willpower and release any worries that you might have. In that case, I think I may need a very big rhubarb pie…

With a historical connection to the Black Death, where rhubarb was used during the great plague, it brings a powerful protective energy. The dried leaves also work well as a magical ingredient.

Rose
(Rosa spp.)

Magical Properties: Love, psychic powers, healing, luck, protection, peace, mysteries, knowledge, dreams, friendship, death and rebirth, abundance

Roses are one of the most recognisable flowers. Whether as a bush, a climber, or in a bouquet of flowers, the rose is beautiful. It also provides us with a complete palette of colours to choose from. Rose flowers bloom between May and September. The petals are incredibly easy to dry; I just lay them out on a large tray and leave them in a cool, dry place. In the autumn, the rose provides us with rosehips. You can use rose thorns for magic year-round.

If you are looking for an herb to represent the Mother aspect of the goddess or for a mystery that needs to be delved into, look no further than the rose. Obviously roses are perfect for any love workings, but they also increase your knowledge and psychic powers. Roses have a strong moon magic connection.

Work with colour magic and use rose petals for spells: pink for friendship, red for passion, white for peace, and yellow for happiness. Rose brings a large amount of feminine energy as well as a connection to death and rebirth. Rose petals in spells or your bathwater can bring balance, love, and relaxation. Rose thorns are excellent for protection spells or curses.

Rosemary
(Salvia rosmarinus)

Magical Properties: Protection, love, lust, mental powers, exorcism, purification, healing, sleep

Rosemary is a good plant for your garden as it grows all year-round. It has woody stems and narrow green leaves. If you are lucky, it will reward you with tiny lilac flowers during the spring and the autumn. Rosemary is a beautiful plant. Everything on the plant carries a scent, even the leaves. After you pick them, you will find scented oil on your hands.

The woody stems make an excellent base for incense blends. Rosemary has been burnt as incense in houses to clear away sickness for a long time. I add rosemary twigs to my smudge sticks in addition to lavender and sage.

Rosemary (in whatever magical form) brings protection, purification, and healing. It is a very useful herb.

Rue
(Ruta graveolens)
Magical Properties: Protection, health, healing, purification, balance, clarity, antianxiety, hex breaking

Rue is a shrub with woody stems that produces yellow flowers during the summer. It has a confusing history; it seems rue was used by wise folk in potions but was also used against witches.

Rue can be used to cleanse and purify. It brings balance and protection, particularly in a sacred space. To ease anxiety and bring clarity of thought and mind, use rue in your workings. Hanging a bunch of rue above your threshold will have the same effect. It is exceptionally good in any health or healing workings because it has a powerful protection energy that is particularly useful when breaking curses and hexes.

Rue is toxic if eaten. The sap can also cause skin burns.

Saffron
(Crocus sativus)
Magical Properties: Happiness, energy, psychic powers, healing, fertility

The tiny *Crocus sativus* gives up its stigmas to provide the saffron we use in cooking. It has a lovely earthy flavour and turns any food a golden-yellow colour. It is often added to curries. You can eat saffron as part of a dish or add it to spell workings to benefit from its magic. I am all for eating in! So were our ancestors—apparently, it was once believed that eating too much of it could cause death from "excessive joy."

Saffron can ease depression and help you gain some motivation. Add a pinch of saffron to your tea to bring in healing energy and increase your psychic abilities. Whether you add it to your spell work or eat it in curries, cakes, or breads, saffron has a warm, happy energy.

Salt

Magical Properties: Cleansing, purification, protection

Salt is a very common item that most people have in their cupboard. Lucky for us, it is an incredibly powerful and useful magical ingredient. According to alchemists, salt has a very strong female energy, the opposite being sulphur (which has a male energy).

Salt brings cleansing, purification, and protection. Hoodoo root workers and anyone working with folk magic will often sprinkle salt in each corner of the room before undertaking any kind of ritual or spell work. Add black pepper, red pepper, or cayenne and you completely boost the protection energy.

Black salt, sometimes called Witches Salt, has a salt base with charcoal and occasionally black pepper added. You can use black salt for cursing and hexing. Throw black salt behind an enemy or on their property to encourage them to move or just to stop bothering you. Black salt is also very good for protection workings and can provide strong personal protection.

Add salt to your bathwater (Epsom salt is a good one for this) to cleanse and purify your body and to release any negative energy.

Self-Heal
(Prunella vulgaris)

Magical Properties: Releasing, cleansing, spirituality,
stress relief, calming, clarity, protection

As the name suggests, this perennial plant is perfect for self-healing. It can be found growing at the woodland edge and over grass- or scrubland. In your garden, self-heal can be an annoying weed: they are self-rooting and will take over if left alone. The plus side to this is that they have pretty purple and white flowers during the summer and both the leaves and flowers are edible.

Work with self-heal to bring about calm and relaxation and to ease stress. Self-heal can also bring people closer together! The flowers can be eaten or used in spell work to provide clarity, particularly if there has been a misunderstanding or miscommunication. For purification and cleansing, add self-heal to your incense blends or floor washes.

Skullcap
(*Scutellaria spp.*)
Magical Properties: Faithfulness, restoring, prosperity, stress relief, peace

From the mint family, *Scutellaria* covers a large group of annual and perennial flowering plants. The flowers resemble tiny medieval helmets, having upper and lower lip parts.

If you feel spiritually or psychically drained, skullcap is the herb to use. It can also pep you up after any exorcism workings. Skullcap relieves stress and brings some peaceful, calming energy into your life.

Skullcap is hepatotoxic (damaging to liver cells) and mildly narcotic if eaten.

Star Anise
(*Illicium verum*)
Magical Properties: Luck, psychic powers, purification,
protection, dreams, spirituality, sleep

Star anise is an ancient herb. The seed pods are picked just before they ripen and then left out to dry in the sun. The seeds are shaped like a star, which is perfect for all sorts of magical correspondence. An added bonus is the yummy aniseed taste as well as a cleansing, refreshing scent.

Star anise makes a brilliant incense ingredient. It burns well and adds purification, protects your home, boosts your psychic abilities, and adds a punch of psychic protection to keep away the nasties. A piece of star anise under your pillow can help to bring about prophetic dreams along with peaceful sleep. Adding a couple star anise to your bathwater provides a cleansing and purifying body wash that will clear your body and soul.

Sweet Pea
(*Lathyrus odoratus*)

Magical Properties: Courage, strength, friendship, peace,
happiness, truth, spirituality, psychic abilities, protection, sleep

The sweet pea plant is a pretty climber with beautiful flowers that have the most amazing scent. Sweet pea does actually come from the pea family, but one important difference is that sweet peas are poisonous if eaten.

Sweet pea flowers carry a very strong fragrance that can bring peace, love, joy, and new friendships. Keep the flowers near you to boost your spiritual and physical strength. The spiritual energy of these gorgeous flowers can also help in workings to bring a connection to spirit and boost your psychic abilities. Sweet pea works well in spells to provide a peaceful night of sleep. The sweet pea is often thought of as a flower for children; not only does it engage their senses, it also provides them with protection.

Sweet pea seeds are toxic if eaten.

Thyme
(*Thymus vulgaris, Thymus serpyllum*)

Magical Properties: Healing, health, peace, psychic powers,
love, purification, courage, releasing, sleep, beauty

Thyme may be a common herb, but it is one that is packed with magic. It has woody stems and tiny leaves with lilac-coloured flowers in the summertime. It is a very low-growing herb. It can be found growing in gardens or in the wild. It favours woods, fields, and heathlands. Thyme smells and tastes divine. You can use it in savoury or sweet dishes.

This is one of my preferred herbs for health and healing. It can be used in incense to cleanse and purify your home, leaving it open for peaceful, loving energy to fill. Thyme can help bring you courage when you need it and willpower when you want it. Take some time (no pun intended) to make thyme tea; it will work with you to let go of things and release the past. Thyme also has this effect when added to your bathwater. If you need a sound night of rest, mix thyme with lavender to create a brilliant sleep pillow.

Turmeric
(Cucurma longa)
Magical Properties: Purification, protection, peace

Turmeric comes from the long tuberous roots of a perennial plant. It is used in cooking to boost flavour but also adds a cheerful yellow colour. Unless you want something stained bright yellow, be very careful when working with turmeric—it has a habit of staining everything it comes into contact with!

Mix turmeric in water and sprinkle it around your house, ritual area, sacred space, or workplace to purify, cleanse, and bless the area. Pop a piece of turmeric root above your doorway or windows to bring in protection. It can also be burnt in incense blends to bring about a peaceful, calming energy.

Valerian
(Valeriana officinalis)
Magical Properties: Protection, purification, love,
sleep, peace, animal spirit, stress relief

Growing in ditches and on riverbanks, valerian is a perennial plant with dark green leaves and tall flower stems. The flowers arrive in pink clusters during July and August. It is, however, the root that is generally used in medicine and magical workings.

To bring protection and a peaceful energy to your home, hang a piece of valerian root above your threshold. Place a small piece of valerian root under your pillow or add a pinch of powered valerian to a sleep pillow to help promote peaceful sleep. Valerian is also very good for calming your nerves and easing any stress you may be suffering from. Burn valerian to cleanse and purify your home. Valerian incense can be used to invoke animal spirits.

Vervain
(Verbena officinalis)
Magical Properties: Protection, love, purification, peace,
sleep, healing, money, inspiration, shape-shifting

This perennial plant can be found growing on grassland or verges. In late summer, it is topped by small white or lilac spikes of flowers. Wait until it has come to the end of flowering before harvesting. Remove any large pieces of stem and grind the rest to create a rough working powder. Druids have used vervain for cleansing and consecrating ritual spaces and in divination. Cerridwen's potion found within her cauldron (we know it as the Awen) was said to include vervain.

Drink a cup of tea made with vervain and it will bring you a connection to the underworld. It will also help with your divination skills as well as your psychic and spirit connection, and will provide you with inspiration. Vervain can aid with shape-shifting. This is a good herb to use for peace, relaxation, or calming energy workings. Vervain is thought to have aphrodisiac qualities, so it also works well in love spells.

Willow
(Salix alba, Salix fragilis)
Magical Properties: Love, protection, healing, cleansing, wishes, release, inspiration, intuition

Nine times out of ten, the draping tree seen on riverbanks with its branches grazing the water is probably a willow tree. The leaves and flowers both appear in April and May. I find the willow to be a very emotional tree. It is influenced by its water elemental presence but is also ruled by the moon, making it a double whammy of emotional energy.

The young branches of willow trees are very flexible and can be used to make small besoms or brooms for sweeping and cleansing ritual areas, sacred spaces, or your home. They can also be plaited together to create witch ladders or tied together for working knot magic. If you stand under the light of the moon and speak your intent out loud as you tie a knot into a young willow branch, the knot will seal your intent. If you mix willow with sandalwood, it makes a good incense to use for releasing and letting go, particularly if burnt during a waning moon.

Witch Hazel
(*Hamamelis virginiana*)
Magical Properties: Protection, divining, balance, helps with grief

Witch hazel is a wonderfully witchy-looking tree with its twisty, turny, crooked branches. Once the leaves fall in autumn, yellow flowers appear and are then replaced with black nuts filled with small seeds.

It is an excellent ingredient to work with to bring about balanced emotions and to overcome grief.

Yarrow
(*Achillea millefolium*)
Magical Properties: Psychic powers, love, alleviates fear, courage,
exorcism, dreams, peace, happiness, divination, protection

Yarrow has big heads of white (or sometimes pink) flowers surrounded by feathery green leaves during the summer and early autumn. Often found in meadows and on the roadside, it can also be found in cultivated varieties that come in different colours: reds, oranges, and yellows.

Work with yarrow to clear away any fears you might have and to bring you courage. If placed under your pillow, yarrow can bring prophetic dreams. Drink yarrow as a tea or add it to your incense blends to help boost your psychic abilities. Keep yarrow in the house or burn it as incense for love, happiness, and peaceful energies. For protection, yarrow can be sprinkled or grown around your property. It can also be worked into a protection amulet.

CHAPTER TWENTY

❦

Bath and Body Care
for Healing

In this section I have given different options for lotions and body care potions. Each recipe is simple to make. If you have never tried creating your own bath and body products, I encourage you to give it a go. Not only will you end up with a beautiful and natural product to use, but creating it will also make your kitchen smell lovely! I've included thirteen basic recipes and provided my personal suggestions for herbs and oils to use. Trust your intuition and be guided by what you need to add.

Body Oil

Massage this oil blend onto your body after you shower. It will nourish your skin, and the scent of the oils will help relieve any emotional issues.

Basic Recipe

> 3 tablespoons base oil (wheatgerm, almond, jojoba, etc.)
>
> 20 drops essential oil

Combine all the oils together and pour into a dark glass bottle. Seal. Your new oil is ready to use! This recipe makes 45 mL (1½ fl oz) and will keep for up to three months.

Suggested Essential Oil Blends

Anxiety Blend
Combine eight drops lavender, eight drops chamomile, and four drops geranium.

Stress Blend
Combine ten drops lavender and ten drops passionflower.

Depression Blend
Combine ten drops orange, five drops bergamot, and five drops rosemary.

Panic Attack Blend
Combine ten drops patchouli, five drops lemon balm, and five drops mint.

Fear Blend
Combine ten drops mint, five drops fennel, and five drops ginger.

Guilt Blend
Combine ten drops mint, five drops star anise, and five drops grapefruit.

Worry Blend
Combine ten drops mint, five drops fennel, and five drops lemon balm.

Grief Blend
Combine ten drops orange, five drops cloves, and five drops marjoram.

Self-Esteem Blend
Combine ten drops rose, five drops lemon balm, and five drops sweet pea.

Obstacles and Blockages Blend
Combine ten drops frankincense, five drops pine, and five drops orange.

Sleep Blend
Combine ten drops chamomile and ten drops lavender.

Menopause and Menses Blend
Combine ten drops frankincense, five drops lemon balm, and five drops coriander.

Transitions and Changes Blend
Combine ten drops lavender, five drops rose, and five drops sweet pea.

Bath Salts

Add bath salts to your next bath for a relaxing, rejuvenating experience. (Part of what makes this so relaxing is actually taking the time to have a bath!)

Basic Recipe

    600 g (21 oz) sea salt

    300 g (10½ oz) Epsom salt

    6 drops essential oil

    1 teaspoon of herbs or flower petals

Make sure you have the bathroom to yourself (no small children knocking at the door or pets scratching to get in!). Maybe light some candles and even pop on some relaxing music. Sprinkle your blend into the bathwater and enjoy!

Suggested Essential Oil and Herb Blends

Anxiety Blend
Combine six drops rose essential oil and one teaspoon dried lemon balm.

Stress Blend
Combine three drops frankincense essential oil, three drops ylang ylang essential oil, and one teaspoon dried lavender flowers.

Depression Blend
Combine three drops lemon essential oil, three drops grapefruit essential oil, and one teaspoon dried thyme.

Panic Attack Blend

Combine three drops lavender essential oil, three drops chamomile essential oil, and one teaspoon dried mint.

Fear Blend

Combine three drops ginger essential oil, three drops mint essential oil, and one teaspoon dried lemon balm.

Guilt Blend

Combine three drops pine essential oil, three drops black pepper essential oil, and one teaspoon dried mint.

Worry Blend

Combine three drops passionflower essential oil, three drops fennel essential oil, and one teaspoon poppy seeds.

Grief Blend

Combine three drops lemon essential oil, three drops cardamom essential oil, and one teaspoon dried marjoram.

Self-Esteem Blend

Combine three drops ginger essential oil, three drops lemon balm essential oil, and one teaspoon dried thyme.

Obstacles and Blockages Blend

Combine three drops coriander essential oil, three drops star anise essential oil, and one teaspoon dried mint.

Sleep Blend

Combine three drops lavender essential oil, three drops sweet pea essential oil, and one teaspoon dried thyme.

Menopause and Menses Blend

Combine three drops patchouli essential oil, three drops frankincense essential oil, and one teaspoon dried mint.

Transitions and Changes Blend
Combine three drops ginger essential oil, three drops lemon balm essential oil, and one teaspoon dried lemon balm.

Bath Melts

Bath melts are super easy to make, and they give you the healing and uplifting power of essential oils while nourishing your skin. And having a bath gives you time out to yourself, which is always precious!

Basic Recipe

> 50 g (2 oz) shea butter
>
> 50 g (2 oz) cocoa butter
>
> 2 tablespoons coconut oil (solid)
>
> 20 drops essential oil

Pop the shea butter and cocoa butter in a glass bowl and place it over a pan of warm water. Leave them over the water until the butters are melted together, then add the coconut oil and essential oils. Mix to combine.

Pour the mixture into ten soap moulds or small cupcake cases. Leave to cool until set.

Keep the melts cool and dry by storing them in the fridge. They will keep for up to three months.

Add a bath melt to your bathwater or use in the shower, letting it warm in the heat of the water and rubbing it over your skin to moisturise.

Suggested Essential Oil Blends

Anxiety Blend
Combine ten drops rose and ten drops chamomile.

Stress Blend
Combine ten drops lavender and ten drops lemon balm.

Depression Blend
Combine seven drops lavender, seven drops rose, and six drops orange.

Panic Attack Blend

Combine ten drops patchouli, five drops mint, and five drops passionflower.

Fear Blend

Combine ten drops rose and ten drops passionflower.

Guilt Blend

Combine ten drops mint, five drops grapefruit, and five drops ginger.

Worry Blend

Combine ten drops passionflower, five drops fennel, and five drops lavender.

Grief Blend

Combine ten drops bergamot, five drops orange, and five drops lemon.

Self-Esteem Blend

Combine ten drops lemon balm, five drops black pepper, and five drops ginger.

Obstacles and Blockages Blend

Combine ten drops bergamot, five drops pine, and five drops ginger.

Sleep Blend

Combine ten drops bergamot, five drops rosemary, and five drops sweet pea.

Menopause and Menses Blend

Combine ten drops frankincense, five drops cinnamon, and five drops star anise.

Transitions and Changes Blend

Combine ten drops rose, five drops ginger, and five drops lemon balm.

Room and Body Mists

Room and body mists are easy to make and smell great.

Basic Recipe

  180 mL (6 fl oz) distilled water

  24 drops essential oil

  Sprig of herbs, flower petals, or spices

To make distilled water, boil water in your kettle and let it cool. Pour it into a spray bottle, then add a few drops of essential oil and pop in a sprig of herbs. Spray the mist around your home or on your body.

Suggested Essential Oil and Herb Blends

Anxiety Blend

Combine eight drops lavender, eight drops lemon balm, and eight drops rose essential oil. Add a few rose petals or a lavender sprig to the bottle.

Stress Blend

Combine twelve drops cloves and twelve drops mint essential oil. Add a few cloves to the bottle too.

Depression Blend

Create a mixture of any of the citrus essential oils, such as orange, lemon, grapefruit, lemon balm, and bergamot. Add whichever herbs or flowers suit you.

Panic Attack Blend

Combine eight drops lavender, eight drops jasmine, and eight drops chamomile essential oil. Pop a few rose petals into the bottle too.

Fear Blend

Combine twelve drops lavender and twelve drops mint essential oil. Add a few rose petals to the bottle.

Guilt Blend

Combine eight drops ginger, eight drops grapefruit, and eight drops star anise essential oil. Add a piece of star anise to the bottle.

Worry Blend

Combine eight drops mint, eight drops lemon balm, and eight drops lavender essential oil. Add a sprig of lavender to the bottle.

Grief Blend

Combine eight drops cardamom, eight drops lavender, and eight drops lemon essential oil. Pop a sprig of lavender in the bottle too.

Self-Esteem Blend

Combine eight drops lemon balm, eight drops cinnamon, and eight drops ginger essential oil. Put a few pieces of crushed cinnamon stick in the bottle too.

Obstacles and Blockages Blend

Combine twelve drops fennel and twelve drops mint essential oil. Place a piece of star anise in the bottle too.

Sleep Blend

Use twenty-four drops lavender essential oil. Place a sprig of lavender in the bottle. This is a good mixture to spritz in your bedroom and on your pillow.

Menopause and Menses Blend

Combine twelve drops frankincense and twelve drops passionflower essential oil. Add a few pieces of crushed cinnamon stick to the bottle.

Transitions and Changes Blend

Combine twelve drops ginger and twelve drops lavender essential oil. Place a few pieces of crushed cinnamon stick in the bottle too.

Cooling Spritz

This spritz is lovely and refreshing for when you overheat, or when you just need to feel a bit refreshed and uplifted. (It's great for menopausal moments!)

Basic Recipe

    90 mL (3 fl oz) distilled water

    12 drops essential oil

To make distilled water, boil water in your kettle and let it cool. Pop the water and the oils into a spray bottle and give it a little shake. Spritz your face or body when you have a hot flash. The oils can also be used in a diffuser to cool and calm the energy in a room.

Suggested Essential Oil Blends

My Favourite Blend

Combine six drops bergamot, three drops geranium, and three drops chamomile.

Pulse Point Balm

This balm can be rubbed on your pulse points (wrists and temples) when you are hit with strong emotions. The calming scent will work its magic to help ease you.

Basic Recipe

    56 g (2 oz) base oil such as almond, coconut, or grapeseed

    28 g (1 oz) beeswax or soy wax

    20 drops essential oil

Melt your base oil and beeswax slowly over a double boiler, stirring occasionally with a wooden spoon.

When the beeswax is completely melted, add the essential oils, stir, and immediately pour carefully into tins/jars.

Leave to cool completely for several hours, then add the lid and store.

Suggested Essential Oil Blends

Anxiety Blend

Combine ten drops chamomile and ten drops lavender.

Stress Blend
Use twenty drops peppermint.

Depression Blend
Combine ten drops sweet pea and ten drops grapefruit.

Panic Attack Blend
Combine ten drops chamomile and ten drops lavender.

Fear Blend
Combine eight drops vanilla, eight drops lavender, and four drops rose.

Guilt Blend
Combine ten drops pine, five drops coriander, and five drops mint.

Worry Blend
Combine ten drops lemon balm and ten drops chamomile.

Grief Blend
Combine ten drops lavender, five drops orange, and five drops cardamom.

Self-Esteem Blend
Combine ten drops rosemary, five drops lavender, and five drops ginger.

Obstacles and Blockages Blend
Combine ten drops mint, five drops rosemary, and five drops grapefruit.

Sleep Blend
Combine ten drops chamomile and ten drops lavender.

Menopause and Menses Blend
Combine ten drops mint, five drops fennel, and five drops frankincense.

Transitions and Changes Blend
Combine ten drops ginger, five drops cinnamon, and five drops black pepper.

Body Powder

Body powders are easy to make.

Basic Recipe

    12 drops essential oil

    6 teaspoons of powdered herbs and/or flower petals

    2 tablespoons sodium bicarbonate (baking soda)

    5 tablespoons arrowroot or corn starch

Add the essential oil to the dried herbs and allow to dry.
Once dry, mix with the baking soda and arrowroot/corn starch.

Suggested Essential Oil and Herb Blends

Anxiety Blend

Combine four teaspoons ground cinnamon, one teaspoon ground cloves, one teaspoon ground rose petals, and twelve drops rose essential oil.

Stress Blend

Combine three teaspoons ground dried mint, three teaspoons ground dried lemon balm, six drops lemon balm essential oil, and six drops passionflower essential oil.

Depression Blend

Combine three teaspoons dried marjoram, three teaspoons dried rose petals, and twelve drops orange essential oil.

Panic Attack Blend

Combine six teaspoons lavender flowers, six drops lemon balm essential oil, and six drops patchouli essential oil.

Fear Blend

Combine three teaspoons ground fennel, three teaspoons dried mint, and twelve drops lemon balm essential oil.

Guilt Blend

Combine three teaspoons dried basil, three teaspoons dried mint, and twelve drops grapefruit essential oil.

Worry Blend

Combine three teaspoons fennel seeds, three teaspoons dried lavender flowers, and twelve drops lemon balm essential oil.

Grief Blend

Combine three teaspoons dried lavender flowers, three teaspoons dried orange peel, and twelve drops bergamot essential oil.

Self-Esteem Blend

Combine three teaspoons dried marjoram, three teaspoons fennel seeds, and twelve drops lemon balm essential oil.

Obstacles and Blockages Blend

Combine three teaspoons dried pine, three teaspoons coriander seeds, and twelve drops bergamot essential oil.

Sleep Blend

Combine six teaspoons lavender flowers and twelve drops passionflower essential oil.

Menopause and Menses Blend

Combine three teaspoons dried chamomile, three teaspoons fennel seeds, and twelve drops patchouli essential oil.

Transitions and Changes Blend

Combine six teaspoons dried lemon balm, six drops ginger essential oil, and six drops black pepper essential oil.

Bath Bombs

This is a recipe to make your own bath bombs to help you unwind and relax, leaving behind all your cares and worries. You can add all sorts of herbs and oils to your bathwater. To make the experience even more fragrant, you could burn scented candles or incense whilst you bathe.

If bath bombs aren't your thing, you can make herbal tea bags to put in the water instead. Add a combination of dried herbs and spices to a square of muslin, tie it with ribbon, and either hang it under the tap in the running water or pop it in the tub.

Basic Recipe

400 g (14 oz) sodium bicarbonate (baking soda)

200 g (7 oz) citric acid

2–3 teaspoons herbs and/or dried flower petals

1 teaspoon vegetable oil or cocoa butter

15 drops essential oil

1 teaspoon water

Lightly grease twenty indents in an ice cube tray or cake pop mould.

Measure out all the dry ingredients and give them a mix together.

If you're using cocoa butter, melt it in a glass bowl over a pan of warm water, then add the essential oils. (If you're using vegetable oil, simply add the oils—no need to heat!)

Pour the oil mixture into the dry ingredients and mix to combine.

Add one teaspoon of water, sprinkling it over the mixture. Give it all a mix until it feels and looks like damp sand and sticks together. If it is too crumbly, add a bit more water, but only do a tiny amount at a time.

Press the mixture into the moulds firmly and allow to set. It will take at least an hour.

Once the mixture has set, turn out the moulds and store your bath bombs in a cool, dry place. They will keep for up to three months.

Suggested Essential Oil and Herb Blends
Anxiety Blend

Combine two teaspoons lavender or rose flowers and fifteen drops passionflower essential oil.

Stress Blend

Combine one teaspoon lavender flowers, one teaspoon dried lemon balm, five drops peppermint essential oil, and ten drops lemon balm essential oil.

Depression Blend

Combine one teaspoon thyme, one teaspoon dried lemon balm, five drops orange essential oil, and ten drops rose essential oil.

Panic Attack Blend

Combine one teaspoon dried mint, one teaspoon dried lemon balm, one teaspoon chamomile flowers, five drops mint essential oil, and ten drops lemon balm essential oil.

Fear Blend

Combine one teaspoon dried lemon balm, one teaspoon dried mint, five drops fennel essential oil, five drops lemon balm essential oil, and five drops mint essential oil.

Guilt Blend

Combine one teaspoon dried grapefruit peel, one teaspoon dried mint, five drops rosemary essential oil, and ten drops pine essential oil.

Worry Blend

Combine two teaspoons dried lavender flowers, seven drops mint essential oil, and eight drops lavender essential oil.

Grief Blend

Combine two teaspoons dried marjoram leaves, seven drops lavender essential oil, and eight drops orange essential oil.

Self-Esteem Blend

Combine two teaspoons dried lemon balm leaves, seven drops rosemary essential oil, and eight drops thyme essential oil.

Obstacles and Blockages Blend
Combine two teaspoons dried mint leaves, seven drops lavender essential oil, and eight drops rosemary essential oil.

Sleep Blend
Combine two teaspoons dried lavender flowers, seven drops sweet pea essential oil, and eight drops passionflower essential oil.

Menopause and Menses Blend
Combine two teaspoons fennel seeds, seven drops passionflower essential oil, and eight drops patchouli essential oil.

Transitions and Changes Blend
Combine two teaspoons dried rose petals, seven drops lemon balm essential oil, and eight drops ginger essential oil.

Body Butter
This is a beautiful homemade, soothing body lotion.

Basic Recipe
> 225 g (8 oz) shea butter, cocoa butter, or mango butter (or a mixture of two of them, or all three!)
>
> 110 g (4 oz) coconut oil
>
> 110 g (4 oz) carrier oil such as olive or almond
>
> 20 drops of essential oil

Pop the butters, coconut oil, and carrier oils into a bowl over a pan of water (or in a double boiler). Bring the heat to medium and stir continuously until all the ingredients are melted.

Remove from the heat and allow to cool slightly, then add in your essential oils.

Put the mixture in the fridge to cool further for about an hour. When it's ready to come out, it should still be soft but starting to harden around the edges.

Using an electric mixer, whisk the mixture for about 10 minutes, until it is light and fluffy.

Spoon into glass jars with lids. Seal.

Put back into the fridge to set. This will usually take about 15 minutes.

Once set, store in a cool, dry place and apply as needed.

Suggested Essential Oil Blends

Anxiety Blend

Combine ten drops chamomile and ten drops rose.

Stress Blend

Combine ten drops passionflower and ten drops peppermint.

Depression Blend

Combine ten drops orange, five drops rosemary, and five drops rose.

Panic Attack Blend

Combine ten drops mint, five drops passionflower, and five drops lavender.

Fear Blend

Combine five drops rose, five drops fennel, and ten drops passionflower.

Guilt Blend

Combine five drops mint, five drops rosemary, and ten drops grapefruit.

Worry Blend

Combine ten drops lemon balm, five drops lavender, and five drops passionflower.

Grief Blend

Combine five drops lemon, five drops orange, and ten drops lavender.

Self-Esteem Blend

Combine five drops fennel, five drops lemon balm, and ten drops rose.

Obstacles and Blockages Blend

Combine five drops frankincense, five drops grapefruit, and ten drops orange.

Sleep Blend

Combine drops thyme, five drops rosemary, and ten drops lavender.

Menopause and Menses Blend

Combine ten drops frankincense and ten drops patchouli.

Transitions and Changes Blend

Combine ten drops ginger, five drops cinnamon, and five drops lemon balm.

Perfume

Making your own perfume is quite easy, and it means you can tailor it to your own favourite scent! Basically, perfume is a blend of essential oils in a base of alcohol (the alcohol helps preserve it). Each scent will fall into three categories: the base, middle, and top notes. The top note is the first scent you get hit with when you smell a perfume, then the middle, and lastly, the base. I would start with your base scent, then add your middle notes, and finish with your top ones.

Base notes are the stronger woody scents, middle notes tend to be the flowery ones, and the top notes are often the more citrusy ones.

The alcohol you choose can change the scent slightly, and the scent of the notes will also change once the mixture has had a chance to rest. It might take a bit of experimentation to get something you are happy with.

Basic Recipe

40 drops essential oil

140 drops of alcohol (vodka works best; use the highest proof you can get)

20 drops distilled water (optional)

Start with a clean 10 mL atomiser bottle.

Carefully count out your drops of essential oil as you add them, starting with your base note, then give the bottle a little shake to blend.

You need to leave the essential oil bottle in a dark place for a week. Yep—unfortunately, patience is key here.

After a week, take your blend out and give it a sniff. If you don't like the smell of your essential oil blend, chuck it out and start again.

If you like the scent, you can now add the alcohol and distilled water (if you choose). To make distilled water, boil water in your kettle and let it cool. Distilled water will dilute your perfume a little, but it can also make it cloudy, so it is optional.

Once the oils are mixed with the alcohol and water, you need to pop it back in the dark place again for three to four weeks.

After three to four weeks, give it a spray. If the alcohol smell is overpowering, you may have added a little too much, or it might just need a few more weeks of hiding in the dark cupboard.

With enough trial and error, you will find a system and scent that works for you.

Suggested Essential Oil Blends

Each of these essential oil blends are split into three: twenty drops base note, ten drops middle note, and ten drops top note.

Anxiety Blend

Combine twenty drops cinnamon, ten drops passionflower, and ten drops lemon balm.

Stress Blend

Combine twenty drops frankincense, ten drops passionflower, and ten drops peppermint.

Depression Blend

Combine twenty drops cardamom, ten drops passionflower, and ten drops orange.

Panic Attack Blend

Combine twenty drops patchouli, ten drops mint, and ten drops lemon balm.

Fear Blend
Combine twenty drops ginger, ten drops fennel, and ten drops passionflower.

Guilt Blend
Combine twenty drops pine, ten drops ginger, and ten drops grapefruit.

Worry Blend
Combine twenty drops fennel, ten drops passionflower, and ten drops mint.

Grief Blend
Combine twenty drops bergamot, ten drops black pepper, and ten drops orange.

Self-Esteem Blend
Combine twenty drops frankincense, ten drops back pepper, and ten drops grapefruit.

Obstacles and Blockages Blend
Combine twenty drops frankincense, ten drops coriander, and ten drops orange.

Sleep Blend
Combine twenty drops bergamot, ten drops lavender, and ten drops chamomile.

Menopause and Menses Blend
Combine twenty drops frankincense, ten drops patchouli, and ten drops coriander.

Transitions and Changes Blend
Combine twenty drops cinnamon, ten drops black pepper, and ten drops lemon balm.

Body Scrub
Body scrubs are good for your skin: they clear away dead skin cells, moisturise your skin, and boost your circulation. They can also help to release negative energy.

Massage the body scrub gently into your skin and rinse off with warm water. I like to use mine in the shower; you can add in the power of visualisation when you are scrubbing and rinsing too. See all the negative energy, issues, and vibes being cleansed away.

Basic Recipe

> 1 tablespoon porridge oats
>
> 1 teaspoon dried flowers
>
> 2 tablespoons base oil (almond, olive, jojoba, etc.)
>
> 8 drops essential oil

Crush the oats and dried flowers to form a powder. This can be done in a blender or by hand with a mortar and pestle.

Mix the base oil and essential oils together.

Combine the oils with the oat and flower mixture to form a paste. If it is too dry, add another drop of base oil. If it is too wet, add some more ground oats.

Store in a sterilised jar with a lid. This recipe makes a 45 mL (1½ fl oz) body scrub and will keep for up to three months.

Suggested Essential Oil and Herb Blends

Anxiety Blend

Combine rose petals, four drops lemon balm essential oil, and four drops cloves essential oil.

Stress Blend

Combine lavender flowers, four drops mint essential oil, and four drops cloves essential oil.

Depression Blend

Combine dried thyme, four drops lemon balm essential oil, and four drops lavender essential oil.

Panic Attack Blend

Combine poppy seeds, four drops mint essential oil, and four drops passionflower essential oil.

Fear Blend

Combine dried lemon balm, four drops fennel essential oil, and four drops mint essential oil.

Guilt Blend

Combine dried mint leaves, four drops ginger essential oil, and four drops grapefruit essential oil.

Worry Blend

Combine fennel seeds, four drops mint essential oil, and four drops passionflower essential oil.

Grief Blend

Combine dried marjoram leaves, four drops lemon essential oil, and four drops black pepper essential oil.

Self-Esteem Blend

Combine dried rose petals, four drops rose essential oil, and four drops fennel essential oil.

Obstacles and Blockages Blend

Combine lavender flowers, four drops mint essential oil, and four drops rosemary essential oil.

Sleep Blend

Combine dried thyme leaves, four drops sweet pea essential oil, and four drops passionflower essential oil.

Menopause and Menses Blend

Combine fennel seeds, four drops coriander essential oil, and four drops ginger essential oil.

Transitions and Changes Blend
Combine dried lemon balm and eight drops sweet pea essential oil.

Bath Infusion

Add this infusion to your bath and it will take you away on a relaxing journey...

Basic Recipe

> 500 mL (17 fl oz) water
>
> 2 tablespoons dried herbs and/or flowers
>
> 10 drops essential oil
>
> 1 tablespoon mineral salts

Boil the water and add two tablespoons of herbs/flowers of your choice. Infuse for 10 minutes.

While that is infusing, mix your essential oils into the mineral salts.

Strain the infusion and add the salt mix. Stir until the salt has dissolved.

Add this mixture to your bathwater.

Suggested Essential Oil and Herb Blends

Anxiety Blend
Combine one tablespoon dried rose petals, one tablespoon dried lemon balm, and ten drops rose essential oil.

Stress Blend
Combine one tablespoon green tea, one tablespoon dried lemon balm, and ten drops lavender essential oil.

Depression Blend
Combine one tablespoon dried rosemary, one tablespoon lavender flowers, and ten drops grapefruit essential oil.

Panic Attack Blend
Combine one tablespoon dried lavender, one tablespoon dried mint, and ten drops passionflower essential oil.

Fear Blend

Combine one tablespoon fennel seeds, one tablespoon dried mint, and ten drops rose essential oil.

Guilt Blend

Combine one tablespoon dried mint, one tablespoon green tea, five drops ginger essential oil, and five drops rosemary essential oil.

Worry Blend

Combine two tablespoons dried lemon balm, five drops mint essential oil, and five drops fennel essential oil.

Grief Blend

Combine two tablespoons dried marjoram, five drops cardamom essential oil, and five drops orange essential oil.

Self-Esteem Blend

Combine one tablespoon dried rosemary, one tablespoon rose petals, five drops ginger essential oil, and five drops lemon balm essential oil.

Obstacles and Blockages Blend

Combine one tablespoon dried pine, one tablespoon dried rosemary, five drops mint essential oil, and five drops star anise essential oil.

Sleep Blend

Combine one tablespoon dried lemon balm, one tablespoon dried lavender flowers, and ten drops lavender essential oil.

Menopause and Menses Blend

Combine one tablespoon dried mint, one tablespoon fennel seeds, and ten drops frankincense essential oil.

Transitions and Changes Blend

Combine one tablespoon black pepper, one tablespoon dried lemon balm, and ten drops rose essential oil.

Foot Bath

Use this foot bath and then massage your feet. (If you'd like, you can find more specific massage instructions in chapter 16). Note: Do not use this mixture if you have just shaved your legs—the vinegar can sting newly shaven skin!

Basic Recipe

> 500 mL (17 fl oz) water
>
> 1 tablespoon dried mint (or two mint tea bags)
>
> 2 drops mint essential oil
>
> 2 drops grapefruit essential oil
>
> 1 tablespoon mineral salts
>
> 1 tablespoon honey (vegans can omit this)
>
> 1 tablespoon apple cider vinegar

Boil the water and drop the dried mint in. Leave it to infuse for 10 minutes. After 10 minutes have passed, strain.

Add all the remaining ingredients and stir until combined.

Add the mixture to a bowl of warm water and soak your feet.

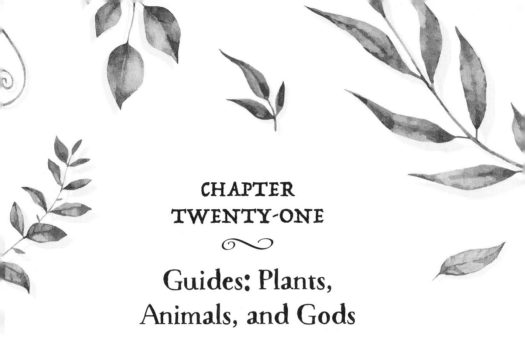

CHAPTER
TWENTY-ONE

Guides: Plants,
Animals, and Gods

Whatever spiritual pathway you are on, it can help to have some guidance. You may already work with plant spirits, animal guides, or deity in some form. If you haven't, then I do encourage you to explore any or all of these avenues. Opening up to connect with spiritual guides of all kinds can be incredibly beneficial, not just for guidance in your life path but also as a means of support. It can really help to know that there is someone (or something) to call upon to help you make decisions, bring focus and direction into your life, or just listen to you.

Sometimes an animal guide will find you; in fact, quite often that seems to be the case. You might keep meeting a certain animal, or you might keep seeing it on media outlets, in shops, or on material items. It will be a huge benefit to you to find out more about the animal—where it lives, what it eats, how it looks after its young, and what energy it can lend to you. There is such a variety of animals, each with their own unique energy to lend to you. Usually there is a really good reason why that particular animal has chosen you.

It can be the same with plant guides. You may keep seeing a particular plant, tree, or herb. Acknowledge its presence and do some research. What do the correspondences of that plant mean you to at this point in your life? The plant world is vast, and each and every individual plant has a unique character and energy, whether it is a tree, bush, fruit, vegetable, or weed.

Deity nearly always finds you. They have a way of getting your attention. If someone makes themselves known to you, treat them with the proper respect. Do your research so that you have an idea of their story, history, and character. Are there similarities to your own life? What do you think they have sought you out for? Each encounter will be a new experience. Work with it. Always be respectful, show your gratitude, and make the most of the journey.

Deity or the Divine comes in many forms. It may be that you work with the Divine in the form of gods and goddesses. Your deity vision may be one of a single god or goddess that encompasses the all. It could be that you see deity as different facets of the whole. You might prefer to work with simpler figures like Father Sky and Mother Earth. Your guidance may just come from the moon and the sun. Whatever form the Divine shows up in, there will be a reason for it.

Allow your guide, in whatever form they appear, to help you.

Animal Guides

Animal spirit guides can be very rewarding to work with. Some people refer to them as a totem animal, messenger, ally, power animal, guide, and fetch, to name a few. I have one main guide: a wild boar who has been with me for many years. But I do find that other animals pop in when I need them for specific issues… When I am dealing with emotions, the seagull appears. When life is hectic and chaotic, pigeon makes his name known. And when dealing with difficult situations, the magpie hops on over.

I have also learnt to watch and listen when any animal starts to appear. Put feelers out to find an animal spirit guide to help you on your journey. You may discover a lifelong guide, or perhaps just one to help you deal with your current issues. You may end up with a whole menagerie of animals, each one with specific areas to help you with. I have provided a meditation to help you along, but do keep an eye and an ear open when you go about your daily life. Guides have a habit of finding you when you least expect it.

Meditation to Find an Animal Spirit Guide

This meditation may help if you are looking for an animal spirit guide to assist you with your present journey or for a specific issue. Be open to whatever comes to you; it might not be the animal you expected.

Make yourself comfortable in a place where you won't be disturbed. Close your eyes and focus on your breathing… deep breaths in and deep breaths out.

As your world around you dissipates, you find yourself in darkness, but you don't feel afraid. As you adjust to your surroundings your eyes focus, and you begin to see the walls of a large cave around you. The air is fresh and sweet, and you can feel a slight breeze.

In the centre of the cave is a small fire, and it sends up sparks that highlight the walls of the cave.

On the far side of the fire, you see a slip of daylight that must be the entrance to the cave.

Just behind you are blankets and cushions, so you grab some. As you do, you realise that behind them is a pool of water, a natural spring or perhaps an inlet from the ocean.

Taking your blankets and cushions, you make a comfortable spot closer to the fire. You sit and take in your surroundings.

You can hear sounds now from outside, possibly the crashing of ocean waves and the sound of birds. Then the breeze brings in the scent of fresh grass and wildflowers.

Sit quietly and think about your life situation at the moment. What would you like help and guidance with?

A sound catches your ear.

Did it come from the cave entrance? Or from the water pool?

You get up and make your way to where you heard the noise.

An animal is waiting to greet you…

It is not afraid of you and you are very comfortable with its presence.

The animal is here to help you. Talk to it; make a connection. Tell the animal what you need help and guidance with.

The animal should reply. It may also agree to journey with you until your issue is sorted.

It's important to talk to the animal, but also listen carefully to what it has to say…

When you are ready, you thank the animal and it disappears into the darkness again.

Come back to the fire and sit for a while. Think about what the animal has said.

When you feel ready, slowly and gently come back to this reality. Open your eyes. Wriggle your fingers and toes.

Eat and drink something.

Jot down any thoughts or images that came to mind during your meditation. It can be useful to refer back to them later.

Honouring Your Animal Spirit Guide

If you found an animal spirit guide to walk with you on your current journey, you may want to pop an image of it on your altar. You may even be drawn to set up a separate altar just for your animal guide. If one has agreed to work with you, then it is only good manners to acknowledge and honour the animal in some way.

If I am working with the energies of a specific animal, I like to put a photograph or picture of that animal on my altar. (I usually find my images on the internet.) My lifelong animal guide, the wild boar, has a small altar all to himself. I have recently added a small candle holder and vase to my main altar that are decorated with bees; this is my nod to my new animal spirit guide.

Animal spirit guides do seem to like attention. If you care about them and do what you can to honour them, you will find them to be very rewarding. They can provide support, wisdom, guidance, and strength.

Animal Spells

The energy of animals can also be used in spell work. Think about the characteristics of a specific animal and use that energy in your magic. When you work with an animal spell, you can use any animal—it doesn't need to be an animal spirit guide you have worked with before. You aren't asking for the animal to join you as a guide, just to lend their unique energy to a particular spell. Each animal has unique energies that can be called upon. Use the following list or be guided by your intuition.

I have listed some suggestions here in case you want to select your own animal to work with based upon their magical energy. For example, try calling upon the dolphin for healing, or connect with the energy of lion for courage. This animal list can also be used if you want to call upon a specific animal to help you as a guide.

- Alligator—confidence, using your own power, survival
- Badger—self-confidence, strength, defence, self-reliance
- Bat—personal transformation, breaking old habits, strength, making changes
- Bear—healing, finding answers within, directions and decisions, personal strength
- Bee—communication, organisation, productivity, healing, renewal, protection
- Butterfly—transformation, happiness, harmony, changes, living in the present
- Camel—patience, dealing with difficulties, perseverance
- Cat—balancing the physical and the spiritual world
- Coyote—survival, finding the truth, dealing with difficult situations, coping no matter what life sends your way
- Crow—balance, survival, changes, growth, dealing with it all
- Dolphin—healing, communication, dealing with emotions
- Dove—peace, calm, acceptance
- Dragonfly—self-discovery
- Eagle—taking risks, leaps of faith, confidence, clarity, balance
- Flamingo—healing, emotions, connections, being true to yourself, balance, confidence in your own abilities
- Fox—going with the flow, evolving to cope with your environment, dealing with change
- Frog—renewal and regeneration, transformation, dealing with changes

- Hedgehog—independence, looking after yourself, confidence, being present in the moment
- Jackal—self-confidence, capability, courage, adapting, taking calculated risks
- Jaguar—self-confidence, independence, strength, facing your fears, empowerment
- Ladybird/ladybug—protection, turning your weaknesses into strengths, inner power, letting go of the past
- Lion—strength, courage, patience, acknowledging your own strengths and weaknesses, balance
- Lizard—perspective, change, focusing on what matters, letting go of the past, being true to yourself
- Magpie—dealing with the unpredictable, embracing opportunities, clarity, seeing through illusions, confidence
- Owl—wisdom from experience and learning, seeing and dealing with whatever you come across, truth
- Panda—self-discovery, being at peace with yourself, learning how to let go of the past
- Peacock—pride in your accomplishments, strength, balance
- Penguin—organisation, control, creating balance
- Phoenix—rebirth, renewal, growth, strength
- Porcupine—control, self-confidence, letting go of the past, protection
- Rabbit—overcoming irrational fears and anxiety, rebirth
- Raccoon—adapting to any situation, protection, taking control, transformation
- Rat—being able to deal with whatever comes your way
- Rhinoceros—self-assurance, protection, intuition
- Salmon—strength, renewal, determination
- Scorpion—strength, protection, power
- Seahorse—going with the flow, letting go, contentment, confidence in your own abilities, patience

+ Seal—changes, being flexible, movement, direction, confidence in your own abilities, dealing with whatever life throws at you
+ Shark—inner work, motivation, power, seeing your true self, movement
+ Skunk—self-esteem, self-assurance, truth, pride in your abilities and image
+ Snake—renewal, changes, letting go of the past
+ Spider—being in control of your own life and destiny, creative energy, strength, decisions, choices, balance
+ Swan—peace, calm, intuition, strength, accepting that which we cannot change, support, focus
+ Unicorn—truth, intuition, dealing with emotions, power, healing, renewal, understanding
+ Vulture—trust, resourcefulness, solutions, dealing with emotional situations
+ Whale—healing, positive attitude, dealing with difficult situations, communication
+ Wild boar—strength, independence, power, self-confidence, self-reliance
+ Zebra—confidence, clarity, problem-solving, individualism

Plant Spirit Guides

The plant world has spirit allies that can be called upon for support, wisdom, and healing. You will meet some of them in the meditations within this book. I have picked specific plants that I believe will be able to help with each individual situation, but the plant world is huge and there are plant spirit guides ready and willing to assist and support you through your individual issues. To help you find one, try the following meditation.

Meditation to Find a Plant Spirit Guide

Make yourself comfortable in a place where you won't be disturbed. Close your eyes and focus on your breathing…deep breaths in and deep breaths out.

As your world around you dissipates, you find yourself outside a large, old, sand-coloured brick building. It is a beautiful day, and the sun is shining.

You look around to take in your surroundings. The building in front of you looks like a temple or a monastery of some kind. You also notice a large wooden door that is slightly ajar, so you make your way toward it.

As you step through the door, you enter a large garden.

You have never seen so many plants, flowers, fruits, and vegetables growing in one place. Breathe in the scents, listen to the sounds of all the birds and bees, and feast your eyes upon the garden.

There is movement and you realise there are what appear to be monks dotted across the garden, all working hard tending to the plants or picking fruit and vegetables. They go about their work in contented silence.

You hear someone approach you and turn to see an old man dressed in a monk's habit. He doesn't speak but beckons you to follow him. He leads you on a walk around the garden.

You are led through beds of herbs, flowers, vegetables, and all kinds of plants until you end up in an orchard full of trees. There seem to be fruits of all kinds: apples, pears, peaches, and some fruits you have never seen.

The monk gestures for you to sit on a nearby bench, so you do. He wanders off now and leaves you on your own. You feel comfortable and are happy to sit quietly with your own thoughts.

When you are ready, you get up and start to walk about under the canopy of trees.

You wander for a while until you reach a small clearing. In the centre is a brick well. Growing around the base is a plant. You make your way over and perch on the edge of the well. You are drawn to reach out and touch the plant. A connection is made.

This plant tells you that it is your plant spirit guide and can help you deal with any issues that you currently have. It gives you its name…

Open up and talk to this plant. In return it shares wisdom and guidance.

In your own time, thank the plant. Then take the bucket from the well, wind it down, and fill it with water. Lifting it out, you tip the water to nourish the plant that you have connected with.

Then you make your way back through the orchard to the bench. Take a last look around and know that you can come back to this place whenever you need to.

Slowly and gently come back to this reality. Wriggle your fingers and toes and open your eyes.

Eat and drink something.

Jot down any thoughts or images that came to mind during your meditation. It can be useful to refer back to them later.

If you are able to grow the plant you met in your garden, excellent! But you can also buy a plant and keep it on your windowsill or, if that is impractical, just find yourself a nice image of the plant to keep on your altar.

Help from Gods

Some of us have gods and goddesses that we work with all the time to guide us, support us, and (in my experience) kick our butts. When dealing with self-care and any negative issues, I usually lean toward my matron or patron deity. However, there are a few deities that lend themselves to this kind of magic. Please do your research before you work with any deity. If you are asking for their help, then it only seems polite and actually sensible to find out all you can about the deity first. They each have unique and individual characteristics and personalities.

There is a school of thought that we should only work with deities specific to the region we live in. I absolutely resonate with that idea. I was born in England and have lived here my entire life, so when I first started on my Pagan journey it made sense to research and work with deities from the Celtic pantheon, which I did. It has been an interesting journey that still continues today. However, over the years I have had deities present themselves to me from pantheons across the globe. Believe me, it is a very bad idea to ignore a deity when they are trying to get your attention. I have worked with deities from most of the areas across the globe without any issues. Just be respectful and do your homework. Know what and who you are working with and how to honour and respect them.

I have given some deity recommendations here. They won't all suit everyone. Mostly they cover self-care, healing, and inner strength. Some of my suggestions are deities that don't stand for any nonsense and are there purely to kick your butt... See which one you are drawn to, or work with the meditation below to find one that is willing to step up. I have not personally worked with all the deities listed; some were suggested by friends who have.

Meditation to Find a Deity

This meditation is intended to help you find a deity that will work with you on your self-care journey. Listen to their guidance and wisdom and take note of any details you see, hear, or feel.

Make yourself comfortable in a place where you won't be disturbed. Close your eyes and focus on your breathing... deep breaths in and deep breaths out.

As your world around you dissipates, you find yourself in a temple. There are stone pillars around you and a mosaic floor beneath your feet. Take in the sights, sounds, and scents.

In front of you is an altar covered with candles, the flames flickering slightly. Dishes of incense are burning and the smoke spirals upward. The altar also has plates with offerings of food and vases of fresh flowers.

In front of the altar is a bench covered with cushions, so you make your way over. Before you sit down, you take an unlit candle from beside the altar, ignite it from a lit flame, and set it carefully with the others.

You sit on the bench and watch the flames dancing and the smoke twisting and turning.

You hear movement and a figure emerges from between two of the pillars. They head over to you. What do they look like?

The figure comes and sits beside you. They ask what you want from them.

You respond...

Listen to them carefully.

You may ask their name. They might tell you, or they might not.
Ask them what you need to do to help with your self-care journey.
Listen.
When you are finished talking, you thank them. As they stand to
go, they hand you a gift.
Once they have disappeared, you look down at the gift. What does
it mean to you?

Slowly and gently come back to this reality. Open your eyes. Wriggle your fingers and stamp your feet.

Eat and drink something.

Write down any advice you were given and do some research on the deity you interacted with.

Deities

Aengus Og

An ancient Irish god and member of the Tuatha De Danann, Aengus Og is the son of Dagda and Boann. He is a god of love and youth and is incredibly handsome and fit. Aengus Og is said to be able to inspire love in anyone he meets.

Call on Aengus Og for self-esteem, self-confidence, and self-love.

Airmid

An ancient healing goddess from Ireland, Airmid is also associated with herbalism. Her father is the healing god Dian Cecht. Airmid deals with healing, herbalism, relationships, learning, and magic.

Call on Airmid for healing, relationships, self-esteem, releasing, and guilt.

Aja

Aja is an orisha from the West African Yoruba religion. She is the spirit of the forest, a healer, and a wise woman ruling over forests, woods, and the animals within. Aja teaches herbal medicine to anyone that wishes.

Call on Aja for healing, worry, stress, and depression.

Aphrodite

Aphrodite is an ancient Greek goddess of love, passion, lust, pleasure, and beauty, but also war. Although she rules marriages, Aphrodite also guides affairs. Self-love is her thing, but she isn't always polite with her responses to requests. She is often compared with the Roman goddess Venus, but I think Aphrodite has a more sassy, sexy vibe.

Call on Aphrodite for self-esteem, love, and guilt.

Apollo

Son of Zeus and twin brother to Artemis, Apollo is an ancient Greek god that can help you with pretty much anything from knowledge to music to healing. Healing is one of his key subjects, although he was known not only to heal but to bring about plagues as well. Being the patron deity of Delphi, he is particularly skilled in prophecy. He can also be found in the Roman pantheon with the same name.

Call on Apollo for depression, healing, worry, fear, and panic attacks.

Artemis

The twin sister of Apollo, Artemis is an ancient Greek goddess of the hunt, forests, and wild animals. She protects womankind and those in childbirth, but she herself is chaste and not at all interested in sexual affairs. She also protects young girls. Artemis is independent and confident, promoting courage and strength. Ancient Romans called her Diana. She also has a little bit of a temper.

Call on Artemis for panic attacks, menopause, menses, self-esteem, fear, stress, and worry.

Belenus

Belenus is an ancient Celtic sun god. I have been working with him for the past year. He is definitely an interesting character; he insisted on being in this book. He brings the magic of fire and warmth and the healing powers of the sun.

Call on Belenus for healing, self-esteem, grief, depression, anxiety, and worry.

Brighid

A feisty ancient Irish goddess, Brighid brings protection, inspiration, creativity, and healing. She is also associated with grief and mourning. Brighid is a solar goddess and brings all the associations you find with the element of fire. She later became the basis for the Christian Saint Brigid.

Call on Brighid for healing, grief, anxiety, stress, depression, panic attacks, fear, and guilt.

Cerridwen

A goddess of healing, creation, harvest, fertility, and transformation, Cerridwen hails from Wales. She can also shape-shift. Her cauldron represents the womb and is filled with Awen, or the liquid of knowledge, wisdom, transformation, rebirth, and inspiration.

Call on Cerridwen for healing, stress, transformation, menopause, menses, releasing, grief, fear, and panic attacks. In fact, Cerridwen is a pretty good all-rounder for any emotional issues.

Dian Cecht

An ancient Irish god, Dian Cecht is associated with healing and restoring the body. Part of the Tuatha De Danann, he was considered to be a physician of the gods. He is also father to several children, most of whom were also healers, including Airmid. His healing claim to fame is being the one to replace Nuada's severed hand with a silver replacement.

Call on Dian Cecht for healing, anxiety, panic attacks, worry, grief, and fear.

Dionysus

Dionysus is probably most well-known as the ancient Greek god of wine. The Romans called him Bacchus—same god, different name. The offspring of Zeus and a mortal woman, he is one of the Olympians. But Dionysus is often seen as an outsider because of his upbringing and early life. He is in this list because he deals with madness and addiction—the curing, of course! Dionysus also embodies a duality of both male and female.

Call on Dionysus for any or all emotional issues.

Durga

Definitely a protection goddess, the Hindu goddess Durga has eighteen arms, rides a tiger, and is a warrior. She carries various weapons and sacred objects. She also provides instruction on the value of truth and teaches how to receive love. Durga beats all negative energy and issues, helping deal with egos and conquering evil forces.

Call on Durga for self-esteem, releasing, self-love, guilt, and worry.

Freya

A Norse maiden, Freya is a goddess of love and war. Supposedly, she is the most beautiful goddess ever—no one can resist her. She gathers slain warriors, taking them to the afterlife. Freya brings love, happiness, and good family ties as well as help with any sexual issues. She is also known for being accompanied by her two cats.

Call on Freya for self-esteem, depression, guilt, releasing, grief, and sleep.

Ganesha

Perhaps the most recognisable Hindu deity, Ganesha is the elephant-headed god of new beginnings. He removes obstacles and blockages and is depicted with one broken tusk (he holds the broken part in one of his hands). His other hand is usually holding sweet treats, of which he is particularly fond.

Call on Ganesha for releasing, worry, removing obstacles, and grief.

Grannus

Grannus is a Celtic god of healing, mineral springs, and the sun. There doesn't seem to be a great deal known about him other than his chain of hot spring spa locations, the waters of which healed everything you could think of. He is often associated with a healing goddess called Sirona, as they worked their healing magic together.

Call on Grannus for healing, depression, anxiety, stress, fear, and worry.

Hathor

Daughter of the sun god Ra, Hathor is an ancient Egyptian goddess of love, happiness, music, success, abundance, and sexuality. She rules all aspects of

womanhood and femininity. Hathor is considered to be mother to all the pha-
raohs. Her talents also include having the knowledge of every child's destiny.

Call on Hathor for menopause, menses, self-esteem, depression, anxiety,
and panic attacks.

Hestia

Hestia is the ancient Greek goddess of family life, home, and the hearth. She
is the best host at parties and keeps alight the sacred flame, providing protection, security, and blessings. In ancient Rome she was called Vesta.

Call on Hestia for stress, anxiety, panic attacks, fear, worry, and sleep.

Inanna

Inanna is the Sumerian goddess of fertility, abundance, sensuality, fertility,
and also war. She was known as the "Queen of Heaven." She is also known
under the name Ishtar.

Call on Inanna for releasing, removing blockages, self-esteem, menopause,
menses, and sleep.

Isis

Goddess queen of ancient Egypt, Isis covers magic and healing. She also protects women and children, marriage, and love. Isis uses her wisdom and sor-
cery to bring about change and transformation.

Call on Isis for healing, menopause, menses, transformation, and all emotional issues.

Kali

Kali is the Divine Mother, albeit in quite a ferocious form. She is the Hindu
goddess of time, sexuality, transformation, and death. She also epitomises
Shakti—feminine energy, fertility, and creativity. Kali destroys in a way that
cleanses and purifies, making way for transformation and rebirth.

Call on Kali for releasing, removing blockages, fear, transformation, grief,
and panic attacks.

Kuan Yin

Ancient Chinese goddess of compassion, Kuan Yin is always listening and will lend a helping hand. She brings healing, light, fertility, feminine energy, wisdom, strength, transformation, and enlightenment.

Call on Kuan Yin for anxiety, menopause, menses, transformation, and all emotional issues.

Lilith

Lilith is often said to be the first Witch and is called the first wife of Adam. Whatever you believe, she has enormous power, strength, and some awesome feminine wiles. Often depicted as a winged demon, she is a strong and powerful goddess who has a voice that will not be silenced. Lilith carries the cause for women.

Call on Lilith for menopause, menses, self-esteem, panic attacks, fear, and worry.

Mary Magdalene

Mary Magdalene is not technically a goddess, but she is a biblical figure who holds feminine energy and can be called upon to help in many areas. She covers all feminine issues, strength, healing, sexuality, fertility, and magic.

Call on Mary Magdalene for menopause, menses, healing, and worry.

Pele

The goddess Pele is a Hawaiian volcano and fire goddess. She is known as "She Who Shapes the Sacred Land." Pele is passion, purpose, and putting things into action. She will bring love, passion, creativity, motivation, energy, cleansing, renewal, fearlessness, and protection.

Call on Pele for self-esteem, depression, anxiety, fear, guilt, worry, and releasing.

Persephone

Daughter of Greek gods Zeus and Demeter, Persephone is the goddess of spring, growth, and happiness. She is also Queen of the Underworld, and in this guise she brings the wisdom of life and death but also magic and divination. In ancient Rome she was called Proserpina.

Call on Persephone for grief, releasing, and depression.

Psyche

Psyche is an ancient Greek goddess and protector of the soul, love, and happiness. She looks after all relationships and represents the transformation that a woman goes through from maiden to mother. She is often depicted with the wings of a bird or butterfly.

Call upon Psyche for menopause, menses, and all emotional issues.

Sekhmet

Often referred to as the Eye of Ra, Sekhmet is the ancient Egyptian warrior goddess. She carries anger and rage with her. Destruction is her strength, but with that comes cleansing, purification, and creation. She is fire, power, and huge amounts of feminine energy. Protector of womankind, Sekhmet also brings balance to life.

Call on Sekhmet for removing obstacles and blockages, releasing, menopause, and menses.

Sulis

Sulis is an ancient Celtic, Romano-British deity often associated with the city of Bath. She is linked to the natural healing springs that can be found there. Sulis is associated with healing, the sun, water, fire, wishes, community, and offerings. When the Romans arrived in Britain, they loved the healing springs; thus the Roman baths were created, tapping into the natural source. The Romans called her Sulis Minerva.

Call on Sulis for depression, fear, guilt, and worry.

Tara (Blue)

Blue Tara is a Tibetan goddess worshipped in Hindu and Buddhist pantheons. With her compassion, she liberates those stuck in emotional turmoil and helps to release mental and emotional blockages. Protecting against and destroying negative issues, Blue Tara also brings in positive vibes.

Call upon Blue Tara for sleep, all emotional issues, and to help release blockages.

Venus

Venus is an ancient Roman goddess of beauty, sex, and love. She is similar to Aphrodite; however, I believe Venus has a more matronly energy than Aphrodite. Sending away negative issues and vibes, Venus dishes out all the good stuff. Seek her out for any sexual issues as well.

Call on Venus for self-esteem, self-love, depression, worry, and panic attacks.

White Buffalo Calf Woman

As a goddess of the Native American Lakota tribe, White Buffalo Calf Woman teaches her people how to work with the land and provide for themselves. She brings life lessons and nourishment and helps you live a full, happy life.

Call on White Buffalo Calf Woman for depression, worry, anxiety, and stress.

Yemaya

Yemaya is an orisha and a goddess of water from the West African Yoruba religion. She is celebrated in many African and South American countries. Yemaya is mother to the moon and the sea. Guarding womankind, childbirth, children, and infants, she carries a huge amount of feminine energy. She heals with compassion and provides emotional support for those that seek it.

Call on Yemaya for guilt, menopause, menses, releasing, and all emotional issues.

CHAPTER
TWENTY-TWO

Chakra Health

I like to work with practical magic, preferring to hold dried herbs in my hands or work with a candle flame. However, I am very aware that the energy in our bodies can become blocked, stagnant, or even whiz around in a hyper state. This is all linked to chakras, which are worth taking a look at.

There are seven main chakras, but countless more which you can investigate if working with chakras interests you. In this chapter we'll be discussing the seven main chakras and the two additional chakras that I work with, the soul and earth star chakras. I like to work with nine chakras, just because I like to be a rebel…

Some people can see chakras, and with practice you may begin to as well. They are often described as a spinning wheel of coloured energy. Each chakra rotates at a different speed and each has its own colour. The main seven chakra colours are like a rainbow: red, orange, yellow, green, blue, indigo, and violet. With the addition of the soul and earth star chakras, there are also white and brown. The size of each chakra wheel will vary from person to person, and the colour and speed of spinning will depend on you and your mental, physical, and emotional well-being.

Some see the energy moving differently. Energy travels throughout your body between each chakra along a pathway called a meridian. So it can be seen as moving directly in a straight line from one chakra to the next, then in a circle back to the beginning again. Others see the energy flowing in a criss-cross system. Think of the caduceus symbol and how the snakes cross over each other in a spiral shape, linking each chakra.

Energy is in all natural things, from a pebble on the beach to the plants and trees around us. This includes crystals, which all carry their own individual energies. Tied in with energy are your chakras. So if your chakras are not balanced, or if the energies are blocked, it can affect how you feel physically, mentally, and emotionally. Conversely, if the chakras are wedged open too much, they will flood your body with too much energy, which is equally as bad. Keeping your chakras balanced may help your mental and emotional well-being as well as aiding in keeping your physical body in tip-top shape.

You can rebalance your chakras using meditation, visualisation, crystals, and pendulums. Using a pendulum to determine which one of your chakras is not working properly helps you identify where to work. Placing crystals on each of your chakras to recharge them can help, and meditation can help cleanse and rebalance them.

Sometimes it can be difficult to relax enough to cleanse your chakras. You may find that one of them just won't budge. If that is the case, look at the mundane. If your spiritual visualisation cannot clear it, then you will need to do something in the outside world to sort it. Chakra energy flow is affected by what we do and how we interact with people and the planet. If you aren't speaking your truth to someone it will block your throat chakra, and no amount of spiritual cleansing is going to clear it until you actually open your mouth and say something!

However, working with a meditation to identify those chakras that are blocked (either open or shut) can help you identify the root of the problem so you can begin to work on fixing it.

Blocked Chakra Exercise

In the next section, there is a chakra cleansing and balancing meditation. It will help you clear any blockages and get the energy flowing freely through your chakra points. However, if you want to find out first which chakras may be blocked, this exercise can help.

Sit quietly. Close your eyes if you wish. Then ask yourself the following questions; be totally honest with your answers. Focus on the area in your body where each chakra is located as you ask the question.

Earth Star Chakra

Do you feel centred and grounded?

If the answer is yes, this chakra is working well.

If you feel lightheaded and airy, this chakra could be blocked.

Root Chakra

Are you in good health at the moment?

If the answer is yes, this chakra is working well.

If you are suffering with ill health, this chakra could be blocked.

Sacral Chakra

How are your emotions? Do you feel balanced and in control of all areas of your life?

If the answer is yes, this chakra is working well.

If you are all over the place and feeling overwhelmed, this chakra could be blocked.

Solar Plexus Chakra

Do you feel confident and proud of yourself? Are you proud of how you work, look, and feel?

If the answer is yes, this chakra is working well.

If you are lacking self-esteem and self-worth, this chakra could be blocked.

Heart Chakra

How is the love in your life? Do you have good relationships? Do you have positive connections with friends and family?

If the answer is yes, this chakra is working well.

If you are struggling with any kind of relationship or having issues with loved ones, this chakra could be blocked.

Throat Chakra

Are you saying what you need to? Are you communicating well with others?

If the answer is yes, this chakra is working well.

If you are not saying what you think, or if you are not getting your point across when you need to, this chakra could be blocked.

Third Eye Chakra

Is your intuition kicking in properly? Do you know things and feel things instinctively?

If the answer is yes, this chakra is working well.

If your intuition is letting you down, this chakra could be blocked.

Crown Chakra

Do you feel connected to the Divine and your inner self?

If the answer is yes, this chakra is working well.

If you have lost your spiritual link and are feeling adrift, this chakra could be blocked.

Soul Star Chakra

Does life feel free-flowing?

If the answer is yes, this chakra is working well.

If you feel there are blockages or obstacles keeping you from letting go, this chakra could be blocked.

To cleanse and balance all your chakras, work with the Meditation for Cleansing Chakras. Spend as much time with each chakra as you need. Some may need a little more work than others.

Meditation for Cleansing Chakras

I have provided a cleansing meditation here, but you could also adapt the Rainbow Garden meditation from chapter 5—it works really well with the chakras.

Make yourself comfortable. I'd suggest lying on the floor or your bed. You can also place some crystals around you if you would like to.

Close your eyes and focus on your breathing. As you breathe in, visualise a bright white cleansing and purifying light. As you breathe out, send out all your negative energies.

See a white ball of spinning light a short distance above your head, as if the clouds have opened up and sent it down to you. This is your soul star chakra. See it spinning and opening up into a pure white rose, the petals unfurling as it spins.

If the flower is having trouble opening or spinning, use your visualisation skills to help it. See a gentle breeze or a soft rain wash over it, then see a white light beaming from the open rose.

Allow this light to flow down into your crown chakra. As it meets your chakra, visualise the light becoming a beautiful violet colour. Open your chakra by visualising it as a lotus flower ... each petal opening and, in the centre, a violet spinning ball of energy.

If the flower is having trouble opening or spinning, use your visualisation skills to help it. See a gentle breeze or a soft rain wash over it.

Then allow the light to travel down to your third eye chakra. As the light meets this chakra, it turns indigo blue and the chakra becomes an orchid flower. It starts as a bud and then opens out and blossoms to reveal a spinning ball of indigo light.

If the flower is having trouble opening or spinning, use your visualisation skills to help it. See a gentle breeze or a soft rain wash over it.

The light then goes to your throat chakra. As the light meets this chakra it turns into a beautiful bright-blue colour and becomes a cornflower. As the petals open, you see a ball of swirling blue energy inside.

If the flower is having trouble opening or spinning, use your visualisation skills to help it. See a gentle breeze or a soft rain wash over it.

The light then moves down to your heart chakra. As the light meets this chakra it turns a bright green colour and becomes a rosebud. As the petals open, you see a ball of swirling green energy inside.

If the flower is having trouble opening or spinning, use your visualisation skills to help it. See a gentle breeze or a soft rain wash over it.

The light moves on to your solar plexus chakra. As the light meets this chakra, it turns a bright yellow colour. As it touches the chakra it turns into a sunflower. The sunflower blooms and in the centre is a spinning ball of yellow energy. This is the centre of your power.

If the flower is having trouble opening or spinning, use your visualisation skills to help it. See a gentle breeze or a soft rain wash over it.

The light travels down to your sacral chakra. As the light meets this chakra it turns a bright orange colour and becomes the bud of a poppy flower. As each petal opens, the poppy reveals a ball of orange spinning energy in its centre.

If the flower is having trouble opening or spinning, use your visualisation skills to help it. See a gentle breeze or a soft rain wash over it.

Next the light travels to your base chakra. As the light meets this chakra it turns a bright red colour and becomes the roots of a tree. As the roots grow, your chakra opens to become a ball of swirling red energy.

This chakra opens to reveal your ability to ground, centre, and remain connected to the earth. Visualise these roots travelling down into the earth. As they do so, they draw energy up into your body.

Spend a few moments watching the colours of energy swirl around as they heal, soothe, and energise your spiritual and physical body.

Allow the colours to join together into a stream and let that energy flow from one chakra to the next, cleansing and clearing. As it reaches your earth star chakra it grounds into the earth, but the energy keeps flowing from the soul star chakra through your body until you are ready for it to stop. When you feel fully cleansed, allow any excess energy to drain out through your earth star chakra and into the ground beneath you.

Once this is done, slowly and gradually come back to the present. Open your eyes. Wriggle your fingers and toes.

Take a moment to steady yourself and come back to this reality fully before standing up.

Eat and drink something.

Earth Star Chakra

The earth star chakra is located approximately twelve to eighteen inches below the soles of the feet, sometimes just called the earth chakra. The earth

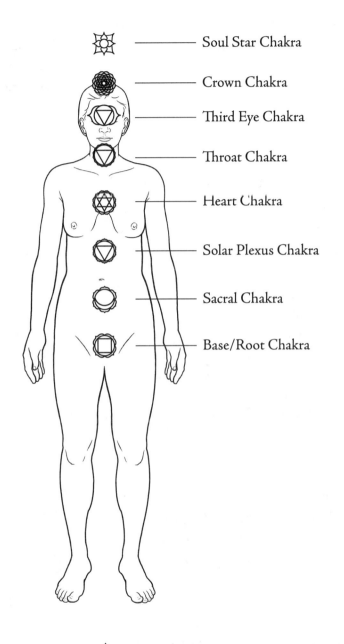

Soul Star Chakra

Crown Chakra

Third Eye Chakra

Throat Chakra

Heart Chakra

Solar Plexus Chakra

Sacral Chakra

Base/Root Chakra

 —————— Earth Star Chakra

star chakra is a big ole grounding one and ties you to Mother Earth. Using any electrical items (laptops, phones, etc.) for a prolonged period of time can cause conflict with this chakra. Spiritual and energy work can also unground you. With this chakra working properly you can stay focused and grounded, keeping your mind and spirit within the real world, helping you to cope with everyday life.

Earth Star Chakra Correspondences
- **Colours:** black, dark brown, deep forest green
- **Crystals:** apache tears, black kyanite, black tourmaline, hematite, smoky quartz, snowflake and black obsidian
- **Flowers/Plants:** anemone, fern, hellebore, moss, tree roots, trunk wood

Base or Root Chakra

Your base chakra is red and is located at the base of your spine. I am of the school of thought that the base chakra can "float" anywhere between the base of your spine and your feet, but go with what feels right to you. It is associated with basic health, security, and survival. Your base chakra is also the key to your kundalini, the fire spirit within your body. It is your link to reality but also controls your sex drive, procreation, fear, acceptance, circulation, support structure, survival, base instincts, confidence, and protection.

Base/Root Chakra Correspondences
- **Colours:** black, red
- **Crystals:** black tourmaline, bloodstone, garnet, obsidian, red aventurine, red jasper, ruby, smoky quartz
- **Flowers/Plants:** lily, poppy, rose, tulip

Sacral Chakra

The sacral chakra is orange and is located just below your navel. This chakra is associated with emotions, vitality, fertility, sensuality, intimacy, reproduction, and sexual energy. The sacral chakra also guides your relationships, your commitment to them, and how you relate to the world outside.

Sacral Chakra Correspondences
+ **Colour:** orange
+ **Crystals:** amber, carnelian, fire agate, fire opal, imperial topaz, orange calcite
+ **Flowers/Plants:** marigold, poppy

Solar Plexus Chakra

The solar plexus chakra is yellow in colour and is located just above your navel. It affects your willpower and is usually your energy centre. This chakra houses your personal power, action, self-esteem, self-confidence, self-worth, willpower, manifestation, creativity, empowerment, and your ego. The solar plexus chakra is the area where responsibility for others, caring for others, personal honour, and courage emerge. This chakra is responsible for the effective flow of energy, not only to this region but throughout the whole body.

Solar Plexus Chakra Correspondences
+ **Colour:** yellow
+ **Crystals:** amber, citrine, gold calcite, gold topaz, sunstone, tiger eye, yellow jasper
+ **Flowers/Plants:** daisy, sunflower

Heart Chakra

Your heart chakra is green in colour and located pretty much where your real heart lies, the centre of your chest. Some see the heart chakra as being pink in colour; go with what works for you. This chakra is associated with affairs of the heart—love, compassion, and affection. This chakra's meaning is all about the concept of "loving," in every meaning of the word.

Heart Chakra Correspondences
+ **Colour:** green
+ **Crystals:** amazonite, chrysocolla, emerald, green aventurine, green jade, green and pink tourmaline, malachite, rose quartz
+ **Flowers/Plants:** anemone, lily, rose

Throat Chakra

The throat chakra is blue in colour and you will find it at the base of your neck. It is associated with your vocal cords, communication, and creative expression. The throat chakra is the area of the body where your communication abilities emerge and is also associated with hearing and truth.

Throat Chakra Correspondences

+ **Colour:** blue
+ **Crystals:** angelite, aquamarine, blue chalcedony, blue lace agate, blue topaz, chrysocolla, sodalite, turquoise
+ **Flowers/Plants:** cornflower/bachelor's buttons, Himalayan poppy

Third Eye Chakra

Your third eye chakra, or brow chakra, is indigo in colour and is found in the spot just between your eyebrows. This chakra corresponds with your inner vision, your psychic abilities, and your imagination. The third eye chakra is your connection to the inner and outer world. This chakra's meaning is all about the concept of "seeing," especially in a spiritual and psychic sense. The third eye, or pineal gland, was believed in ancient times to be where "the sight" was located.

Third Eye Chakra Correspondences

+ **Colour:** indigo, a combination of red and blue
+ **Crystals:** amethyst, azurite, charoite, lapis lazuli, lepidolite, quartz crystal, sapphire, sodalite, sugilite
+ **Flowers/Plants:** hydrangea, geranium

Crown Chakra

The crown chakra is violet in colour and can be found at the top of your head. It is associated with enlightenment and your connection with the Divine and your higher self. The crown chakra relates to spirituality, selflessness, empathy, intellect, thought, and humanitarianism.

Crown Chakra Correspondences

+ **Colours:** shimmering white, violet
+ **Crystals:** amethyst, chalcopyrite, danburite, diamond, moonstone, purple fluorite, quartz crystal, selenite, sugilite
+ **Flowers/Plants:** lily, lotus, peony, rose

Soul Star Chakra

The soul star chakra is situated above the highest point of the physical body. It is approximately a hand's width above the head (around six inches), although this can be up to two feet in some people. The white light of spiritual cleansing and healing, the soul star chakra relates to infinite energy, spirituality, supreme Divine wisdom, and spiritual compassion. It also is associated with the origin of enlightenment and ascension. This chakra encourages you to let go.

Soul Star Chakra Correspondences

+ **Colours:** clear, white
+ **Crystals:** amethyst, blue kyanite, charoite, clear quartz, Herkimer diamond, indigo kyanite, selenite, sugilite
+ **Flowers/Plants:** lily, rose

CHAPTER
TWENTY-THREE

Turning to Nature:
Moons, Elements, and Seasons

Mother Nature provides us with so many beautiful and wonderful creations, all of which can help us in a magical way. From the power of the moon and her phases to the elements and seasons, each one has a magical energy that can help release your negative emotions and replace them with positive energy. Just look at the moon shining in a dark sky sprinkled with stars, or stand in a meadow full of flowers with the sun on your face. Both these situations (and many more) can make your heart sing.

Draw upon the bounty that Mother Nature provides. She is more than happy to lend you any positive energy that you need in whatever form.

The seasons, the elements, and the planetary phases have a very strong effect on how we feel. Work with the ebb and flow instead of fighting against it. Learn how each one interacts with you and your emotions. Magic is out there; you just need to tap into it.

Working in Harmony with the Moon Phases

The moon is powerful; she possesses serious amounts of energy that will affect your mood and state of mind. I mean, the moon moves entire oceans, so messing with your emotions is pretty simple for her (although I don't think she does it on purpose).

Try keeping a moon diary for a while and see how the different phases make you feel. How does it affect your physical energy? Your moods? Your emotions? Write it all down and then, when you have enough information, see if there is a pattern. Your findings will help you work with the energy and go with the flow.

I have included some correspondences below for each moon phase to help you get a grip on the ebb and flow. Try the meditations to help you ease your emotional issues, working with the corresponding moon phase to add to the power.

Waxing—New Beginnings

When the moon is on the up, beginning her climb from darkness to the crescent, your energy may echo hers. I often find this is the time when I get stuff done. My mood is usually quite good as well; I'm riding the waxing wave. The waxing phase is good for working with the planning stages of new ventures. This is the time for job hunting, house hunting, self-improvement, health, protection, courage, emotions, optimism, boosting your energy, communication, love, and any new beginnings.

+ **Goddess:** Maiden
+ **Colours:** green, orange, red, silver, white

Waxing Moon Meditation

Make yourself comfortable in a space where you won't be disturbed. Light some incense if you wish. Close your eyes and focus on your breathing... deep breaths in, deep breaths out.

As your world around you dissipates, you find yourself in a courtyard. There are stone pillars all around you. You look up to see that the structure has no roof; it is nighttime and you can view the inky dark sky, scattered with silver stars. There is light coming from just a slither of the moon, peeping into the courtyard where you stand. You hear an owl hoot in the distance. A warm breeze touches your skin.

There are flaming torches fixed to the walls so you can see clearly within the stone structure. Take a look around you.

At one end there appears to be a long stone table, so you head over.

On the table is a large, empty wooden bowl and lots of dishes. Each one contains what appears to be dried herbs, roots, plants, and flowers. Investigate and see what you find. Scoop up handfuls and take in the scent. Do you recognise any of them?

Select several of the bowls of plant matter and take them over to the empty wooden bowl. Scoop out handfuls or pinches of each one that you like and mix them together in the empty bowl.

What does the scent smell like once they are combined? Does it need anything else? If you need to add something, do so.

You realise the other end of the table is filled with dark glass bottles. Investigate ... They are perfumes and essential oils of all kinds. Which ones are you drawn to?

Take the ones you like over to your bowl of mixed plant matter and add a few drops of each.

What does the final mixture smell like?

You hold the bowl up so that the light from the waxing moon shines down and fills the bowl with Luna energy.

This is a bowl of beginnings, of new and fresh energy. Feel it wash over you.

What areas of your life will you use this new energy for? State your intent.

When you are ready, place the bowl back on the table.

Look up and send your blessings of thanks to the waxing moon.

Take a last look around and know that you can return to this place at any time.

Slowly and gently come back to this reality. Wriggle your fingers and toes and open your eyes.

Eat and drink something.

Jot down any thoughts or images that came to mind during your meditation. It can be useful to refer back to them later.

Full Moon—Energy

The full moon can cause all kinds of chaos with your emotions. The word "lunatic" is derived from "Luna," and this is no surprise. Not only does the full moon affect my emotions, I often find that it affects my sleep as well. Waking in the early hours and not being able to settle again is a regular thing for me during the full moon. The upside is that it also brings a big punch of power, so you may find this is the point in the month when you step into your superpowers. Work with the full moon for courage, luck, motivation, friendships, strength, progress, patience, protection, centring, relationships, family, changes, transformation, and goals.

+ **Goddess:** Mother
+ **Colours:** blue, orange, white, yellow

Full Moon Meditation

Make yourself comfortable in a space where you won't be disturbed. Light some incense if you wish. Close your eyes and focus on your breathing... deep breaths in, deep breaths out.

As your world around you dissipates, you find yourself in a courtyard. There are stone pillars all around you. You look up to see that the structure has no roof; it is nighttime and you can view the inky dark sky, scattered with silver stars. There is light coming from just a slither of the moon, peeping into the courtyard where you stand. You hear an owl hoot in the distance. A warm breeze touches your skin.

There are flaming torches fixed to the walls so you can see clearly within the stone structure. Take a look around you.

At one end there appears to be a long stone table, so you head over.

On the table is a large wooden bowl full of herbs and oils. Take the bowl and breathe in the scent.

On the end of the table is a candle; the flame flickers slightly in the breeze. Next to the candle is a large copper bowl filled with glowing charcoal.

Beside the table is a chair. You pull it close and sit down.

Take a handful of the herb mixture and throw it onto the hot coals.

It fizzes and sputters for a brief moment and then burns, sending up a dancing spiral of coloured smoke. The air fills with the most beautiful scent.

Sit quietly and watch the smoke. Look for any patterns or images...

Throw another handful of plant mix onto the coals and look up to the full moon.

This incense carries the energy of the full moon; ask for courage, guidance, and energy to succeed in your goals. Set your intent.

Allow the smoke to dispel and the coals to grow dark.

Look up and send your blessings of thanks to the full moon.

Take a last look around and know that you can return to this place at any time.

Slowly and gently come back to this reality. Wriggle your fingers and toes and open your eyes.

Eat and drink something.

Jot down any thoughts or images that came to mind during your meditation. It can be useful to refer back to them later.

Waning Moon—Releasing

As the moon slides from full down to the other side of the crescent phase, you may notice your energy levels waning too. The waning moon might also affect how you feel on the emotion front. Work with the waning moon energy for removing and banishing, letting go of old habits, and releasing unwanted emotions. This energy is lovely for dealing with changes, decisions, health and healing, self-improvement, enlightenment, and protection.

- **Goddess:** Matriarch
- **Colours:** blue, pink, purple

Waning Moon Meditation

Make yourself comfortable in a space where you won't be disturbed. Light some incense if you wish. Close your eyes and focus on your breathing… deep breaths in, deep breaths out.

As your world around you dissipates, you find yourself in a courtyard. There are stone pillars all around you. You look up to see that the structure has no roof; it is nighttime and you can view the inky dark sky, scattered with silver stars. There is light coming from just a slither of the moon, peeping into the courtyard where you stand. You hear an owl hoot in the distance. A warm breeze touches your skin.

There are flaming torches fixed to the walls so you can see clearly within the stone structure. Take a look around you.

At one end there appears to be a long stone table, so you head over.

There is a wooden bowl half filled with an herb mixture and a copper bowl full of ashes.

Take the bowl with the ashes and hold them up to the waxing moon.

This is a bowl filled with releasing and banishing, letting go of that which no longer serves you.

Tell the waning moon what you wish to release from your life. State your intent.

Then take the ashes over to the edge of the courtyard. You find a small stream of water running down the hillside. Tip the ashes into the water and watch as it carries them away. Let it take your troubles with it.

You go back and take up the bowl half-filled with herbs and hold it up to the waning moon. Ask for positive energy to fill the void left by releasing.

Then walk to the edge of the courtyard once more and tip the herbs onto the soil there.

When you are ready, place the bowl back on the table.

Look up and send your blessings of thanks to the waning moon.

Take a last look around and know that you can return to this place at any time.

Slowly and gently come back to this reality. Wriggle your fingers and toes and open your eyes.

Eat and drink something.

Jot down any thoughts or images that came to mind during your meditation. It can be useful to refer back to them later.

Dark Moon—Guidance

When you cannot see the moon in the sky at all (although she is still there, I promise), you are dealing with a dark moon. This is definitely a quiet time that is good for reflection and inner work (not really the moment for a big party). Work with the dark moon energy for breaking addictions, change, removing obstacles, letting go of the past, and self-love.

+ **Goddess:** Crone
+ **Colours:** black, blue, purple

Dark Moon Meditation

Make yourself comfortable in a space where you won't be disturbed. Light some incense if you wish. Close your eyes and focus on your breathing… deep breaths in, deep breaths out.

As your world around you dissipates, you find yourself in a courtyard. There are stone pillars all around you. You look up to see that the structure has no roof; it is nighttime and you can view the inky dark sky, scattered with silver stars. You hear an owl hoot in the distance. A warm breeze touches your skin.

There are flaming torches fixed to the walls so you can see clearly within the stone structure. Take a look around you.

At one end there appears to be a long stone table, so you head over.

On the table is a copper bowl and a jug that looks to be filled with water. You pull up a chair and sit down.

Pour the water into the copper bowl. Watch as it ripples and shimmers.

Beside the jug is a small glass bottle. You pick this up and pour a few drops of the contents onto the water. It appears to be dark ink and makes patterns and images across the surface of the water.

This is a bowl filled with the energy of the dark moon. Look up to the sky and ask for her wisdom and insight.

Now look at the surface of the water. What do you see?

After a while, add a few more drops of ink to refresh the images.

If you have questions, ask them. Read your answers from the images on the water.

When you are ready, look up and send your blessings of thanks to the dark moon.

Take a last look around and know that you can return to this place at any time.

Slowly and gently come back to this reality. Wriggle your fingers and toes and open your eyes.

Eat and drink something.

Jot down any thoughts or images that came to mind during your meditation. It can be useful to refer back to them later.

The Elements

Nature not only provides a cornucopia of plants, flowers, and food to work with; she also gives us the elements. They are there to help—use them. When you invite them into your ritual, really see and feel them arrive. Use all your visualisation skills and senses. For earth, see dark rich soil, mountains, rocks, and caves in your mind. As you invite air in, feel a breeze on your skin and see trees blowing in the wind. Fire is an easy one to visualise; flames from a bonfire are perfect, but also smell the smoke and feel the heat on your face. Water is oceans, rivers, and waterfalls; feel raindrops on your face.

Work with the elements to help you deal with any issues.

Earth can bring grounding and stability but also assists with home life and finances. Practical exercises include putting your hands and feet in soil, hugging trees, gardening, and going for a walk in nature.

Air rules intellect and how your mind functions. Work with this element to help retrain your way of thinking. Practical exercises include focusing on your breath and your breathing and going outside in the wind.

Fire brings passion and creativity but also helps burn away the old and the negative to make way for new patterns of thinking and different habits. Practical exercises include having a fire pit or bonfire, soaking up the sun (not too much! And don't forget sunscreen), or watching a candle flame.

Water is all about the emotions. Get a grip on this element, and it will seriously help you to rein in the wayward emotions and feelings. Practical exercises include standing in the rain, taking a bath or shower, going to the ocean, or washing your hands or face.

Meditation to Meet the Elements

Make yourself comfortable in a place where you won't be disturbed. If you can sit outside to do this meditation, even better.

Close your eyes and focus on your breathing...deep breaths in and deep breaths out.

As your world around you dissipates, you find yourself standing barefoot in a field. The sun is shining and the sky is blue. The field around you is a dark, rich soil, recently tilled and ready for planting.

Wriggle your toes in the earth. Feel the warmth of the soil on your feet. Take a walk around the field slowly. Feel your connection to the earth.

The earth is grounding and stability, so tell it what you need. What areas of your life need stabilising? Talk and then listen for a response…

As you stand quietly, you feel a light breeze on your face, then on your arms and around your whole body. The wind has picked up quite quickly and is blowing gently but firmly.

Throw your arms out wide and allow the air to embrace your body. Let the wind bring clarity of thought and inspiration. Talk to the element of air. It will listen… and then it will answer you…

Just as suddenly as it started, the wind disappears and the sun warms your face once again.

You walk a little further around the field and see a bonfire in one corner. Lots of old, dead, and dry grass has been piled up to be burnt. See the flames and feel the heat of the fire as you approach. The fire has passion and creativity; it has the ability to tear down that which does not serve and leave a clean slate. Tell the fire what areas of your life you need to clear out. It will listen… and reply to you…

As you finish listening to the fire, you feel spots of rain on your skin… slowly at first, and then you look up to see the sky has filled with dark clouds. The heavens open with cool, refreshing rain.

Stand and allow the water to soak you or run about and splash in the newly made mud. The element of water has the ability to cleanse and refresh; tell it what emotions you need to clear. It will listen… and then it will reply…

Just as soon as it started, the rain stops.

The earth is muddy beneath your feet now, but the sky is blue once again and the air is fresh and sweet.

Take a long look around and remember all the wisdom that the elements shared with you.

When you are ready, slowly and gently come back to this reality. Wriggle your fingers and toes and open your eyes.

Eat and drink something.

Jot down any thoughts or images that came to mind during your meditation. It can be useful to refer back to them later.

Seasonal Effects

Outside influences can affect your mood and your emotions. The time of year, the seasons, and the weather can all have a huge impact on how you feel. Realising how you are affected by it all and learning how to work with it rather than fight against it can be really beneficial.

Spring is fresh and alive; the whole earth is waking up. Often we get clear blue skies and bright sunshine. All around us life is stirring. Seasonal energy can reflect upon us and hopefully bring a positive feeling. Go with it. Get outside and enjoy that energy as much as you can.

Summer energy can be extremely uplifting and powerful. The sun has an enormous amount of positive and passionate energy to share. This is the time of year to be outside as much as possible. Unless it is a heatwave—then perhaps enjoy it in short bursts.

Autumn has its own special magic: the turning of the leaves on the trees, the artist's palette of colours across Mother Nature. This is the time to reflect, to plan out your downtime over the next few months, and to tidy up any loose ends or unfinished projects. Make sure you take the time to get outside and kick up those leaves!

Winter is one of my favourite seasons, but it doesn't suit everyone. For me it is about staying in and keeping warm. One of my favourite places to be is curled up on the sofa under a blanket, reading a good book, with a mug of hot cocoa and a bowl of steaming stew. Winter is a time to work on your inner self, to look inwards, and to spend some solitary time with yourself. Pamper yourself. Look after yourself.

Work with the seasons using meditation or decorate your altar as each season changes. Bring nature indoors to help you connect. I've included some meditations and correspondences that can help.

Spring

The spring season is all about new beginnings, growth, and fresh starts. Work with that energy to create a clean slate and to set new intentions for your mind, spirit, and soul.

- **Goddess:** Maiden
- **Element:** air
- **Colours:** pastels such as light green, pale blue, pale pink, white, and yellow
- **Symbols:** chicks, daffodils, eggs, lambs, tulips
- **Magic:** clarity, communication, illumination, knowledge, movement, new beginnings, travel

Spring Meditation

Make yourself comfortable in a place where you won't be disturbed. Close your eyes and focus on your breathing… deep breaths in and deep breaths out.

As your world around you dissipates, you find yourself standing on a dirt pathway. The sky above you is a pale blue, flecked with wispy clouds. The sun is out but there is still a crispness to the air. To the left of the pathway is a wide-open field. The ground looks uneven and is covered with grasses of all kinds. In the centre of the field you can see sheep, and when you look closely you see that there are a few lambs springing around the mothers. Listening carefully, you can hear the sheep bleating to each other.

To your right is a river that stretches along and bends around the edge of the field. The water is deep and dark but flowing gently. Moored to the side of the river are several brightly painted houseboats. They bob gently in the water.

The other side of the river is banked with trees. The branches are dark against the skyline, but you can see they are all covered with beautiful white and pink blossoms. You watch as the breeze sends a shower of petals down onto the surface of the river to be carried away.

A noise catches your ears and you turn to see a mother duck swimming gracefully along the river, followed by several tiny ducklings all in a line. Watch as they come toward you and sail on past.

You are drawn to walk across the field, heading toward the sheep.

One of them appears to be lying down, so you investigate further.

She is about to give birth; she appears to be coping and not in any distress. She even seems comfortable with you being close by.

Watch as the energy of spring takes on its role and a baby lamb arrives into the world…

Spend some time watching the mother clean her lamb. It suckles for milk.

This is the energy of spring: new beginnings and the growth of new life.

Think about what you would like to birth—new ideas, projects, a new beginning, a fresh perspective…

Make your way back to the riverbank and sit on the edge. Take your shoes and socks off and dip your toes in the water. It is incredibly cold but so refreshing. Allow the water to wash over your feet, to cleanse and purify. Let it take any negative energy away with it…

When you are ready, come away from the river edge and stand up.

Take a long look around you… the ducks and ducklings; the trees with their blossom; the lambs in the field; the river as it meanders along, going with the flow of life; and the fresh, new energy of spring.

Give thanks for what you have and for the new adventures you are ready to embark upon.

Slowly and gently come back to this reality. Wriggle your fingers and toes and open your eyes.

Eat and drink something.

Jot down any thoughts or images that came to mind during your meditation. It can be useful to refer back to them later.

Summer

The summer season is bursting with promise. Work with the energy of summer to make things happen and to bring in power and energy to support you.

+ **Goddess:** Mother
+ **Element:** fire
+ **Colours:** gold, orange, red, yellow

+ **Symbols:** flames, flowers, sun
+ **Magic:** change, courage, creativity, energy, passion, power, protection, rebirth, strength

Summer Meditation

Make yourself comfortable in a place where you won't be disturbed. Close your eyes and focus on your breathing… deep breaths in and deep breaths out.

As your world around you dissipates, you find yourself standing on a dirt pathway. The sky above you is a clear azure blue; there is not a cloud to be seen. The sun is out and feels warm on your skin. To the left of the pathway is a wide-open field. The ground looks uneven and is covered with grasses of all kinds, scattered with a beautiful array of brightly coloured wildflowers. You can hear the buzzing of bees and see butterflies flitting between each flower. In the centre of the field are some sheep, each of them looking a little naked, and you realise they have had their heavy woolly coats sheared to keep them cool in the summer heat.

To your right is a river that stretches along and bends around the edge of the field. The water is deep and dark but flowing gently. Moored to the side of the river are several brightly painted houseboats. They bob gently in the water. Each roof is covered with pots of cheerful summer plants.

The other side of the river is banked with trees. The branches are full of bright green leaves. You listen carefully as you hear the perched birds calling to each other.

Laughter sounds and you turn to watch a small boat with a couple of children in it, weaving its way downstream. They are having a huge amount of fun.

Turning back, you decide to walk into the field a short way and spy a clearing ahead. The grass here is flatter and looks comfortable so you sit down, then lie back. The clearing is surrounded by bobbing flowers and tall grasses. You lie quietly and watch the bees as they whiz across the clearing from flower to flower. Butterflies skip and hop across your eyeline.

Soak up the sun and watch the insects as they make the most of summer's bounty.

This is the energy of summer: warm, laughter-filled days with nature showing us her very best.

Think about your life and the bounty that it offers to you. What can you do to jump on the wave of summer energy?

When you are ready, you stand up and walk back to the pathway by the river. The birds are still singing, and a warm breeze brushes past you.

Give thanks for what your life has to offer you.

Slowly and gently come back to this reality. Wriggle your fingers and toes and open your eyes.

Eat and drink something.

Jot down any thoughts or images that came to mind during your meditation. It can be useful to refer back to them later.

Autumn

The autumn season is ready and waiting for you to reap what you have sown. Bring in your own harvest and give thanks for all that has been provided.

- **Goddess:** Matriarch
- **Element:** water
- **Colours:** brown, dark green, orange, red
- **Symbols:** cornucopia, leaves, nuts, wheat sheaf
- **Magic:** abundance, balance, cleansing, gratitude, peace, protection, purification, relationships, transformation

Autumn Meditation

Make yourself comfortable in a place where you won't be disturbed. Close your eyes and focus on your breathing... deep breaths in and deep breaths out.

As your world around you dissipates, you find yourself standing on a dirt pathway. The sky above you is blue with a few scattered clouds. The air is warm but has a crisp feel to it.

To the left of the pathway is a wide-open field. The ground looks uneven and is covered with grasses of all kinds waving their seed heads in the breeze. In the centre of the field are some sheep lazing around munching on the grass.

To your right is a river that stretches along and bends around the edge of the field. The water is deep and dark but flowing gently. Moored to the side of the river are several brightly painted houseboats. They bob gently in the water. Pots of herbs adorn the roof of each one.

The other side of the river is banked with trees. The branches are covered in the most beautiful array of coloured leaves: reds, oranges, and yellows. A wisp of wind whips through them and shakes a kaleidoscope of coloured leaves down onto the surface of the water.

You take a walk along the dirt pathway, leaving behind the coloured barges and the sheep in the field. As you walk you look around at the scenery. There are so many trees displaying their autumn colours.

As you turn a corner in the pathway you come across a small wooden bridge that leads across the river, so you make your way over to it. Stepping onto the bridge, you walk to the centre and turn, leaning your arms on the rail to look over into the water. It splashes and bubbles as it tumbles over itself, weaving ever onwards.

A leaf from one of the trees on the bank is picked up by a gust of wind and delivered to your feet. Bend down and pick it up. What type of leaf is it? What colour? Make a wish on that leaf. What do you want to harvest from your own life? What are your true desires? Send the wish into the leaf and then drop it into the water.

Walk quickly to the other side of the bridge and watch as the leaf floats out from under the bridge. Watch it as long as you can. It bobs along, being taken on a journey by the water.

Spend a few moments thinking about the abundance you have in your life and what you can reap now from the ideas and plans sown back in the spring. What happened and what didn't? Assess your situation and think about what changes you need to make, if any.

When you are ready, turn back and walk once again along the dirt path, back to the barges and the field of sheep.

Give thanks for what you have received in your life.

Slowly and gently come back to this reality. Wriggle your fingers and toes and open your eyes.

Eat and drink something.

Jot down any thoughts or images that came to mind during your meditation. It can be useful to refer back to them later.

Winter

The winter season is all about self-care and inner work. It is a time to hibernate, to withdraw, and to focus on rebuilding yourself so you are ready for when spring comes around again.

- **Goddess:** Crone
- **Element:** earth
- **Colours:** black, dark brown, midnight blue
- **Symbols:** bare twigs, pebbles, snowflakes
- **Magic:** abundance, grounding, manifesting, prosperity, protection, stability

Winter Meditation

Make yourself comfortable in a place where you won't be disturbed. Close your eyes and focus on your breathing... deep breaths in and deep breaths out.

As your world around you dissipates, you find yourself standing on a dirt pathway. The sky above you is grey with a few heavy-looking clouds. The air is cold and crisp, but you are dressed for the cold weather.

To the left of the pathway is a wide-open field. The ground looks uneven and the grass is covered with frost. Tall, dark seed heads stand up proudly here and there, spiking the skyline.

To your right is a river that stretches along and bends around the edge of the field. The water is deep and dark but flowing gently. Moored to the side of the river are several brightly painted houseboats. They bob gently in the water. Their roofs are covered in a layer of sparkling white frost.

The other side of the river is banked with trees. The branches are dark and bare, skeletons of their former selves.

As you take in your surroundings and the breathtaking beauty of nature in her winter slumber, you feel something on your skin...

Tiny snowflakes begin to fall. The snow is light at first but becomes heavier.

You decide to walk along the dirt pathway, your feet crunching on the crisp, fresh, snowy ground.

Watch as the snow lightly coats the branches of the trees and begins to make a perfect blanket over the field.

As you turn a corner in the path, you see a small wooden hut. It is closed in on one side with the other open to the field. You make your way over and enter.

Inside is a large wooden bench with a few cushions and a pile of blankets. You make yourself comfortable. Then you notice a large flask and a mug, so you help yourself to a steaming cup of hot chocolate.

Sit quietly in the warmth, watching the snow fall onto the field. There is quite a thick blanket now, covering the grass below. Think about all the life that lies below the surface of the soil... all the plants and insects in their winter hibernation, sleeping quietly, gaining strength and energy over the cold winter months so that they are ready to emerge renewed and refreshed in the spring...

Then think about your own life. What can you do this winter to nourish your spirit, body, and soul? This is a time to withdraw and replenish. What actions can you take to look after yourself more?

Take all the time you need. Then, when you are ready, leave the warmth behind. The snow has stopped falling now. You make your way back along the pathway to the edge of the field and the houseboats.

Give thanks for the friends and family in your life.

Slowly and gently come back to this reality. Wriggle your fingers and toes and open your eyes.

Eat and drink something.

Jot down any thoughts or images that came to mind during your meditation. It can be useful to refer back to them later.

CHAPTER
TWENTY-FOUR

Finding and Holding
Your Focus

In this fast-paced world, it can be really easy to lose focus. We can end up floundering and flapping about with no real idea of where we are going or what we are supposed to be doing. Having a focus or a direction can really help keep things on track. It can balance emotions and centre your mind. Hopefully the spells, rituals, and meditations within this book will bring your focus into being. But in case you need a little more help, here are some everyday ideas and suggestions that can also help.

Ditch the Tech

Our world is stuffed full of technology. In principle this is a good thing, but I also believe that too much of it is overwhelming. We are constantly bombarded with media, news, visual and audible stimuli, and—basically—never a moment's peace. This isn't healthy.

I was shocked to find myself completely reliant on my mobile/cell phone. It was never more than a few inches away from me: in my bag when I was out, on my desk when I was working, or beside me when I sat watching TV in the evening. And each little notification, each little "Bing!", drew my attention away from what I was doing. As soon as I woke up, I was reaching for the phone. When I went up to bed early to read a good book, I found that half the time I was mindlessly looking at the phone instead.

I also caught myself, on more than one occasion, aimlessly scrolling through social media for considerable amounts of time. I wasn't even taking notice of what was on it. It had become a habit, a bad one, and quite frankly, a pointless waste of time. I try now to only check social media a couple of times a day, both to take proper notice of what is on there and to limit the time spent.

In my home, we have always had the rule that no phones are allowed at mealtimes, but it didn't seem like this was quite enough. I now try to have "phone-free" periods of time, and in the evening when spending time with my family, I leave my phone on the hall table, away from where I am sitting.

Honestly, the world will not end if you aren't on social media for five minutes.

Tarot for Daily Balance

Tarot (and oracle) cards are excellent to read for guidance. I also like to work with them as a focus point for meditation and in spell work. You don't need to be able to read tarot or oracle cards to be able to use them for spells and journeys. Choose a tarot or oracle deck that you are drawn to. Take a look at the images; your first impression is important.

I have several tarot and oracle card decks. (Collecting them becomes addictive.) I have two sets that I use just for readings. I also have a specific set that I use just for spell work. The images are basic and the keywords are stated clearly on the cards, so they make a perfect focus for spells or journeys.

As always, I would advise to use whatever deck you are drawn to, focus on the intent or issue, and shuffle the cards. Then spread the deck out facedown and pick a card, or turn the cards faceup and pick one that you are drawn to.

If you prefer to be guided by the general meanings of each card, here are some suggestions:

+ Action—The Chariot, Ace of Wands, Eight of Wands
+ Addiction—The World, Judgement, Strength, Temperance
+ Change—The Magician, Eight of Wands, Wheel of Fortune, Judgement, The World
+ Courage—The Star, Strength, The Chariot
+ Decision—The Star, The Hermit, Justice, Nine of Wands, The Chariot

+ Emotion—Ace of Cups, The World, The Sun
+ Health—Strength, The Star, The World, The Magician, The Sun
+ Health (physical problems)—Strength, The Star, The World, Three of Cups
+ Motivation—The Magician, Eight of Pentacles, Ace of Wands
+ Obstacles—The Chariot, Strength, Two of Cups
+ Protection—The Star, Temperance, The Chariot, Four of Wands
+ Releasing—The Moon, Judgement, The World
+ Stress—The Hanged Man, Temperance, Four of Cups, Ace of Cups
+ Transformation—The Chariot, The Magician, Judgement, The High Priestess, Strength, The World, Temperance

Individual cards, or a combination, can be used in spell work to help amplify and focus the energy. Add one or two into any of the spells included within this book or use the cards to create your own.

For meditation, select a card that you want to draw energy from and sit quietly with the card in front of you. Focus on the image—really dive deep into the picture and allow your mind to wander around the imagery and landscape of it. Talk to the people/person in the card's picture. See what wisdom they can offer to you.

Pop a tarot or oracle card on your altar and use it as a focal point to draw strength and energy from.

It's the Little Things

Turning your life around for the better can be a challenging and frightening task. My advice is to start small. Don't write out a huge list of goals; just work on one small thing a day.

There are lots of easy, everyday ways to make positive change. Say "good morning" to one person on your way to work or hold open the door for someone. Making a difference is really rewarding; you get a warm, fuzzy feeling and it may well be the highlight of that person's day.

Household chores can seem overwhelming too, but again: start small. Make your bed every day after you get up. These days, with quilts, it is seriously easy and only takes a second. Coming home later and seeing a nice, tidy bed rather than a messy one is a small victory. Wash up straight after dinner. It is a boring chore, but getting up the following day and seeing a kitchen full of dirty dishes is disheartening and starts your day off on the wrong foot.

Every house will benefit from a good spring cleaning, but this can be a mammoth task. First things first, you don't have to do your thorough cleaning in the spring—any season works! Break down the chores into bite-size chunks and tackle one a day.

Take a moment each morning and breathe. This is a new day; this is your chance for a new start. Focus and set your intention for the day.

Make Yourself Happy

Ultimately—and even though you probably don't want to hear this—you have the key to making yourself happy. It is the responsibility of no one else. You are in control; you really are.

There will be outside influences that you can't change completely. We all have to earn money, for instance, and most jobs are a means to getting cash in the bank rather than being "dream" jobs. However, we can all make changes to our lives; even tiny ones will have a ripple effect. Drop a tiny, pea-size pebble into a pond and you still get a ripple that reaches outwards.

Blaming others and everything else for your situation will not help; it's just shifting responsibility … Not even shifting it, really, just shifting your perception of it, because in reality the responsibility lies at your own feet. You are the one that can change things. You are the one that can take control. You are the one that can make a difference. Yes, it will take hard work (lots of hard work probably), but it will be so worth it for the results.

Wallowing in self-pity works for a while, but it soon becomes seriously boring. (Seen it, done it, got the T-shirt.) And whilst I absolutely appreciate that getting yourself out of it is difficult, it can be done. Then you can start on the road to recovery/enlightenment/living/insert-any-positive-vibe-here.

> *Do what makes your heart sing.*
> *Do what works for you.*
> *Trust your intuition.*
> *Even baby steps in the right direction count.*
> *Never give up.*

Learn from your mistakes. (You will make them. We all do.)
Failure happens, but what you do after that is important.
This is your life. You only get one shot (well, in this incarnation any-way), so make it count.

A Final Reminder

You are never alone, particularly with this online world. There is always some-one somewhere that will listen.

You are important.

You are amazing, no matter what you think on a bad day. Remember that you are just experiencing that … a bad day. Underneath it all, you are amazing.

There is nothing that cannot be sorted, dealt with, or handled in some way.

Don't give up. It is OK to have a day off and start again the next day, or even the next week.

Be kind to yourself and be gentle. Learn to trust your intuition.

You are not broken. You do not need to be fixed. You just might need a bit of TLC and some fine-tuning.

Index